H. J. Reed 2017

EXEMPLARY JUSTICE

By the same author

Intensive Inquiries
The Air Marshals (Macdonald)
The Prosecutor
The Splendid Pauper
The Mad Motorists
The Whisky Barons (Jupiter)
The Royal Whore (Hutchinson)
The King Who Lost America (Jupiter)
The Follies of King Edward the Seventh (Lexington)
Quotations for Speakers and Writers, etc. (Newnes)

EXEMPLARY JUSTICE

ALLEN ANDREWS

HARRAP LONDON

Written for
BOB ANDREWS

First published in Great Britain 1976
by GEORGE G. HARRAP & CO. LTD
182–184 High Holborn, London WC1V 7AX

ISBN 0 245 52775 3

Composed in 10 on 11 pt. Baskerville and printed in Great Britain by Billing & Sons Limited, Guildford, London and Worcester

Contents

Illustrations

Justification

This is the story of an investigation into thirteen separate confederacies of murder, and into the central conspiracy which planned these murders and achieved the desired result: the death of fifty Allied aircrew officers as a deterrent to ten thousand others in prisoner-of-war camps within Germany. In a mass break-out from Stalag Luft III, a prison camp at Sagan in Silesia, seventy-nine officers escaped, three reached Great Britain, seventy-six were recaptured, and fifty of these were shot in degrading circumstances by the personal order of Adolf Hitler.

For a full year the British authorities did not know where to place responsibility for these acts, but a slow accumulation of intelligence seemed to clear the Luftwaffe, in whose custody the prisoners had been before escaping. Eventually the order to seek out and detain an unknown number of unidentified murderers was issued to the Royal Air Force seventeen months after the crimes were committed. The trail was cold. The terrain was vast—no less than the expanse of the former Greater Germany, corrupt and disorganized in the chaos of defeat. The wanted men belonged to a body, the Secret State Police or Gestapo, which held and exercised every facility to provide its members with false identities and forged identification papers immediately they were ordered to go on the run at the moment of national surrender.

The small detachment (an overall total of five officers and fourteen NCOs) of the Special Investigation Branch of the Royal Air Force which took on this task was active for three years until its authority was dissolved by the decision of the British Government to begin no more trials against war criminals after 31st August 1948. But even then its senior officer continued to find guilty men as they emerged cautiously from cover, and he urged pressure on the German civil authorities to take up the responsibility for their prosecution. The last man was sentenced twenty-four years after the crime was committed. In all seventy-two murderers were identified, sixty-nine were accounted for. Inevitably, therefore, there may be three faces still smirking when this narrative is presented.

'His Majesty's Government . . . are firmly resolved that these foul criminals shall be tracked down', the British Foreign Minister had assured Parliament in June 1944. 'They will be brought to exemplary justice.' This was one of the few occasions when an ambitious pledge made by a belligerent in the passion of indignation had an immediate discernible effect on an enemy, and was moreover abundantly fulfilled. The visible sequence was that the German High Command abandoned acquiescence in internationally illegal orders against Western prisoners of war after Mr Eden's public warning; the Gestapo made elaborate efforts to cover up the crimes already committed; and the individual criminals in hiding betrayed peculiar fear, even three years after the crime, when they saw that the investigators homing in on them wore the blue uniforms of the Royal Air Force, rather than the familiar khaki of most of the occupation forces.

At the subsequent trial in Hamburg invitations were extended to the Governments of Australia, Belgium, Canada, Czechoslovakia, France, Greece, Lithuania, New Zealand, Norway, Poland and South Africa to send official observers to the court, since officers from these eleven countries—the majority having flown in Royal Air Force squadrons—fell with the British in the massacre. The guilty were identified and punished, and the culmination of the Foreign Secretary's desperate threat of retribution seemed effected.

A sanguine presentation of the completed case would therefore parade the fulfilment of the pledge as the achievement of *exemplary justice*. Yet this interpretation may reasonably be contested. In technique it was a copybook detective operation, utilizing experience and courage, intuition and routine, in a dazzling combination of the virtues of Sherlock Holmes and Police Constable Plod; and this is the main concern of the narrative that follows. As a monument of significant impact, however, the edifice of effort remained uncrowned. The *example* was not stressed at the time. 'Justice' was belated, its consummation was diffused amid subsequent headlines, and perhaps it needs this book to be registered at all. Few observers had the endurance to sit through the long trial, and the outcome was given little publicity. Yet the simplicity of the judgment delivered at that time merits renewed emphasis today.

The Stalag Luft III murders were continually referred to at the Nuremburg trial of the major war criminals, and the established guilt of Göring, Keitel and Kaltenbrunner in the initial conspiracy was one of the findings which ensured their condemnation to death. But the incident of Sagan, no doubt deservedly, was smothered by the vast overlaying charges of breaking treaties to wage aggressive war, murdering and enslaving civil populations by the million, the additional incredible accomplishment of genocide, and the plunder and destruction of civilized communities on a scale unwarranted by any military necessity. The issues raised, however, at the Hamburg trial for the Sagan crime were uncomplicated, clear and salutary.

The main defence of those accused of the Stalag Luft III murders was that they were obeying higher orders which had been issued to enforce a political deterrent. That defence was overridden and confounded by the tribunal at the time of the trial. The rejection has been questioned since—in my view wholly wrongly—from two points of view. The young cynics who have never been in a national war, but are working off their righteousness, idealism and aggression through other means, say that all the Old Gang were wrong, and the tribunals which judged defeated 'war criminals' represented those who were as guilty, but had not been charged. (Goering himself had pre-empted this plea when he was given his 24 000-word indictment in a cell at Nuremburg, and remarked that he had been compiling similar documents for his enemies. 'The victor will always be the judge,' he said, ' and the vanquished the accused.')

The more positive revolt against the attempt to put a prop of case-law in support of a tottering table of decency has been that the same 'Sagan' defence has been resurrected since, and is pleaded today as justification for political killings and military massacres which still stand condemned by international law as plain murder —in Mr Eden's phrase, 'cold-blooded acts of butchery'. Some remarkable parallels between the Stalag Luft III investigation and later events illustrate this.

There is an hour of intimacy between an interrogator and even the most rugged prisoner once a formal confession of guilt has been made and recorded. Squadron Leader F. P. McKenna, an experienced peacetime criminal investigation officer, sometimes responded to this during the German inquiry by prompting a discussion on the morality of what had been done. He himself was a religious man, but he was not directly pursuing the other man's conversion through self-confrontation. He learned more about the criminal—and therefore more about the crime, and the crimes that were still unsolved—from what was divulged in this interval of relaxation, before the prisoner began to plan the tortuous tactics of a juridical defence.

'How could you do it?' McKenna asked ex-Kriminalsekretär Emil Schulz, who had admitted the murder of Squadron Leader R. J. Bushell on the side of the autobahn near Kaiserslautern, 29th March 1944. 'There was Roger Bushell, shot in the spine, fallen to the ground, turns on his back rocking in agony with his knees drawn up, rocking back and forth in absolute agony. And you get down on the ground, steady your pistol in the crook of your elbow, wait till his temple comes round against it, and then you pull the trigger. You say it was the *coup de grâce*. I call it wilful murder. How could you do it?'

Schulz reflected and answered. He was an undistinguished career policeman who had worked his way up through three ranks in the Gestapo. 'I never fought at the front', he said. 'I have never killed a man before or since. I tried to get out of this killing, but I was told to remember that the man was a terror-flier, and to think what our wives and children had to suffer in the German cities.' (Bushell, a Spitfire pilot, had in fact been shot down over Dunkirk in an engagement with five Messerschmitt 110s on 23rd May 1940, long before the Luftwaffe Blitz on Britain and two years before the Allied bombing offensive on Germany.) 'I knew that what I had been ordered to do was wrong. I said so, and was told to get on with it. What else could I do? If I'd not done it, someone else would have done it. If we had all refused, we could have been shot. But I have always expected to answer for this . . . this deed I never wished to do. And now it is the end of the road.'

> *The 'Sagan defence' at My Lai, 16 March 1968: evidence of Pfc Simpson*[1]
> 'This lady got up and she had her back turned to me, and my platoon leader, Lieutenant La Cross, told me to shoot her, and I said: "Well, you shoot her. I don't want to shoot no lady." So he said: "I'm giving you a direct order to shoot and if you don't shoot her then you can be shot yourself." So, as she was putting her foot in the door, I shot her about five or six times, and then I went there and turned her over, and there was a little dead three-month-old baby in her arms, which I had thought was a gun, and this kind of cracked me up.'

'How could you do it?' Squadron Leader McKenna asked the former SS Sturmbannführer Johannes Post, who had admitted the murder in a field outside Kiel of the Australian Squadron Leader J. Catanach and at least one of his three brother officers who had been killed almost immediately afterwards. Post had shot Catanach in the back, but not by surprise. It was a point of pride with him to announce to his victim, as long in advance as possible, what he was going to do, although in this case it was strictly against his orders from Berlin. Post was of about the same age as Schulz, thirty-five at the time of the crime, blond and broad and masterful. His SS military rank was equivalent to Major, his police rank equivalent to Inspector. Well over a hundred killings were alleged against him.

'How could you do such a thing as this?' asked McKenna. 'How could you be so inhuman?'

'Inhuman!' said Post. 'I was dealing with sub-humans. Yet I always gave them a full night's warning before I shot them, so that they could prepare to meet their fate. For the glory of the Führer I have killed any number of sub-humans. I have liquidated non-Aryans, gypsies, vagrants, Jews and politically unreliables. The

[1]Interrogated by Richard Hammer, reported in *The Listener*, London, 8th April 1971.

Führer has shown his appreciation by personally awarding me the highest political decoration in the realm. For the glory of the Führer I only regret that I have not killed more. People like you', he said, pointing at McKenna's aircrew brevet—the interrogator had flown Lancasters in Bomber Command. 'I wish I had had the chance to wipe out more people like you, who have left our cities in ruins and killed our women and children. These terror-fliers I disposed of were of no more good to the Reich than all the other sub-humans whom I sent on their journey to Heaven [*Himmelsfahrt*] for the glory of the Führer who has presented me with the Order of the Blood.'

An uncanny echo of the ratiocination of the then dead SS Major Post came a generation later at the trial of Lieutenant William Calley, United States Army, who, according to the witness Private Simpson, had at My Lai

> 'This grave, this massive ditch. I think it was about fifty people at a time. They would put two machine guns on each side, and put two people with automatic rifles, and he would stand over them, and he said "Shoot 'em." So he just killed all of 'em, all fifty of 'em, and then they would make another pile of 'em, and put 'em in a ditch, and then get another fifty.'

At his court martial Lieutenant Calley admitted the killings, but said he had acted under orders. His attorney, George W. Latimer, suggested that the victims were 'not human', but 'an enemy with whom no one could speak or reason'.

The other echo of the Stalag Luft III investigation dogged McKenna through his Service career, and sounds across the world today. It is the principle of intimidation through terroristic murder, by indiscriminate killing, or the slaughter of hostages, or the death of a random man haphazardly sentenced by a so-called 'court' which has never seen him nor even knows his name. 'Political killing!' McKenna once exploded. 'People say it's in a different category from crime. If murder is immoral, this is wrong. I've had to examine youngsters on the mortuary slab before their elbows have stiffened, when they're still warm and the smell of cordite hangs over their bloodstained flesh, ten minutes after being slaughtered on the street. People have said to me: "These were political killings, you can't call them crimes." I have said: "Here's this young corporal from the office, he's just got off the Service bus at the top of the street, he's waylaid by three thugs with firearms and they shoot him from below when he's coming round the corner carrying his kit. Do you call that a political act, to kill this innocent lad?"—"Oh, yes. It's for freedom, striking at establishment and authority. It's quite sound."—It's not a view that I can subscribe to.'

There is a tendency for murder to achieve major significance only when it is conducted on a massive scale. This gradation of morality was vehemently resisted not only at the Hamburg trial but at the Nuremberg trial, where the shooting of the fifty officers from Stalag Luft III was continually raised as a matter of marshals' honour and an issue of international concern, although there was every encouragement for its submersion. In the calendar of inhumanity, this incident was, whatever its ignominy, undoubtedly of minor dimensions—perhaps its most striking significance is that, in the face of appalling difficulties, *this crime, of all the war crimes, was fully requited.* Its scale was a disadvantage to the investigators. Flight Lieutenant A. R. Lyon,[1] commenting on the frustrating difficulties he experienced during inquiries in the eastern zones of the former German territories, said, 'It is probably true that neither the Poles nor the Russians really believed our motives in making this investigation. To them the murder of fifty officers was a matter of such triviality, when compared with their own civilian and military casualties, that they simply could not see why we were making so much fuss about it. I believe they thought we were spies, using the investigation as a pretext for our presence, and this accounts for their complete lack of co-operation.'

Innumerable cases had been cited at Nuremberg of the torture and extermination not only of complete local populations but of vast contingents of prisoners of war, particularly those from the eastern territories, who were regarded—in the official German term, which by its very acceptance damns a doctrine—as subhumans, fit only for slavery and death. But there were no racial restrictions on butchery. In France 642 villagers and children, the entire population of Oradour-sur-Glane save ten who were left for dead, were burned to death or, breaking out of the church, machine-gunned to death by a detachment of the SS Division Das Reich; by one decision of Himmler, 200 000 French men and women in concentration camps and forced labour camps were put to death when the Allies advanced on the western front; and Poland, as an individual nation desperately poised between the Germans and the Russians, lost in one operation 200 000 souls derisively excommunicated as expendable in the Warsaw Rising, besides the 15 000 officers mown down at Katyn.

Flight Lieutenant Lyon himself, interrupting his Royal Air Force investigation for an interrogatory interview with Rudolf Franz Hoess, observed to him, 'They say, Hoess, that while you were commandant of Auschwitz you were responsible for the murder and cremation of about two and a half million Jews'. Hoess, displaying a certain sense of shock, quickly corrected him: 'Oh, no, Herr Hauptmann. It must have been three millions or more.' Lyon had omitted the half-million who, without preliminary gassing, had been allowed to die from starvation and disease. The statistics were revised when Hoess was put on trial in Warsaw, and he admitted responsibility for the death of 4 000 000 Jews, 300 000 other camp

[1]Officers are named throughout in the rank they held at the time of the incident referred to.

inmates, and 12 000 Russian prisoners of war, illegally held in his concentration camp. He was hanged on the Auschwitz gallows.

In cynical terms of sensationalism, can the Stalag Luft III crime and investigation stand out alongside these horrors? I have written this book *only because the Royal Air Force traced and exposed the killers.* The Service appointed its Special Investigation Branch as an arm of that law—international law—which has suffered from a surfeit of advocacy and a damning dearth of enforcement. Enforcement was in this case so complete that its success virtually created an advanced point of principle through the qualitative change: international law *can* be effectively implemented—do not be diffident in drafting more where it is called for, and assigning effort to back it up. But the success of this achievement was denied acknowledgment. In spite of the intense emotion which the Stalag Luft III murders contemporaneously prompted in Great Britain and the Commonwealth, and a profound acceptance that the grave words spoken by Mr Eden in Parliament represented a more than ephemeral statement of values, the former Foreign Secretary and Prime Minister, when he came to write his memoirs as the Earl of Avon, KG, PC, MC, did not mention the subject, or the pledge, or its fulfilment; and Sir Winston Churchill similarly omitted any reference. It was lost amid the thousand miseries of war.

It deserves better. This painstaking, and initially hopeless, judicial process concerning a too swiftly forgotten affair of fifty murders went some way towards the re-establishment of a principle and the recognition of a restraint written internationally into the laws of war. It is worth the chronicling. The baldest recital of the tension of its interlinking inquiries stiffens the sinews. The climax, in my view, summons up the blood, and vindicates a pride in this dogged, unostentatious pursuit whereby the Royal Air Force, through its investigations branch, declared a belief in values which are relevant now.

It was a remarkably civilian-style police operation, in the sense that the Royal Air Force investigators used no 'militaristic' violence in their interrogations, even though they were dealing exclusively with Gestapo officials who had used every degree of torture in their own careers. An exception—which is clearly recorded here if only because of its rarity—is the occurrence of what under British law is a technical assault, in that a woman was threatened, but not touched. There was one physical assault (not by a member of the Royal Air Force) which is also recorded, along with its ironic consequence. One sergeant-major in a British military gaol indulged his indignation at the Stalag Luft III murders by beating a prisoner accused of some of them. The result, through a complicated series of circumstances, was that although the prisoner's confederates were hanged, this man was reprieved from a death sentence and released under amnesty comparatively soon: which was not what the sergeant-major intended.

This book does not seek to raise a pretentious cenotaph for fifty flying men who, when their own daring clashed with a political decision, became isolated from a hundred thousand other Allied aircrew who died in the Second World War. Rather it lays a lily on their monument dedicated to the patient pursuit of justice which their deaths provoked, and that has no known memorial.

The chronicle could never have been presented without the co-operation—for which I express my sincere thanks—of Air Commodore B. C. Player, CBE, Provost Marshal of the Royal Air Force at the time when the book was researched and written; Air Commodore G. Innes, MBIM, his successor and co-adjutor; Air Commodore H. M. Shephard, CBE, his predecessor, without whose fighting faith the book would never have been written; the late Air Commodore H. M. Massey, CBE, DSO, MC, Senior British Officer at Stalag Luft III, who gave his unique photographs to the Imperial War Museum; Group Captain E. B. Haslam, MA, FRHistS, with Mr E. H. Turner and the staff of the Air Historical Branch of the Ministry of Defence; Group Captain H. M. A. Day, GC, DSO, OBE; Group Captain W. V. Nicholas, CBE; Group Captain L. G. Brown, OBE; Squadron Leader F. P. McKenna, OBE; Squadron Leader A. R. Lyon; Flight Lieutenants J. W. Bowes, BEM, S. H. Courtney and H. E. Harrison; Sergeant M. J. Symonds, RAF; Mrs Joyce Andrews, an untiring aide; the Earl of Avon, KG, PC, MC, DCL, LLD; Mr Colin Bagnall; Mr Jan Bobinski; Mrs Annelise Derrick; Mr H. H. Edmonds of the Ministry of Defence; Mr Paul André Ramseyer of the Swiss Embassy in London; Mr Simon Wiesenthal of the Dokumentationszentrum, Vienna; and David Williamson, Esq., OBE, QPM, Chief Constable of Renfrew and Bute. Thanks are due also to the Keystone Press for permission to reproduce the photograph of men in the dock.

The public records to which I have been given generous access are Crown Copyright, and I gratefully acknowledge the permission granted to use them and to make verbatim quotation. I myself, however, am solely responsible for the accuracy of the statements made and the opinions expressed, which do not necessarily reflect the views of H.M. Government.

A. A.

1 Escape is no longer a sport

It began in mist.

The escape occurred in deep snow. The killings were done in squalor on roadside verges, and the falling men found deathbeds of slush or frost or dew, often marked by their own urine. But the investigation began in mist, and continued so for a long time.

Eichacher sauntered through the flat area of huts and bedraggled garden plots. He paused almost imperceptibly in the rising mist alongside a weather-shielded board. He drove his thumb into the board and walked, self-consciously casual, on to the gates, where he submitted to the routine of being checked and counter-checked by guards who knew him familiarly. Then he strode with quickening pace and decelerating pulse, out of the chill and menace of the mist into the comparatively golden intimacy of his quarters in the German staff compound. His actions had been almost imperceptible, and yet perceived. Eichacher's movements were an entry in the log of the Duty Pilot, the Royal Air Force officer-prisoner who had been placed on watch to record the arrival and departure of every German into and out of the north compound of Stalag Luft III, according to the system which had been energetically recommended by the escape supremo 'Big X', Roger Bushell, Squadron Leader, Royal Air Force, now dead, and diligently perfected by his security aide 'Big S', Tom Kirby-Green, Squadron Leader, Royal Air Force, now dead.

Eichacher was the man who usually pinned up the announcements on the notice-board at Stalag Luft III. Because he held rank in the Luftwaffe and not in the Gestapo, and because the Luftwaffe wanted to emphasize to the Royal Air Force that they had had no hand in recent events, Eichacher tried to be inconspicuous during certain activities. He contrived to time the fixing of any notice referring to the shooting of the fifty for grey periods like dawn and dusk, when he could slip away before hearing the pointed comments of the officer prisoners of war. Consequently it was not until morning was bright on 24th July 1944, just four months after the mass escape, that most of the British and Allied air-crew officers in the north compound of Stalag Luft III were reading the bald announcement, printed in that form of English which was available to the German High Command, which ran:

THE ESCAPE FROM PRISON CAMPS
IS NO LONGER A SPORT

A copy of that notice was eventually placed in the hands of the Judge Advocate General in London, whose Military Department was patiently compiling a dossier of all relevant events preceding and following the killing of the fifty officers from Sagan. A pledge had been made that the murderers would be hunted down and brought to justice. This flimsy sheet was to be one of thousands of documents in the files that eventually condemned the guilty men.

Intrinsically it was not very important, except to show that the OKW,[1] which had issued it as a circular, reiterated responsibility for the prevention and punishment of escapes by prisoners of war in spite of the efforts of Himmler, as Head of the Security Services, to gain control of this area; in spite, also, as was already known to British Military Intelligence, of individual members in the German High Command who were frantically passing the buck for the murders to Himmler and the Gestapo in order to save their own professional military honour. The Judge Advocate General's department filed a minute that publication of this notice incriminated Field-Marshal Wilhelm Keitel, Chief of the High Command under the Supreme Commander Hitler, as originator of the order to kill the fifty from Sagan.

But the document had an additional, emotional importance. Criminal investigation is carried out by men. It would be foolish to demand that they become personally involved in every crime, yet it is an axiom of morale that the last ounce of energy is put in by people who care. The officers investigating the Stalag Luft III killings cared deeply, not only because they were what they themselves would have called 'good coppers' who wanted to see justice done, and not entirely because of the political and public abhorrence of the crime—but also because the victims were their own comrades, from squadrons they knew, wearing insignia which they shared, using the same slang and singing the same songs. By the standards of those who have never worn uniform their sympathy was naïve. Perhaps for the same reason, their gut-reaction was intense. These investigating officers have since mentioned their simple revulsion at that flat threat: 'Escape is no longer a sport'. It became a phrase that was grimly repeated, and potently repeated, when deep reserves of effort had to be whipped in during the chase.

[1]Oberkommando der Wehrmacht, High Command of the Armed Forces.

23.7.1944. THE ESCAPE FROM PRISON CAMPS IS NO LONGER A SPORT. That announcement had been posted in every prisoner-of-war camp in Germany where English was read. The weight of its intimidation was clear. The fact that fifty escaped Royal Air Force officers had been shot on recapture had now become international knowledge, which Germany had been forced to share with her own armed forces and civil population—where the reception ranged between extremes of disquiet and jubilation. The reservations were most keenly felt by the military, and not always in self-centred fear of reprisals. Under international law all prisoners of war had the right to escape, and under the military usage adopted by both Germany and Great Britain all officer prisoners of war had the duty to escape: a duty so pressing that it was forbidden for an officer to give his parole not to escape, except for recognized short periods when it was convenient to both sides. The authorities administering prisoner-of-war camps similarly had an internationally recognized right to prevent escapes, and to use firearms against people in open flight, but to impose no more than a short sentence of solitary confinement on those who were recaptured.

In the camp at Sagan the bleak announcement on the notice-board could not be expected to be given anything but a sullen acknowledgment. The prisoners had lived with its message for some time. Twelve days after the break-out, the Senior British Officer had been officially informed that forty-one of his men had been shot 'whilst resisting arrest or trying to escape after re-arrest'.[1] On the following Sunday a memorial service was held in the prison camp. Each of the 1400 officers in the congregation had sewn a black diamond on his sleeve. Sixty-one officers were still missing, forty-one were said to be dead, and no one knew the names of those who had died or those who lived on. It was Easter Day, a poignant festival for those who believed in the Resurrection.

For since by man came death, by man came also
the resurrection of the dead.

For as in Adam all die, even so in Christ
shall all be made alive. . . .

The last enemy that shall be destroyed
is death.

In later communiqués the death roll had finally been declared at fifty. The Gestapo began to send the victims back, cremated

[1]The figure was, in fact, inaccurate because one Gestapo District Chief had had orders to kill his man, the forty-first on the list, on the following day. The appointed day was Good Friday, and the Gestapo leader, who was a practising Christian churchman, was wrestling with his conscience about committing such a deed on such a day. He compromised by having the officer shot on Maundy Thursday, but some seven hours after the death had been counted in the Sagan total.

to conceal all evidence of the cause of death. When Eichacher pinned up his notice the last consignment of the forty-six urns and four boxes containing the ashes of the murdered men had recently been received. The remains lay in a store in the camp sick-quarters, and the German Commandant had agreed that stone should be made available for the construction of a memorial. The decency of his decision had been appreciated by the prisoners, and officers had given the temporary parole required before they could work on clearing the pines and birches in the cemetery area, outside the wire, where in an open high altar they were to seal the ashes of the men with whom they had striven and hoped.

It was a time of intense emotion in a place where all too often the drab days flattened into months of dispirited abasement. Death itself was, willy-nilly, a drama. But minds were also racing with expectancy. Rome had fallen. The D-Day invasion was seven weeks old. The raucous overhead loudspeakers installed to transmit the official German newscasts had not been able to smother the fact that the breakthrough in Normandy had at last been achieved, and the liberation of Paris was in sight. Only four days previously the speakers had broadcast the shock announcement of the bomb against Hitler. On the day of the publication of the High Command circular the prisoners—and the German public—had been given for the first time an official Berlin version of the killing of the fifty Royal Air Force officers: the mass break-out, said the Tannoy, had been deliberately planned by the Allied General Staffs as the detonator of massive political and military revolt inside Germany; the fifty had been shot whilst resisting arrest or attempting further escape; taking offence at Mr Eden's contemptuous rejection in the House of Commons of this explanation, the German Foreign Office had cancelled its previous agreement to give Great Britain further details of these deaths through the diplomatic link with Switzerland, the Protecting Power.

The officers in Stalag Luft III had known for four weeks all about Mr Eden's indignant rebuttal. They had taken it down on the day it was uttered, using the powerful radio receiver which they had built and sunk into the floor of a latrine hut, jauntily cellared beneath a sanitary pan.

Escape is no longer a sport. The prisoners in the camp accepted this. Realistically, they would agree that actively technical, characteristically adventurous and high-spirited officers in captivity after air combat would have been inclined to attempt some reckless escapes as a form of sport—if it had not been for the quite rigorous control exercised through the Escape Committee headed by Big X. Escape discipline in Stalag Luft III was in fact a matter of high responsibility, as was all internal security. The nightly BBC broadcasts, taken down by two shorthand-writers in the latrines, were escorted to each hut in the camp and formally read there after a full muster of counter-sentries had been posted, with the precise control, if not the pomp, of the Ceremony of the Keys in the Tower of London. It was in this mood of responsible discipline that. after the mass break-out of 24th March 1944 and the subsequent slaughter, the new Big X had promptly organized work on the *next* escape tunnel, the 101st to be dug in Sagan, which was now being pushed out from a trapdoor entrance beneath the auditorium of the camp theatre hut. When the threatening notice was posted this tunnel already extended beyond the wire, but had not yet reached the cover of the farther trees.

Whether, in the conditions of the time, another *mass-escape* would be carried through depended on decisions not yet taken. The Escape Committee, in consultation with the Senior British Officer, laid down the policy. The officers in Stalag Luft III were in fact in very tenuous contact with London, though to nothing like the extent alleged by the German Foreign Office of maintaining fluent liaison with Allied General Staffs, or possessing the capability to break out on orders and start mass insurrections. The address of a brothel in Stettin where no questions would be asked for a couple of nights was about the height of communication they could hope for, and there was always the chance that in the interval after transmission the whore-house would have been raided. The intelligence organization known as IS9[1] occasionally got through to them by clandestine means information about safe houses in enemy territory, and more rarely delivered physical aids to escape. But in the autumn of 1944 IS9 let it be known to Stalag Luft III that, in the prevailing circumstances, escape need no longer be considered the duty of an officer. To that extent the German intimidation exercised by the shooting of the fifty officers and the subsequent public warning to prisoners of war may be said to have succeeded.

IS9's instructions for caution did not, however, get through to five incorrigible escapers from Stalag Luft III who on recapture after the March break-out were not shot and not returned to Sagan, but were sent to the Gestapo concentration camp of Sachsenhausen/Oranienburg. They were Wing Commander H. M. A. Day, Major J. B. Dodge, and Flight Lieutenants S. H. Dowse, B. A. James and R. L. N. Van Wymeersch. They all made further escapes, and were recaptured. 'Wings' Day finally succeeded on his ninth escape attempt. He achieved liberty two days before Hitler's death and nine days before the German capitulation. A veteran of the First World War, and holding the DSO and OBE, he had served only forty days in the second war before being shot down on a daylight reconnaissance. Yet, on his belated emergence, he addressed himself to the last week of hostilities with vigour. After fighting alongside the partisans in the streets of northern Italy, he burst through the German lines from the rear in a commandeered car. Through his prompt warning, an American flying column was sent up to Hitler's

[1]Intelligence School 9, a cover-name.

alpine Southern Redoubt, and it rescued from the death sentence already passed on them a group of fifty hostages (from which Day had escaped) including Pastor Martin Niemöller, the German Protestant leader; Kurt von Schuschnigg, the Catholic Austrian ex-Chancellor; and Léon Blum, the Jewish and Socialist French ex-Premier: a notable bag for any Nazi execution squad. Wing Commander Day was awarded the George Cross.

At about the same time as Day's eruption, Major John Bigelow Dodge, who had influential connections of kinship both with American diplomats and with Mr Winston Churchill, was, after months of solitary confinement in Sachsenhausen, repatriated by the German Foreign Office. He was sent to England with a message, in a last-ditch attempt to persuade the British Prime Minister to accept a conditional German surrender to the American and British forces only, with no German territory to be ceded to the Russians. But the Germans had misjudged the speed at which they were hurtling into defeat, and had hung on to Dodge too long. So, while Dodge was still en route in Switzerland, Heinrich Himmler, arrogating the leadership of the German people to which he was only third in succession, offered through Count Bernadotte of Sweden the unconditional surrender of Germany to the American and British forces—or unconditional save for one proviso: that the Western Allies should march across Germany to beat the Russians.

This proposal was then unknown to Hitler, who still had a week to live. News of it—ironically picked up from a BBC London broadcast through a balloon aerial antenna above the Berlin bunker—was conveyed to Hitler five days later, and Himmler's 'treachery' almost caused the Führer to die of apoplexy two days before he put the revolver in his mouth. Dodge did pass the German message in London to the American Ambassador John Winant at dinner with Winston Churchill on 4th May, four days after Hitler's death. But by that evening Field-Marshal Montgomery had taken the German High Command surrender of all forces in north-west Germany, and General Jodl was preparing to meet General Eisenhower in Reims, where the total unconditional capitulation was signed. Major Dodge, though American-born, had won the DSC as a Royal Navy sub-lieutenant at Gallipoli in 1915 and the DSO as a 24-year-old lieutenant-colonel commanding a battalion of the Royal Sussex Regiment in France in 1918. He had limbered up for his five escapes of the Second World War with an escape from the Bolshevik Secret Police in 1921. He was awarded the Military Cross.

In the office of the Judge Advocate General in Spring Gardens off Trafalgar Square, what victory fever could be diagnosed in those rather sterile chambers was heightened by the extraordinary coincidence of Day's escape and Dodge's repatriation long before the department could hope for any sight or interrogation of the other survivors of the Stalag Luft III break-out. Sagan itself was known to have been overrun by the advancing Russians in February 1945, but the prisoners of war had been hurriedly evacuated and set on a series of forced marches in the depth of winter through disintegrating Germany. Tracing them, identifying the very few survivors of the escape, getting them home and rested and mentally composed for interrogation—all this was a task that was hardly going to be completed by the first week-end after the cease-fire.

But Day and Dodge were back in town, alert and radiating leadership—'bright-eyed and bushy-tailed', as an intelligence officer said of one of them at his de-briefing. Their experiences provided invaluable information. They had made the escape. They had met some of the murderers. Each of them had travelled with a companion who had finally been shot. Dodge had been put in gaol in Hirschberg, where he had been in touch with a considerable number of recaptured officers from Sagan, of whom four were known to have been killed. Day had been taken to Berlin for his final interrogation before remittal to Sachsenhausen, and in the Security Police Headquarters there had met face to face the Number One on the Wanted List which the Judge Advocate General had already compiled: Artur Nebe, national head of the Kripo.[1] However, apart from their personal contacts with the slayers and the slain, Day and Dodge had known the planning of the escape as intimately as anyone, and they had a general knowledge of some of the getaway routes planned by some of the escapers who had been caught. These routes, if adhered to, were a factor in the determination of where the deaths had occurred, and these locations in their turn gave some leads to the identity of the possible killers.

Hints and information touching this kind of detail were of first-rank importance. When the news of the Sagan killings first came through it was generally assumed, even by Mr Eden in his denunciation in the House of Commons, that there had been a mass butchery. The public never cancelled this mental image of fifty officers being herded into a prison yard and mown down. The Judge Advocate General's staff had slowly learned of a different outcome. It was clear that many of the victims had been caught on the frontiers of Germany and killed in those areas. But there was much conjecture and little certainty. After fourteen months of jigsaw-piecing there were isolated nodules of cohesion, islands of understanding. The general pattern of events was still largely guesswork.

The Sagan murders, at the time of their being revealed, fell into the province of the United Nations War Crimes Commission which had been set up on 20th October 1943. Seventeen nations and Free Governments in exile were represented on this commission. The Soviet Union was not a member, having established its own war crimes organization—a dichotomy which was to plant broad minefields discouraging the fullest co-operation over the following

[1]Kriminalpolizei, Criminal Police, almost always shortened to Kripo, as Geheime Staatspolizei, Secret State Police, became Gestapo.

years. But the general principle of the pursuit of justice against war criminals had been firmly agreed at the Moscow Conference of the Foreign Ministers of Great Britain, the United States and the Soviet Union, 19th–30th October 1943.

The crime of the Stalag Luft III murders was thus in the province of an as yet untested commission of justice. But convincing grounds for a future prosecution had to be established. The occurrence was initially a Royal Air Force affair. It had then been elevated to become a matter of political status, and the justification for useful menaces in the continuing propaganda war of nerves. When the politicians and propagandists had no further use for it any artificial fury could be expected to evaporate: it would have fulfilled its function; and for this very reason—that, in the RAF phraseology, there was no future in it—no politically sponsored fact-finders were set on to the inquiry to establish a case for the prosecution. Royal Air Force feelings, however, were deeper than the propagandists', and coincided with the intentions of those who wanted to establish a rule of international law. But again, there were no criminal investigators who could be called on from some pool controlled by international lawyers, and the case fell back again to the Royal Air Force. From the beginning, therefore, the Stalag Luft III investigation was committed to the activity of the Provost Marshal's Branch of the Royal Air Force, working with RAF officers on the staff of the Judge Advocate General, and drawing all the aid and information possible from any communicative source of intelligence.

Before the end of the war, using only evidence available at a time when research in the field was denied, sufficient facts had been gathered for the Treasury Solicitor to present the file to the United Nations War Crimes Commission. The Commission assessed the case as of a prima facie strength which justified its immediate acceptance for eventual prosecution. Consequently it was passed to the Judge Advocate General's office for full investigation and preparation. This reclassification was made on 29th March 1945, when all the principal witnesses to the murders were still in German hands.

The Royal Air Force did have, however, access to four witnesses of the escape which preceded the murders, and one of these witnesses could give invaluable and authoritative evidence of events inside Stalag Luft III after the murders. Three officers had got cleanly away from the camp and out of Germany. Two of these were back in England in less than a week, long before the murders were even known. They were the Lieutenants of the Royal Norwegian Air Force, seconded to the Royal Air Force, Jens Muller and Peter Bergsland—though the latter, possibly covering his true identity to protect his family in Norway, was always known in the camp as Rocky Rockland. Muller and Bergsland had had priority in the order of exit from the tunnel, along with some thirty other fluent German-speakers who were due to catch fast trains.

They had changed at Küstrin for Stettin, where they found some

Swedish sailors who smuggled them aboard their ship and hid them during searches, and they had landed in Sweden after a day's voyage. The third man was Flight Lieutenant Bram (Bob) Van der Stok, of Dutch nationality. He made four changes of train to get to Holland, went underground for weeks at a time in his own country and in Belgium and France, and after four months arrived in England via Portugal.

The three returned officers could give minor details of escape plans which were relevant to the fate of the dead fifty; but they were not experienced escape organizers who had had to approve, and sometimes improve, the plans of the fifty, as Day and Dodge had been. Moreover, through their very success, the three who came back could give no details of the names and places of recapture of the officers who had been taken. However, almost a year before Day and Dodge returned, the Germans had incredibly presented the British with an eye-witness of the escape, descriptions of some Germans who could reasonably be assumed to be involved in the murders and an informative analysis of the contradictions of the German versions of the murders. They had repatriated the Senior British Officer of the North Compound of Stalag Luft III, from which all the escapers had come.

Group Captain H. M. Massey, DSO, MC, had been Senior British Officer, apart from a spell in hospital, for the year covering the digging of the large-scale tunnels until the mass escape. It had been impossible for him to take active participation; a foot which he had damaged in action during the First World War had taken its third crippling knock when he had been shot down over the Ruhr, and he was severely lame. Because of this injury a medical board had agreed on his repatriation in exchange for a wounded German flyer. Politically, although the decision had been reached before the escape, its fulfilment was a most damaging move from the point of view of those Germans who wanted to cover up the Sagan crime. They were presenting the British—who were already swearing retribution—with first-hand evidence of the announcement of the deaths of the officers, the embarrassment of the Luftwaffe, the intense activity of the Gestapo at Sagan—and, above all, with second-hand evidence of the *reports of the gaol experiences of the murdered officers*, as smuggled from solitary confinement by those survivors who were returned to the camp before Massey left.

That this was a grave political blunder from the point of view of the German Government of the time cannot be doubted. Whether it was connived at by German officers disgusted or remorseful at the previous slaughter cannot be precisely affirmed. Two officers later claimed credit for letting the repatriation go through, knowing its consequences. One of them, Max Wielen, Chief of the Criminal Police in the area which included Sagan, did not mention the matter until he was fighting for his life at his trial, and boxing with all the guile and experience of forty years passed on the other side of the dock rail. His claim may be discounted. Major-General Adolf Westhoff, Head of Prisoner-of-War Affairs in the German General Staff, declared after his capture that he wilfully concealed from his superiors (that is, in practical terms, from the head of the High Command, Field-Marshal Keitel) the fact that Massey was listed for repatriation, and Westhoff repatriated him on his own responsibility. His motive, he said, was 'simply that I had for weeks been brooding over and searching for a chance of being able to evade or sabotage Hitler's order. . . . I acted because I already hoped then that, on publication of the particulars about the Sagan case, the British Government would not remain silent, and thus Hitler would be forced to see that the measures ordered by him would have to be altered. After the statement in the House of Commons, no case became known to me—as far as I can remember—in which the Gestapo shot escaped prisoners of war.' This is special pleading, made after defeat, but it deserves consideration.

The additional miscalculation made by the German authorities was the freedom of action of the Protecting Power (Switzerland) after the murders.[1]

The Swiss representative was in Stalag Luft III before the last of the fifty had been killed. He expressed immediately and officially his personal belief that the prisoners could not have been shot whilst trying to escape. And he finally submitted to London in the diplomatic bag a full report of the Court of Inquiry held later in Sagan by the new Senior British Officer, which gave very valuable summaries of the evidence of the escapers who had survived.

It is probably more accurate to define the German political

[1]By 1944 the Swiss Foreign Office had charge of eighty-five missions and representations on behalf of the Western Allies, and forty-one on behalf of Axis countries. On the strength of its policy of permanent neutrality, its status as Executive Power of the Red Cross Convention, and its role as principal Protecting Power in the Second World War, Switzerland virtually created its own precedents where discretion was permitted as to the potential of the Protecting Power, and naturally applied its supervising privileges reciprocally —'against' Great Britain as a country holding prisoners of war, and 'for' Great Britain as a belligerent with some nationals held in Germany as prisoners of war. In 1944 in Germany alone, Swiss inspectors visited two thousand prisoners-of-war detachments on forty-two separate tours. They examined barracks, sampled food, checked the weight and health of prisoners, heard complaints, and brought deficiencies and violations to the attention of the detaining Power. They particularly intervened against the use of manacles and other unlawful forms of discipline, and insisted on attending any criminal trials of prisoners. Where capital sentences were imposed, they worked to achieve a stay of execution and the exchange of the convicted person. It is understandable, therefore, that the Gestapo intensified its normal methods of secrecy when dealing illegally with prisoners of war.

thinking on this aspect not as miscalculation but as sheer ignorance arising from inexperience of any objective reporting on the decisions of a dictatorship. Today it requires some mental effort to appreciate that there had been no checks or controls or reference either to political experience or morality applied to any whim of Hitler's for eleven years, since the day—of which the Sagan escape notched a grim anniversary—on 24th March 1933 when the Reichstag handed over its legislative functions to the Nazi Government. Since that time, although the Reichstag had met to adulate Hitler, it had never held a debate, never divided for a vote, never even listened to a speech except from Hitler, telling it what to do—and this grand legislative function had been reserved for passing three decrees, outlawing the Jews.

In eleven years nobody had ever publicly argued with Hitler, nor amended his 'laws' by so much as a comma, nor even criticized him. The notion of a foreign country's representative at large in Germany with power to report to a belligerent nation may have seemed so fantastic that it was never seriously considered by Hitler, and therefore tactfully never brought to his notice. But the Führer's military subordinates were professional officers who were not only morally aware that Germany had been the first to sign the 1929 International Convention on Prisoners of War, but materialistically alert to the advantage of having a Protecting Power superintending the treatment of German prisoners of war in Great Britain and elsewhere. It is small wonder that those who knew the truth of the Sagan killings not only feared but *expected* reprisals, against their own sons in many cases, when the public storm broke.

The German High Command knew from the beginning that what the Gestapo could get away with against Germans, and what they hoped to get away with against conquered civilians, they were extremely unlikely to get away with against identified combatants of recognized belligerent forces. And even that small, qualified prohibition must be considered an advance in international conduct.[1]

But in 1944 very few people in Germany knew the truth about Sagan. Experienced officers did guess, and fear. The murders had been classified Top Secret from the start, with no orders to be written and one essential teleprinted death warrant to be burnt when it had been read. The contradictory thinking that made an intimidatory reprisal into a State secret is characteristic of the paranoiac nature of the whole affair. Keitel said that Hitler wanted fifty officers shot, and in his next sentence ordered his immediate subordinate, the general in charge of prisoner-of-war affairs:

> As an intimidating example the names of those shot are to be posted up in the Camp, so that everyone can see them. The urns

[1]The Germans mainly recognized, at least formally, international conventions defining the laws of war and the treatment of prisoners, especially those which had not been signed by Soviet Russia, whose citizens were accordingly labelled and treated as barbarians.

are to be returned to the Camp and buried there. I forbid that anything be recorded in writing concerning the shooting, or that any talks concerning this matter take place with any other Department, not even the Foreign Office. I hope, however, that the prisoners of war will get such a shock that in future they will not escape.

Very few knew the full facts, therefore, even in Germany. *No one*, it will be appreciated, knew the truth in Great Britain in the summer of 1944. The Foreign Secretary's statements[1] made assumptions of fact which were not justified later. Mr Eden could only promise that the truth would be pursued, the unknown criminals would be found.

It began in mist. The torches of those who were pursuing the truth could illuminate only small areas of visibility. The officers who eventually found the criminals were remote in their own separate activities of war, not yet assigned to the chase. There were five of them, and on the night when the Luftwaffe NCO Eichacher pinned up the General Staff's last derisive notice to the survivors of Stalag Luft III they were occupied in characteristic ways.

Wing Commander Wilfred Bowes was completing Stage One of the initiation rites he applied to taking over a new appointment at the headquarters of the Royal Air Force Special Investigation Branch in Princes Gate Court, a commandeered block of flats in Exhibition Road, South Kensington. That is to say, he was putting the fear of God into all his subordinates, using the remnants of a Geordie accent and a prime line in expletives. This prepared them for Stage Two, when he would support them through thick and thin against criticism or disapproval from any other source. Bowes was a stocky man aged forty-two, with a battered and pugnacious face. He was said, in the Service phrase, to have been in the Royal Air Force since Pontius was a pilot. Actually he had joined during the first year of life of the separate Service, after concealing his true age, and saw his first action in the Chanak Peninsula in Turkey. As a flight sergeant in the RAF Police he had headed the nucleus of the newly formed SIB, the criminal investigation department of the Service, and was later commissioned. He was a tenacious, if unorthodox, interrogator, with an unconcealed contempt for civilian detective procedures, particularly those of Scotland Yard. His swift clearing-up of a barrack-room larceny is a fair illustration of his intuitive method. He had the thirty men in the barrack-block concerned standing by their beds, and went round to each one, holding short, innocuous conversations about football, their families, or their opinion of the food in the mess. Then he ordered one man to be taken to his office, where the airman immediately confessed.

Squadron Leader Francis P. McKenna, then an aircrew sergeant, was receiving Communion in the chapel at Mildenhall. It was the

[1]See Appendix II, page 211.

evening of his first operation as flight engineer and second pilot in a Lancaster bomber of 622 Squadron. On his way to the chapel he saw his navigator, who asked, 'What's this in aid of?' 'Well, we may not come back', said McKenna. 'I've not been to Mass for years,' said the navigator, 'do you think I should go?' 'Come and make your peace', said McKenna. He was a dour, dry-humoured Lancastrian with pale grey eyes under George Robey eyebrows, a very athletic man of thirty-eight who had been a detective sergeant in the Blackpool Police. He had been locked in this reserved occupation until the high rate of Bomber Command losses caused a change in the rules, and he was able to volunteer for aircrew. He had had civilian flying experience, but was five years too old to be considered as a pilot. In July 1944 he was probably of all the investigators the most personally aware of the Stalag Luft III tragedy. He had known three officers held in Sagan, and two of them had been shot. He had heard, in a room full of aircrew, a BBC broadcast of Mr Eden's solemn words: 'His Majesty's Government . . . will never cease in their efforts to collect the evidence to identify all those responsible. They are firmly resolved that these foul criminals shall be tracked down to the last man, wherever they may take refuge. When the war is over they will be brought to exemplary justice.' McKenna said to another former policeman—the crew-room was full of action-starved ex-coppers at that stage of the war, 'He doesn't know what he's talking about. Track them down to the last man, in war-busted Germany, when they'll have the best sets of false papers the Gestapo can provide!' He could not foresee his future role, when he was to be the top-scorer for arrests of wanted men.

Flight Lieutenant Stephen H. Courtney was stomping about in the mud behind Caen, in Normandy, in conditions of heavy rain and ground-fog which were badly hampering the 2nd Tactical Air Force, to which he was attached as Warrant Officer in charge of the RAF Police Unit. It was seven weeks after D-Day. The ground-fighting was fierce, and he was limping badly with no hope of treatment because the overworked field hospitals were refusing casualties unless their injuries were bloodier than his. He was an energetic, hefty man of twenty-eight with an easy manner, very concerned with the welfare of his men, hard to identify with the solicitor's practice in Exeter to which he meant to return.

Flight Lieutenant Arthur R. Lyon was shaking off the exhaustion which a prolonged day of interrogation had caused him. He was a tall, slim, pipe-smoking man, also twenty-eight, with a flair for languages, who had passed top of the competitive entry to go on for graduation at the Hendon Police College, the controversial 'officer-material, Police Sandhurst' founded by Marshal of the Royal Air Force Lord Trenchard in 1934. He had served as a station inspector in various Metropolitan divisions, including a year in the East End during the London blitz, before joining the Intelligence Service of the Royal Air Force. As a fluent German-speaker, he was working in ADI(K),[1] a unit charged with the interrogation of captured members of the Luftwaffe who were thought to have specialized knowledge of new aircraft, armament, electronic equipment and tactics. Since most of the Luftwaffe prisoners of war were what the RAF called 'good types'—meaning that they gave as little under interrogation as, for example, the recaptured prisoners of Stalag Luft III volunteered—the job had its frustrations. Lyon, an extremely polished conversationalist, had been talking in German for some hours that day with a 'good type' who had answered with nothing but his number, rank and name in what ultimately became nerve-racking monotony with the third-degree on the wrong side of the table. Lyon had reported to his Group Captain, who merely vouchsafed this dialogue:

'Well, Dickie, what did you get out of him?'

'Nothing, sir.'

'What? Not a sausage?'

'No, sir. Nothing.'

'Go back and see him again.'

Compliance with that order, on a heavy, sunless summer evening, had demanded some degree of fortitude, and produced its own degree of lassitude, to which only a serious gin and tonic seemed the appropriate answer.

Flight Lieutenant Harold E. Harrison, then like McKenna an aircrew sergeant, was also, like McKenna, preparing for his first operational flight. He was a handsome, fair-haired, fresh-faced young man of twenty-one, who had had no career for the war to interrupt, had enlisted as soon as possible, had trained in North America and was now navigator of a Lancaster in 115 Squadron, Bomber Command. He had a facility in the German language which he vaguely hoped he would not have to use as a prisoner of war. But the prospect of being recruited as a ruthless limb of the law because of it had not yet sullied his mind.

Of these five men, McKenna was the first whom the Special Investigation Branch put into the lists against the 'foul criminals' indicated but not named by the Foreign Secretary. In character McKenna was perhaps the most complex. He had a very strong sense of mercy, as well as of justice. Seventeen years in the police force had not blunted his compassion, except in the active area of his professional duties. Here he had developed his own rather complicated detective competence based on personally framed routines, much conjecture about criminal thinking, and eternal vigilance—with the minimum dependence on outside specialists. This self-reliance made him prickly to the extent that he could not suffer fools in his own profession as gladly as villains outside it: but since, in either camp, he was inclined to strike first and talk later, the interests of justice were not betrayed.

[1]Air Directorate of Intelligence (K).

McKenna had a robust enthusiasm for sport and a candidly expressed sense of fear. His phobia was the sea, alongside which he had lived all his life. His nightmare was coming down in it. He might therefore have been expected to volunteer for some more landlocked Service than flying aircraft in Bomber Command, and he could never have agreed with an alternative more fervently than at the briefing for his first operational flight on 23rd July 1944. The crews sat facing the map in the briefing-room. The Wing Commander came in. 'This is where you're going tonight, you lucky people,' he said, and the top of his pointer touched the map at Mildenhall, went east to the coast at Cromer, and moved inexorably across the North Sea to Kiel. McKenna stared at the map and pictured the expanse of dark water. 'Oh, God Almighty, we'll never make it', he told himself. 'What's wrong with the Ruhr, flak and all?' He received Communion, drew parachute and survival kit, joined Q Queenie at its dispersal point. His pilot took off and they rendezvoused over Newmarket, climbing and circling to 15 000 feet until the sky seemed full of Lancasters—there were 750 of them with 3 000 tons of bombs destined for Kiel that night. The stream headed east. An aircraft in trouble dropped like a lift in front of their nose, bouncing them with the turbulence from its propellers. They ran in straight for twenty miles approaching Kiel. The aircraft soared and the floor banged as the bomb-door springs flew back when the load went down. McKenna pushed the throttles wide open, and his pilot shoved the stick forward all the way for the steep dive that was to take them below the rest of the flak. They eased out and away, throttled back for optimum fuel consumption on the cruise home, and McKenna kept his eyes all the time on the black sea below. 'If I'm to go through this for twenty-nine more ops, I shall only survive as a physical wreck', he told himself. And next time they sent him to the Ruhr!

After half a dozen trips his crew were transferred to 15 Squadron, and they took the role of Master Bomber, leading in the force. He was commissioned as an officer. He finished his tour by Christmas and, being switched to non-operational duties, worked with the Service Police. Because of his detective experience he was posted to SIB headquarters in London with orders to report to Group Captain Nicholas and Wing Commander Bowes.

He made his number at Princes Gate Court. In the waiting-room he met an acquaintance from the past, Flight Lieutenant Tommy Hill, who as a Service Police corporal in Blackpool had won the George Medal after an incident there. Hill greeted him, and was making other introductions when the door opened. A wing commander came in with papers in his hand which evidently displeased him, and with some ferocity he reprimanded an officer in front of the others. No one seemed to take any notice. The wing commander retired. Shortly afterwards he stood at the door again and fixed his eyes on McKenna.

'You,' he said across the room. 'Come here.'

'Excuse me, Tommy,' said McKenna, and he walked casually across.

'Who the bloody hellfire are you?'

'McKenna, sir.'

'Come with me.'

They walked into his office. 'Are you trying to pull my bloody leg?' asked Wing Commander Bowes.

'Me, sir? A pilot officer to a wing commander? Please give me more credit. I'm not trying to take advantage of anyone.'

'Where are you from?'

'Blackpool, sir.'

'I can hear that. Where are you from in Civvy Street?'

'Blackpool, sir, CID Blackpool.'

'Oh. Mr Bloody Sherlock Holmes, eh?'

'No, sir.'

'Did you do any good in the civil police?'

'I had some success, sir.'

'All right. Dismiss.'

McKenna came out of Bowes's offices and went back to Tommy Hill. 'What's the matter with that one?' he asked.

'Matter? Nothing. He's as good as gold. His heart's there.'

'Where?' asked McKenna.

'Oh, he's allowed to bollock anybody. The point is that nobody else can. He's absolutely loyal to his staff. If we make a boob he'll bollock us plenty, but no one else is allowed to criticize. You'll like Freddie Bowes.'

'I'll learn', said McKenna.

VE Day came, but at that stage of the summer there seemed no prospect of an end to the full war. McKenna was promoted to Flying Officer and, two months later, to acting Flight Lieutenant. He was working smoothly at jobs which were very similar to his detective tasks in Blackpool. Between barbed remarks at his CID background, Wing Commander Bowes sometimes called him Mac.

One morning Bowes sent for him. 'Come on, Sherlock, here's a nice job for you. A car taken from the officers' mess at Croydon ran into a tram at Thornton Heath at eleven last night. Two officers and two girls ran away. One of them left an officer's side cap with no identification marks. Solve it, Sherlock. Take Sergeant Evans.'

McKenna found the sergeant, signed for a car, and drove to Croydon. On the journey Evans said, 'We've not got much to work on here, sir.' McKenna said, 'Well, we can't approach a job in that frame of mind; let's just get stuck in.' 'You were CID, sir,' said Evans, 'do you mind if I watch?' McKenna said, 'You can do more than that. I'm not too familiar with Service Police procedure. Who do we report to at RAF Croydon?'

They got the necessary permission to come abòard, and saw the owner of the car. He had been very attached to it, but it was now a total write-off. They saw the mess secretary and the barman. The barman said the mess had been full of officers and guests, but he did remember two young officers with two blonde girls. They left between 9.30 and 9.45.

McKenna and Evans went back to their car. 'Put yourself in their position', said McKenna. 'A quarter to ten at night, two girls, no car, what do you do? Take a car from the park. Where do you go? Towards the bright lights. Which way to the West End? Turn left. So we turn left.' And he drove left out of the station gates.

'Quarter to ten. Too early for the bright lights to be really blazing. Had a few drinks, but probably not tanked up. What do we do? Aha, a pub within a quarter of a mile.' And McKenna pulled across to the public house called The Propeller.

The barmaid remembered two officers and two girls coming in at about ten. Didn't hear any Christian names used. Remembered that the officers both wore pilots' wings. Both had the ribbon of the DFC, too, but one was wearing it the wrong way round.

'Wrong way round!' said McKenna. 'What do you mean?'

'Well, he had it *after* his other medal ribbons', said the barmaid. 'The other boy had it in the centre as usual, with his Father, Son and Holy Ghost towards his shoulder.'

'Cheeky', said Sergeant Evans, as they went back to the car. 'But what do you make of it, sir?'

'An Allied air force', suggested McKenna. 'He would wear his native decorations first and foreigners afterwards. Now, turn towards London. What do we do? Look at the petrol. Perhaps we'd better get some before everything closes down for the night. Here's a service station.'

They called at the filling station. 'We are looking for two blonde girls who may have called here with two Air Force officers last night.' 'Now, that rings a bell', said the attendant. 'I wasn't on duty last night, but I do know of two blonde girls who go to the officers' mess at Croydon. I think they're sisters. I know the house where they live, but not the address. You turn left here, go right and left, and at a T-junction you'll see a house with some very distinctive curtains, like a lot of bouncing balls.' He described the curtains in more detail. 'Thank you very much,' said McKenna, and drove on, keeping an eye open for the left turn. Sergeant Evans was looking distinctly brighter.

They found the house, and McKenna knocked. After an interval a girl came to the door. She was blonde, and she would have been pretty if she had not had two black eyes. 'My name is Flight Lieutenant McKenna, and I've called on behalf of the Station Commander to express his regret for what happened last night. We want to know how you are, and if there's anything we can do.' 'Oh, that's very kind of you', said the girl, 'thank you very much. I'm not too bad really.' 'And how is your companion?' McKenna went on. 'It was your sister, wasn't it?' 'Yes.' 'Could we see her and pass on the

Station Commander's regret?' 'Well, come in, have a cup of tea.'

Over a cup of tea McKenna confided to the girls his immediate problem. 'I want to return the cap that one of your friends left at the scene of the accident, and I don't know which of them to give it to. Do you have any idea whose it could be?' And he produced the side cap.

'Well', said the second sister, 'it must be Bill's because the Dutchman had a peaked cap.'

'Oh, fine. Then there's no problem. Bill . . . Bill, who was it?'

'Don't know their last names', said the girl with a giggle. 'Just Bill and Jan.'

McKenna and Evans got back to RAF Croydon while lunch was still being served in the officers' mess. They waited in the car outside until two officers came out chatting. Both wore the ribbon of the DFC. One, wearing a peaked cap and the shoulder-flash NEDERLAND, had the decoration placed after other ribbons. The other carried no cap.

'Could I have a word with you for a few moments?' asked McKenna.

The English officer looked surprised. 'We've recovered your cap', said McKenna. 'This is it, isn't it? Please try it for size.'

The officer automatically placed the cap on his head, and it fitted.

'Now, about last night,' said McKenna. 'Do you want to tell me all about it, or do I have to tell you? What I do have to tell you is that I'm an RAF Provost Officer and this is an RAF Police Sergeant. Do you want to tell me about it?'

'I'd rather not here', said the officer. 'Can we go to my room?'

There was a succession of formalities, including a visit to the Station Commander and another to the civil police. At four o'clock McKenna and Evans arrived back at Princes Gate Court. They were met by Wing Commander Bowes. 'Look, Mac,' said Bowes, 'I've got a deep job for you. How long do you think you'll be having to work on this Croydon case? Can you estimate it?'

'Well, sir,' said McKenna, 'to be perfectly honest, I don't intend to waste another minute on it.'

'What do you mean?'

'Well, I've covered all the ground I can. I don't see any point in going further.'

Bowes flushed a little. 'Come off it. You've got to pursue these things right to the flaming end, you know. You can't talk about seeing no point in going further. You're not in the civil police now.'

'No, sir, I quite agree. But once you've squared it up and got the story pretty well watertight, what else is there to do but leave it to the Provost Marshal and the Legal Branch?'

Bowes was beginning to look cagey. Sergeant Evans had moved away and was keeping his hands rigidly on the seams of his trousers to stop him thrusting them in his ears.

'Don't talk in bloody parables to me, Sherlock. How far have you got?'

'Well, we've identified the two officers, we've seen the two girls, and we've got statements from all concerned.'

'Are you joking?'

'No, sir.'

Bowes looked at the clock on the wall. 'You flannelling bastard!' he said. 'Better come in and tell Nicky. He'll be delighted.' They went in to report to Group Captain Nicholas.

Nicholas slid a heavy parcel towards McKenna from the corner of his desk.

'I want you to take this pile of bumf to your billet, go through it all carefully, and come back and tell me what you think of it. I don't want to see you before then. I'll give you up to a week.'

'What is it, sir?' asked McKenna.

'The Stalag Luft III statements and appreciations, up to yesterday's date.'

McKenna said nothing.

'You know the Stalag Luft III case?' the group captain queried. 'All it involves? "Those foul criminals shall be brought to justice"?'

'He doesn't know what he's talking about', McKenna heard in his mind—the echo of one copper talking to another in an aircrew room half a lifetime ago. But all he said now was:

'Yes, sir.'

'And the SIB is going to do it', said Wing Commander Bowes, with a savage passion which did not distort his craggy red face but rather purified it.

DITTO

Wing Commander Bowes kept in his desk, as a spur to action if such a stimulus ever became necessary, perhaps the most cynical German archive that was ever collected during the Stalag Luft III inquiry. It consisted of five sheets of a register found in Munich, where German police and military records had been stored, and had been overlooked during the panic-stricken destruction of documents which coincided with the American advance on the city. The cover read: '15 June 1944. Decrease of strength in Air Force Prisoner-of-war Camp No. 3: Return No. 315'. The main pages were headed: 'Strength decrease through death.' They carried fifteen columns which, clumsily typed and sometimes misspelt, gave details of fifty officers: their nationality; prisoner-of-war number; name; date and place of birth; particulars of father, mother and next-of-kin; rank; arm of service; service number; date of capture. The fourteenth column read: 'Wounds, injuries, death (place of burial)'. The fifteenth column read: 'Remarks (e.g. strength increases from other camps, shot whilst trying to escape or mutiny)'.

Against the first name in the list there had been typed, in the fourteenth column, 'Beerdigungsplatz: Sagan—*Place of burial: Sagan*', *and in the fifteenth column,* 'Bei Fluchtversuch erschossen—*Shot whilst trying to escape*'.

For all names below the first in the list the German typist had declined to extend himself. Nothing had been entered in the fourteenth and fifteenth columns. Later a series of marks indicating ditto *had been inked in. For Brettell (British), Bull (British), Bushell (South African), Catanach (Australian), Christensen (New Zealand), Espelid and Fuglesang (Norwegian), and all the others in the long file of death it had not been worth the clerk's effort even to type the lie. 'Shot whilst trying to escape'.*

Ditto *seemed to Bowes the ultimate in contempt for these fallen men. He scanned the list often. He made a sixteenth column to take in, at the appropriate time, the names of the Germans who had shot each man, and the date the killers were accounted for. When consecutive entries concerned the same crime, the same murders, he scorned to write the sign for* ditto. *Jimmy Catanach and Arnold Christensen, consecutive entries in the register, had died in the same field, within minutes of each other, along with Hallada Espelid and Nils Fuglesang. When the time came Bowes carefully wrote against the German* ditto *the full names of the murderers, the dates of their arrest, and the dates of their execution, or suicide. Having completed the record for one victim, he painstakingly copied the relevant details against the next name.*

2 Survivors' tales

McKenna had taken a room in Fulham at the house of a retired policeman whose wife had been killed in the bombing. He lugged the parcel home, and sat down to read. It contained statements from Group Captain Massey, the repatriated Senior British Officer from Stalag Luft III; the reports from the Swiss Protecting Power; early Intelligence appreciations; the results of interrogations of German prisoners of war, captured in 1944, who had been found to have had some connection with Stalag Luft III or with the *Grossfahndung*, the great hue-and-cry in search of the escapers operating in March and April 1944; a chronology of events as seen from Sagan, compiled by the Senior British Officer who succeeded Massey, and forwarded to London through the Swiss; the sworn statements of survivors made at an official Court of Inquiry held at Sagan and, through brash enterprise, also forwarded to London in the Swiss diplomatic bag. Finally there were the narratives—more circumstantial because the narrators could be questioned by experienced interrogators—of all the survivors who had eventually come home to Great Britain after the war; with a sworn statement from the Frenchman Flight Lieutenant Van Wymeersch who, after his stay in Sachsenhausen and his subsequent escape, had no home to go to, his father having been shot as a member of the Resistance. There was nothing in writing from any Australian, Belgian, Greek, Lithuanian, Pole or South African, because all the recaptured officers of these nationalities had been shot.

McKenna read through these files repeatedly. From what details were available he tried wherever possible to build a mental picture of individual traits of character or achievement among the fifty officers who had been killed; for it seemed to him degrading to the dead, and even unhelpful to the investigation, to consider them as the numbered, labelled identical urns of grey ash which had been sent back to the camp. Retabulating all the evidence before him, he compiled as complete a chronology as he could. For the first time he began to appreciate the complexity of events.

Roger Bushell, the brooding, saturnine South African-born squadron leader who had been 'exiled' to Stalag Luft III after four previous escapes in Germany had been planning a mass break-out from Sagan for a year. As Big X, he had organized the simultaneous digging of three long tunnels, code-named Tom, Dick and Harry so that the word 'tunnel' should never be overheard by any German. Tom was discovered and dynamited by the camp authorities. Dick was eventually used as a repository for equipment used on Harry. Harry was ready in March 1944.

It ran from a shaft dug 28 feet down below a trapdoor in one of the huts, and extended for 360 feet to pass under the wire at a depth of 20 feet—still deep enough, it was hoped, for the sound of the digging not to be picked up by the microphones which the Germans had buried in the soil. Harry was ventilated by air-pumps designed by the Norwegian Jens Muller, and illuminated by electricity, the equipment being stolen and the current tapped from the camp supply. Over three thousand bedboards and floorboards had been commandeered, undetected by the guards, and carpentered by a team headed by the Australian squadron leader 'Willy' Williams for manufacture into box-frames, roughly 21 inches square, to shore up the passage. An underground trolley-railway running on rails of filched beading-laths served the whole length of the tunnel, using two interchange stations which were naturally named Piccadilly Circus and Leicester Square.

Six hundred officers had a hand in the tunnelling and the many escape services. The officer in charge of the entrance shaft, a Canadian flight lieutenant named Pat Langford, could, in emergency, close the trapdoor (sealing in the tunnellers) and swing a red-hot camp stove over it in twenty seconds. Lieutenant Clement McGarr, a South African, and Flight Lieutenant George McGill, a Canadian, commanded tunnelling parties of seventy-five workers each. The most energetic beavers in the tunnel were Flight Lieutenant Johnny Bull, Squadron Leader Tom Kirby-Green, who also headed Security, Flight Lieutenant 'Cookie' Long and Flying Officer Harry Birkland, a Canadian who had insisted on working naked until his boss decided that the sand-scars on his knees and elbows would tell too many tales if he were suddenly strip-searched by the guards. Birkland had to go back to winter vests and long johns, like all the others.

Al Hake, an Australian flight lieutenant, ran a factory which made two hundred compasses out of melted gramophone records and magnetized sewing needles. Flight Lieutenant Tim Walenn, behind the cover of a huge P/O Prune moustache, ran the forgery department, known as Dean & Dawson after the travel agents, which produced four hundred forged passes, identity papers, and even forged personal letters and industrial orders on embossed business notepaper which could establish identity. Every 'printed' and 'typed' character in all these forgeries was painted by hand, even the typewriting mistakes. Flight Lieutenant Gordon Brettell, once a racing driver, used his sensitive hands to cut the rubber stamps for these passes out of linoleum and boot heels, and embossed the hand-made writing paper from the back of a toothbrush. All these necessities were carefully stored for the great day in a complex of safe-deposits maintained by Flight Lieutenant Mike Casey.

A young Belgian flight lieutenant with the Croix de Guerre, Henri Picard, was one of the most meticulous artists in this band of fifty forgers and their security stooges. Genuine photographs for the passes were taken in his clandestine studio by Flight Lieutenant 'Chaz' Hall (who was also the expert weather forecaster) with a camera brutally blackmailed from a compromised German guard by the Czech flight lieutenant Ernst Valenta, complying with an unrelenting order from Roger Bushell.

A pillar of the forgery department was the Lithuanian flight lieutenant Romas Marcinkus—but Marcinkus was a pillar of every department. He was the principal pumper of information from soft Germans. He was intelligence expert for the Baltic and the Low Countries; intelligence and language adviser to the forgery department; and grand Know-All on the economics, military dispositions and transport opportunities within Germany. Using an enormous file of German newspapers which the Camp Censor kindly allowed him, with a Baedeker and a railway time-table which the Censor was not consulted about, he compiled an exhaustive dossier of the week-to-week changes in everyday German life, locations of industry, and above all the railway timings which were essential to any 'compleat' escaper. Marcinkus could read between the lines, for instance, and know that Aachen had suffered heavy recent bombing raids. All travel into seriously bombed areas was banned until communications were restored: therefore it was not only futile, but an invitation to arrest the holder on suspicion, for Tim Walenn to issue a (forged) railway pass to go to Aachen.

Others in the intelligence network were the New Zealand flying officer Arnold Christensen, specializing in Denmark, from which his father had emigrated; the French lieutenant Bernard Scheidhauer, and the omniscient Ernie Valenta. A very busy map department, which produced over a thousand detailed and extremely accurate four-colour maps, had the Polish flying officer Adam Kolanowski on its strength. Another Polish flying officer, Jerzy Mondschein, worked in the tailoring department, which produced from blankets fifty full civilian suits for those going by train and other upper-class escapers, and showed the remaining 150 how to dye or shave uniforms into something sufficiently different. The tailors' best effort was the manufacture of a detailed German Army uniform to be worn by another Pole, Flying Officer Pawel Tobolski.

A considerable stock of genuine German money was slowly accumulated, by devious means, so that tickets and sustenance could be bought, and emergency bribery provided. There was also a food factory which supplied to each of the two hundred who were expected to escape ten days' rations of a concentrated fudge made of sugar, cocoa, Bemax, condensed milk, raisins, oats, margarine and chocolate. It proved a highly indigestible mixture when it had all to be disposed of in a hurry before strip-searching of the 120 who were destined not to get out of the tunnel.

The mass break-out was planned for 24th March. It was a moonless night, and a Friday. The next night was also moonless, but the late trains would be running on Sunday timetables, which were inefficient. The weather was bad, but Bushell decided that the occasion had to be seized, because he did not believe that his security could hold out for another month.

Already Bushell knew of ominous happenings. Exactly a month earlier, on another moonless night, Hauptmann Pieber of the Luftwaffe, the well-intentioned Camp Adjutant, had warned Flight Lieutenant Harry Marshall—one of his favourites, and a hardened escaper—that there must be no mass escapes, never more than six at a time, since the Gestapo had threatened to take matters into their own hands in the camps if such a thing occurred. Just before the escape, Oberst von Lindeiner-Wildau, the Camp Commandant, had called Group Captain Massey with his senior officers, chaplains and doctors to a conference and had given a sincere, though veiled, warning against mass escapes.

What Bushell did not know—but McKenna, reading the files retrospectively, now knew—was that there had been an additional sequence of three menacing events.

In February the area officer responsible for prisoner-of-war security, a Berlin-controlled inspector called Brünner, had called on the Commandant at Sagan at the Commandant's suggestion, because von Lindeiner-Wildau sensed that an escape was imminent and wanted to avoid its consequences. Brünner came for less than an hour, which he passed entirely in conversation with the Commandant, and without any inspection of anti-escape measures within the camp, which it was his duty to check, and which the Commandant had urgently asked him to complete. He did not order that the microphones for detecting tunnelling activities—which had been taken out of action for maintenance and improvement of the system—should be switched on for the emergency which the Commandant feared. It had been earlier experienced in the camp that when the Germans knew of a prisoner-of-war activity such as a tunnel they did not always pounce on it, but waited until it was more mature, and involved more people. Brünner's inactivity gave rise to a suspicion in the Judge Advocate General's department in London that it was higher German policy to encourage the escape and then take strong countermeasures—and the Commandant, knowing or suspecting this, sincerely tried to dissuade the prisoners from escaping.

This theory was supported by the fact that, also in February 1944, the German High Command had issued an order known as Stufe

Römisch III[1] decreeing that any recaptured escaped prisoner-of-war officer, 'whether it is an escape during transit, a mass escape or a single escape', was not to be returned to the military authorities, but handed over to the Security Police; and this hand-over was not to be revealed to other prisoners of war, to the German military authorities, the Protecting Power or the International Red Cross—the report was merely to be that he had never been traced. This treatment was mandatory for officers of all nationalities except British and American, and the latter were to be put into police prisons while their cases received individual consideration.

In the next month, March 1944, this order was amplified by the Gestapo in a secret circular entitled Operation Bullet [Aktion Kugel] which said that all recaptured officers held under Stufe Römisch III were to be handed over to the Gestapo in secret and transported to Mauthausen concentration camp for extermination—again, with no formal record of their fate being passed on to their own people, or to the German military authorities, or to the international supervising Powers. It has been learned since the German capitulation that the execution methods at Mauthausen ranged from the Gestapo pistol in the nape of the neck to a hidden explosive device built into an ordinary-looking height-measurer, which was fired when officers, ordered to strip for medical examination, stepped on to the platform for their height to be registered.

It was against this complicated background of preparation and menace that the escape took place.

There were three unforeseen factors which impeded its success.

The first was sheer error, uncharacteristic after the meticulous planning over the last twelve months. The tunnel was halted several feet short of where it should have reached. It was not through pressure of time. It could have been extended with three days' effort during the excavation. It was a miscalculation. The exit shaft came up into open ground. The result was a serious delay in getting each man away from the exit and into cover. The cumulative delay kept half of the would-be escapers away from any taste of freedom—but also, of course, from any taste of Hitler's vengeance.

The second impediment was caused by accident. It proved far more difficult than could reasonably have been foreseen to open the exit shaft at the surface. That mishap cut the time available for escape by over an hour.

The third factor was a decision by Air Chief Marshal Sir Arthur Harris to bomb Berlin on the night of the escape. Berlin was a hundred miles north-west of Sagan, which was directly affected by diversionary flights coming down from the north, less predictably by the normal bomber stream converging on the capital. But on this particular occasion unforecast high winds scattered the bombers from their narrow line of battle and swept them east of Berlin.

[1]Literally, Grade Roman III, a code title.

The Commander-in-Chief Bomber Command had, throughout the winter, doggedly fought the Battle of Berlin in a long, poker-faced confrontation with the Air Staff, who were unconvinced of its value. Harris finally had to concede defeat in this intended knock-out blow against Germany, because his losses from German night-fighter attacks became insupportable. He decided to make his last throw, on 24th March 1944—and he lost again. He put up 791 bombers, and 72 did not return. (Göring sent 100 bombers that night—all the *Terrorfliegen* he could muster, since he had concentrated on night-fighters—over London and south-east England, which experienced their heaviest raid for a considerable time.)

Stalag Luft III had been unaffected by air-raid warnings for some weeks. The disorganization of this last raid ate savagely into the escape-time available.

Even an operation as vast as the D-Day invasion could be postponed because of adverse conditions. This was not possible with the escape from Stalag Luft III. The date-stamps on the forged passes were one of the most critical factors—simply because they were not roughly stamped on in a second, as with genuine passes, but needed far more care when they were applied. With four hundred passes, a whole year's production, capable of being ruined by bearing the wrong stamp, the date decided for the break-out had to be final.

Bushell had to make this decision a fortnight ahead. What was more dangerous from a security angle was that the two hundred officers chosen to make the escape attempt had to know the decision a fortnight ahead, and even know the order in which they would leave the tunnel. The reason for this was that the escapers had to be fitted out with the correct clothes for the roles they were playing, they had to be given time to learn their route, and they had to be word-perfect in their cover stories to cope with the numerous occasions when they would be challenged en route, not necessarily out of suspicion but because that is what citizens of a police state had to get used to.

Selection of two hundred escapers out of six hundred eligible officers—the total who had worked on the whole project—was a delicate enough process in itself. In all realism, it had to be accepted that it was also a highly vulnerable act from the security point of view. Even with a camp of such high morale as Stalag Luft III, *nothing* had to be rated as inconceivable—even the fact that a disappointed officer might inadvertently or otherwise over-react—and therefore even the selection was done in a somewhat cabalistic fashion, with no one being told more than he needed to know. There were, after all, eight hundred other officers in the camp who had not entered the escape project, and their concentration on other activities was a necessary part of the cover for the six hundred. They had learned to ask no questions, express no surprise, and to respect the authority of their Little X and Little S, the subordinate officers in charge of Escape and Security in each separate hut. Roger

Bushell's memorable advice to a newcomer to the Stalag had been, 'If you see me walking round the camp with a tree-trunk sticking out of my arse, take no notice, ask no questions. I'll be doing it for a good cause.'

What could not be entirely eliminated was the fact that the camp was a living organism, with an organic psychology expressing gloom or optimism according to tiny changes of mood in its cells. Big X could repress the symptoms of mood in individuals with all his powerful prestige. But the camp was burning with escape fever, however damped down it was by personal effort. The sensitive Commandant *knew* that something serious was afoot, and made every effort to penetrate the secret. Security was at its most delicate stage. But all the time the long tunnel called Harry stretched out beyond the wire, undiscovered.

The Escape Committee had reserved the first thirty places in the order of exit for those whom they considered had the best chance of making a clean getaway. They allocated these to good German-speakers and those who needed to be out early to catch trains making connections to such distant places as Berlin, Stettin, Danzig and Munich. The rest of the escapers, known as the 'hard-arsers', had to walk. Some were carrying suitcases, and they went first after the train travellers. The others had a few necessities hammock-rolled in a blanket. It was known from the start that many would be caught, but there was a known and calculated cover from the thousands of displaced persons and transient forced labourers—whose clothes were very similar to the dyed adaptations of uniforms worn by the hard-arsers—at that time common on the roads of Germany. And the disorganization in the Reich caused by the attempt to catch the vagrant escapers was considered a useful contribution to the Allied war effort.

The seeded thirty were nominated. The names of the other 570 applicants were written on tickets for a series of complicated lotteries. In addition, four places were reserved for the camp administrative staff and four for the entertainment officers. Their activities had been too restrictive to allow them any great opportunity to work on the practical preparation of the escape, but had been highly necessary to keep the camp running on a level of normality.

The names of the thirty priority escapers went into a lottery to decide the final order of their exit. Then the names of forty officers who had been the key workers on the actual tunnelling were put into a hat, and twenty were drawn. Then the names of the thirty most active workers in the entire escape organization were put in, and twenty were drawn. All the losers in previous lotteries were then put in again with the complete list of applicants to escape, and the draw went on until a total of two hundred had been chosen, all in a precise order of exit. One marshal was allotted to every ten officers, and it was his duty to see that each of his men was supplied with the necessary clothing, papers, money, food, ration cards, maps and compass, and had a session with an intelligence expert to correct the plausibility of his cover story.

The escape began. There were heart-breaking snags. The exit shaft was jammed, and when the surface was at last broken through it was found to be short of the trees among which it should have emerged. Bushell grimly decided to carry on, but the pace was slowed. Towards midnight the air-raid alarm sounded, and the electric lighting went out. The grease-lamps with which the tunnellers had always worked in the daytime were installed. The trolleys, hauled by men in Piccadilly Circus and Leicester Square, again ran up and down the 21-inch square passage, where a broad man had to hunch his shoulders, lying prone, to pass through. Around one o'clock there was a complete hold-up. A frame in the first section of the tunnel had been knocked out and had brought down a heavy fall of sand. Flight Lieutenant Long, then hauling from the Piccadilly station, crawled back, reset the frame, and spread the considerable pile of sand between the railway lines. He worked feverishly, but the delay lasted half an hour. Almost as soon as it was rectified there was a tunnel collapse in the second section, and Long crawled up to remedy that, an operation which expended another twenty minutes. When it was known that dawn was breaking the officers in charge announced that Number 87 would be the last man through the tunnel, to be followed by a closing-up party who would try to reseal the exit shaft in order to give the escapers a chance through its belated discovery. But, while the last eight escapers were still in the tunnel or crouched in the exit shaft, a shot was heard. A sentry had stumbled across the hole in the ground. Seventy-nine men had got out, but three of them gave themselves up immediately to save the life of the eightieth, in the very mouth of the tunnel, whom the sentry was about to shoot. It was 4.55 a.m., 25th March 1944.

There followed three hours of murderous chaos—murderous because the infuriated and humiliated German guards had their fingers on the triggers of revolvers, tommy-guns and machine-guns—while a full muster of the camp was called and a photographic check of every prisoner was completed to ascertain who had escaped. The total was seventy-six, excluding the officers in the shaft and the three in the snow round the exit, who were immediately sent to solitary confinement.

During the roll-call an officer on the Stalag Luft III staff made forty-two telephone calls to the points which had, by regulation, to be given immediate notice of an escape. Besides superior offices in the Luftwaffe Prisoner-of-War Command, these included all local railway stations and aerodromes—for in previous escapes from the camp officers had tried to take over suitable aircraft: however, the calls were not prompt enough to prevent a number of escapers catching local trains at about six in the morning.

The most effective telephone message was to the head of the

Criminal Police of the area, SS Obersturmbannführer Max Wielen at Breslau. Wielen immediately instituted a *Kriegsfahndung*, a war emergency manhunt. He quickly upgraded this order to the top level, of *Grossfahndung*, the national hue-and-cry, which switched into the operation all available forces of the police, the SS, the Armed Forces, the Hitler Youth, and even Air Raid Precaution personnel. This fine network of scores of thousands of searching men was charged to examine the papers of everyone encountered. It was a highly competent organization. Allied Intelligence knew the results of a previous *Grossfahndung* which had been instituted after an escape of forty-three British and American flyers. Altogether, some 14 000 persons were arrested: 809 prisoners of war who were living in comparative security after previous escapes; 8 281 foreign workers who had deserted from their places of employment; 4 825 criminals and other persons wanted by the police.

In the early afternoon following the dawn escape, the two officers most closely concerned with regional prisoner-of-war security arrived at Sagan. They were the SS Major Brünner and Captain Absalon. Brünner returned to Breslau that day, but Absalon and two subordinates remained at the camp for a week and revisited it afterwards. The Commandant, Colonel Lindeiner, had already formally requested that he should be court-martialled following the break-out, but he was told that he was under arrest in any case. He learned that sixteen recaptured officers were already held in Sagan civil police station, and telephoned the Criminal Police there asking that they should be returned to the camp, according to existing procedure. He was told that he had been superseded in command, and no orders from him would be accepted. Later he learned that the officers in question had been removed some thirty-six miles to Görlitz gaol and, in the words of a local *Bürgermeister*, 'laid out'.

While the 64-year-old Colonel Lindeiner was under immediate arrest he suffered from a heart attack. Much later he was tried by court-martial and sentenced to a year's fortress imprisonment. Before his appeal was heard he had a nervous breakdown, and his recovery delayed the promulgation of the sentence into the period of collapse of the Germans before the Russian and Allied armies. He did not, in fact, serve the sentence.

On the evening following the escape, Saturday 25th March 1944, Major-General Adolf Westhoff, a high officer of the German General Staff, was travelling to the headquarters of the High Command at Berchtesgaden with Major-General von Graevenitz, whom he was about to succeed as general staff officer in charge of prisoner-of-war affairs. Halfway through the night journey they were informed of the mass escape from Sagan. When they met Field-Marshal Wilhelm Keitel, Chief of the High Command, he was extremely excited. He said that he had just come from an interview with Hitler, who already knew about the escape, and in his rage had ordered that the officers should be shot on recapture. Göring, as Head of the Luftwaffe, Himmler, as Head of Security, and Keitel, with ultimate control over all prisoners of war, had had a furious quarrel in front of Hitler, each blaming the others for the escape. Himmler stormed at Keitel that it would take an operation by sixty to seventy thousand men of the Home Guard alone to recover the officers. When Hitler repeated that they were to be shot anyway Göring pointed out that an all-out massacre could never be covered up, and would result in reprisals against Luftwaffe prisoners in Allied hands.

Hitler yielded slightly. 'Then more than half are to be shot', he decreed. Himmler fixed fifty as a suitable number, and set up the machinery for dispatching them, ruling that the matter was to be kept at Top Secret level and confined within his own Security department. When Keitel gave Westhoff and von Graevenitz this news he elaborated his own part in the affair and said that the bodies of the murdered officers were to be cremated and returned to Stalag Luft III as a deterrent. Both Westhoff and von Graevenitz pointed out that the suggested shootings and the proposed cremations were equally contrary to the Geneva Convention. Later, in spite of Keitel's order that nothing concerning this matter should be put down in writing, Westhoff wrote a summary of the conversations at Berchtesgaden and sent it to Keitel for his confirmation that this was what had occured. Keitel returned the minute with but one alteration, an amendment to Westhoff's note that the officers were to be shot. He crossed out the word 'shot' and wrote in the margin 'I did not exactly say "shot", but "handed over to the Gestapo".'

Himmler called his second-in-command of Security, Dr Ernst Kaltenbrunner, who prepared the text of a top-secret teleprinter message which was to be sent to Gestapo headquarters in the areas where escaped officers were recaptured. It laid down that the officers were to be taken by road in the direction of Sagan and shot en route. A report was to be sent in that they were shot while trying to escape.

The general order was that recaptured officers would on arrest be held by the Criminal Police, and fifty of them would later be handed over to the Gestapo to be killed. Kaltenbrunner conveyed this to Müller and Nebe, the men immediately subordinate to him in Berlin as the heads of the Gestapo and Kripo respectively. Nebe was to make the selection deciding which officers were to be shot. Nebe sent for the records and photographs of all seventy-six officers who had made an effective escape. The Security Headquarters in Berlin had a duplicate card-index of every officer prisoner of war of the rank of colonel and above; but all captured aircrew, of any rank, were considered outstanding personages, and their records were held in Berlin as well as at their prison camp.

Although many of the escaping officers were still making their way by various means to the frontiers of Germany, some half of the total had already been caught comparatively near to Sagan, and were held in Kripo gaols within the Breslau administrative district. Nebe sent for Wielen, head of the Breslau Kripo, to come to see him in the Kripo headquarters in Berlin.

An account by Wielen of this interview was available. Wielen had later been ousted by political in-fighting at Breslau, and had been transferred to Cologne. He was captured by the British before the end of the war, after their advance over the Rhine. He had been interrogated on the Sagan murders, and had made a statement. There was as yet no corroboration of what he reported, and it was likely that he was incriminating himself as little as possible. He said that Nebe told him in Berlin to hand over any nominated prisoners to the head of the Breslau Gestapo, Dr Wilhelm Scharpwinkel, who would take over the shootings. Wielen said he had strongly protested but Nebe had replied that the responsibility would lie with the Gestapo.

Within Sagan camp the Royal Air Force officers had naturally only very limited knowledge of what was going on. By 6th April six recaptured officers had been returned to Stalag Luft III and placed in solitary confinement. At ten o'clock that morning the Senior British Officer, Group Captain Massey, was summoned to the office of the new Commandant, von Lindeiner's successor. Massey arrived with Squadron Leader Murray, his interpreter. The Commandant stood and read from a statement he held:

'With reference to the recent escapes from Stalag Luft III, Sagan, I am ordered by the German High Command to state that forty-one of the escapers were shot while resisting arrest or in their endeavours to escape again after having been rearrested.'

Breathless with personal shock, Squadron Leader Murray had some difficulty in conveying this announcement in English.

Group Captain Massey asked for a repetition. Then he said:

'How many were wounded?'

The Commandant quoted the statement yet again, and said that he could not amplify it.

Group Captain Massey persisted in his question. 'How many were wounded?'

'None', said the Commandant.

On that afternoon eight more officers were escorted to the camp by Luftwaffe guards and placed in solitary confinement. The total then was 79 escaped; 3 caught at the tunnel mouth; 14 returned to Sagan; 41 reported dead; 21 unaccounted for. Soon afterwards another officer was brought back to Sagan.

On 11th April Group Captain Massey left Sagan on the first stage of his repatriation. On 15th April the new Senior British Officer, Group Captain D. E. L. Wilson of the Royal Australian Air Force, was given a list of the names of forty-seven officers shot, not of forty-one as had been expected. On 17th April the camp was visited by M. Gabriel Naville, representative of the Swiss Protecting Power, and Group Captain Wilson gave him a full report. By 12th

May three more names, making a total of fifty officers killed, were given to the Swiss, who later communicated them to the British Foreign Office. Over the next two months forty-six cremation urns and four boxes containing ashes were delivered to Stalag Luft III. On 23rd June 1944 the Secretary of State for Foreign Affairs, Mr Anthony Eden, made a second statement to the House of Commons,[1] and said that the German Government had assured the Protecting Power that a final communication giving full details would be forthcoming. On 22nd July Hitler sent for the cover-up statement which the German Foreign Office had been preparing, after urgent inquiries to the Luftwaffe Command about a matter concerning which they had been given no details at all. Hitler read the draft statement, and tore it up. He wrote a substitute statement himself, and tore that up. Then he instructed his Foreign Minister, Ribbentrop, that in view of Eden's insolent remarks about the previous report, Germany refused to make any other statement on the subject.

Over the next months the officers of the Judge Advocate General's Military Department collected from secret sources what intelligence they could about the Sagan crime. Over the next year they collated the statements of the survivors. It was not a comprehensively informative document.

At a quarter to nine on the night of 24th March 1944 Johnny Bull went down the shaft, followed by the first pairs of escapers. They were Flight Lieutenants Henry Marshall, a pillar of the tunnel committee, and Ernst Valenta; Roger Bushell with the Frenchman, Bernard Scheidhauer; and two South Africans, Lieutenants Johannes Gouws from the Orange Free State and Rupert Stevens, London-born but domiciled in Cape Town. Bull had to trolley by hand up the tunnel for 120 yards to knock through the last feet of soil at the top of the far shaft in order to open the tunnel. The planks shoring up the roof here had become jammed, and the exit was not clear until a quarter-past ten. When Bull finally shovelled his way through to the cold night air, and cautiously took a sight of the terrain, he was shocked to discover that the exit shaft was five yards short of the cover of the trees, and dangerously near the stilts of one of the guard-box pylons, where a sentry above was weaving his searchlight over the huts of the silent camp. Bull came down, devised a new drill for passing the signal to a waiting man to indicate when it was safe to come out, then climbed out of the shaft and crawled into the woods trailing a rope which was to be pulled to pass the all-clear.

One by one he marshalled twenty men out of the tunnel. As he was expecting his relief—to enable him to crawl to freedom himself—the air-raid siren sounded.

The searchlights went out as the main switch was slammed off in camp headquarters. But the tunnel, which had been lit by borrowed electricity, was in darkness too. Wing Commander Day, who was

[1]See Appendix II, p. 212.

at the bottom of the entrance shaft, took home-made tallow lamps along the tunnel and reorganized the procedure.

Johnny Bull's relief came through to take the signal rope, and Bull moved off into the wood to form the nucleus of a party of twelve, with Flying Officer Jerzy Mondschein as their language expert and travel courier. Their intention was to take a train from a small station south of Sagan to Bober-Rohrsdorf, on the outskirts of Hirschberg and comparatively near the Czech frontier. Eventually the party was completed and they moved off to find the station. Besides Mondschein of the tailoring department, there were Willy Williams the head carpenter; Pop Green, a flight lieutenant with a 1914–18 MC; Major Dodge; Lieutenant Poynter, RN, of the Fleet Air Arm; Flight Lieutenant B. A. ('Jimmy') James, a seasoned escaper; a cheerful Greek flyer named Sotiris Skanzikas and called Skan; an Australian flight lieutenant, R. V. ('Rusty') Kierath; two Poles, Flying Officer Kazimierz Pawluk and Flight Lieutenant Antoni Kiewnarski; and a Scots-Canadian flight lieutenant, James Wernham. Because of the delays of the night they had to wait for a train until nearly six o'clock in the morning. They left it three hours later, and separated into smaller parties.

Bull, Kierath, Mondschein and Williams stayed together. They got well south of Hirschberg and then took to the mountains to cross the Czechoslovak border, which was still maintained as a reinforced defence line because of the troublesome unwillingness of the Czechs to accept incorporation into the Greater Reich. On that day the four men ran into a military mountain patrol and were captured. They were seen only once more by any witness whose evidence later reached London. The Czech flight lieutenant Tonder and his travelling companion, Flying Officer John G. Stower, had emerged from the tunnel as Numbers 21 and 22 in the exit order and, having no need to wait for the formation of a large party, had trudged off south. Because of the juggled start caused by the re-arrangement of the exit drill and the air-raid warning. Tonder knew that they would have to wait hours for a train, and they altered their previous plans and decided to carry on marching. They walked south for three nights, and then reverted to the railway. But the search was at full pressure by then, and they were arrested when their papers were challenged on the train.

They were taken to Reichenberg gaol, within Czechoslovakian territory. Here they met the other four. Tonder's private conclusion was that their friends had been very shaken by interrogation, and that Squadron Leader Williams, at least, had been told that he would be shot. Johnny Bull, Rusty Kierath, Jerzy Mondschein and Willy Williams were taken from the gaol at four in the morning of the fifth day after the escape. Their ashes were later returned to Stalag Luft III with the town Brüx stamped on each urn as the place of cremation, and the date marked as 29th March 1944.

Tonder was later subjected to intensive Gestapo interrogation regarding his contacts in Czechoslovakia, and was kept in various gaols until December 1944. Tonder never saw Stower after his first interrogation, though he talked to him through the cell wall during the day after the departure of the other four. Johnny Stower had already notched one brave escape from Stalag Luft III through Czechoslovakia, and had actually penetrated Swiss territory unknowingly before inadvertently wandering back into German hands. He was taken from Reichenberg at eight in the morning of 31st March 1944. An urn bearing his name and giving that day as the date of his death, but with no place of cremation, was later delivered to Sagan.

Of the remaining eight in Mondschein's original party, Jimmy Wernham and John Dodge travelled together into Hirschberg and tried to buy fresh railway tickets at a suburban railway station. They were refused tickets, and they went into the town, where they were more successful at the main railway station. They were sitting in a train, awaiting its six o'clock departure, when Gestapo officials asked for their papers and arrested them. In Hirschberg gaol they met others from their party—Jimmy James, Pop Green, Lieutenant Poynter, RN, Kazimierz Pawluk, Antoni Kiewnarski, and Skan Skanzikas. Dodge and James were removed to Sachsenhausen, Green and Poynter were eventually returned to Stalag Luft III. But Wernham and Skanzikas were taken from Hirschberg in the morning of 29th March 1944. Their urns were sent to Sagan marked with the next day as the date of their death and with no place of cremation. Pawluk and Kiewnarski went in the afternoon. Their urns announced 31st March 1944 as the date of their death, but gave no place of cremation.

When Johnny Bull went down the tunnel on the night of the escape he was immediately followed by Flight Lieutenants Henry Marshall and Ernst Valenta, and they were the first away. They had intended to go by train from Sagan to Breslau, take another train to the Czech frontier, and walk over the border. Once there Valenta expected to find friends among the Czech Resistance. The delay in everyone's departure resulted in their arriving at Sagan station to find that they had missed three convenient trains, and they decided to walk straight south. They trudged through deep snow until nine next morning, and then hid up for the day in a fir plantation. It snowed all day, and they were suffering from cold and exposure when they set off again after dark. At four the next morning they were challenged by Home Guards and were arrested. When they were taken to the local lock-up they found three brother officers already there. They were Flight Lieutenants Shorty Armstrong and Paul Royle, and Edgar Humphreys, who had been rigorously stripped and searched. Later they were all taken to the civil gaol at Sagan, where there were other recaptured officers led by Chaz Hall, the photographer and weatherman. After another day, there were nineteen officers in the cells. They were then loaded aboard a lorry and taken away from Sagan, to Görlitz gaol thirty-six miles south. More recaptured men were crowded in here, until eventually there were thirty-five.

Twelve of these officers survived, and what was known of the fate of the other twenty-three was recorded from their statements. They were all very harshly interrogated, though without physical violence. Flight Lieutenant Mike Casey, the strong-box treasurer of all the forged papers, was told that he would lose his head. The Canadian Flight Lieutenant George Wiley was told that he would be shot, as were Tom Leigh, an Australian-born RAF flight lieutenant, and Flight Lieutenant Cyril Swain, a Shropshire man. Flight Lieutenant Ernie Valenta was told that he would never escape again, and Flying Officer Adam Kolanowski, the Polish cartographer, would not disclose what was said to him but seemed very depressed after interrogation. Flight Lieutenants William Grisman and Harold Milford were told that they would never see their wives again. Flight Lieutenant Alastair Gunn, from Perthshire, was told that he would lose his head. Flying Officer Denys Street, the son of Great Britain's Permanent Under-Secretary for Air, Sir Arthur Street, whose familiar signature was subscribed at the foot of so many King's Regulation amendments, was also warned that he could be shot.

All these threats were carried out. On 30th March 1944 two of the survivors saw through their cell windows three large cars draw up, with ten guards in the uniform Chicago-style civilian clothes affected by the Gestapo. Six officers were put into the cars. They were Squadron Leader Ian Cross, who had made one unsuccessful escape before, Flight Lieutenants Mike Casey, George Wiley, Al Hake and Tom Leigh, and Flying Officer John Pohe, a jokey New Zealander from Wanganui who signed all his official forms for the Germans as Porokoru Patapu and gave his nationality as Maori. Al Hake, the Australian compass-maker, could hardly walk. He had contracted frost-bite during the hard days after his escape from Sagan. Those watching from the windows thought he was being taken to hospital. The urn bearing his name and ashes was sent to Stalag Luft III with those of his companions. The inscription stamped in the base declared that they had died on 31st March 1944 and had been cremated at Görlitz.

The next day ten officers were taken away by civilians. They were Flight Lieutenants Edgar Humphreys; George McGill, the tunnel team leader; Cyril Swain; Ernie Valenta, the busy intelligence man; Chaz Hall; Pat Langford, the quick-action wizard of the trapdoor; Brian Evans; and Flying Officers Adam Kolanowski, Bob Stewart and Harry Birkland, the toughest tunneller of them all. The plates on their urns showed later that they had been cremated at Liegnitz, fifty-five miles to the east, and well away from Sagan, but no date was shown.

Two days later four officers were taken back to Sagan by rail under Luftwaffe escort. They did not then appreciate that to have a uniformed guard spelt comparative safety. They were put into solitary confinement at the camp, but they were eventually able to make their reports at the Court of Inquiry which the Senior British Officer set up inside Stalag Luft III.

On 6th April 1944, thirteen days after the escape, eight other officers were sent back to Sagan in a truck with Luftwaffe escort. Görlitz gaol was almost quiet then. For, in the dark before dawn that day, six more prisoners had been taken away. None of the survivors saw them go, merely knew that they had gone. These six were Flying Officer Denys Street; Lieutenant Clement McGarr of the South African Air Force, who had led the second-shift tunnelling team which took over from McGill's; and Flight Lieutenants William Grisman, of Hereford, who had led a party of 'hard-arsers' west through the woods outside Sagan only fifty minutes before the escape was discovered; Alastair Gunn of Auchterarder; Harold Milford of Streatham; and John Francis Williams of Ewell, who had all been in the same party since they walked together out of the woods at Sagan, and died together in a place unknown. The six urns were marked to show cremation at Breslau (now Wrocław), ninety miles east of Görlitz gaol, but the date was not stated.

One man remained in Görlitz. He was Flight Lieutenant James L. R. ('Cookie') Long. The tunnel had been his particular pride, and he had made two emergency repairs when the roof fell in during the night of the escape. When he had finally consented to leave he had walked for the rest of the night with one small party, hidden up at dawn, and walked for the next night along the railway line towards Frankfurt an der Oder. He hid in a barn for that day, and after dark went to a marshalling-yard to try train-jumping. No train slow enough to be boarded passed that night, and he went back to his barn. Finally he started walking, but he was arrested by a Home Guard Patrol. After passing through a gradation of civil gaols, he was finally brought to Görlitz. Here he ominously moved daily down the line of cells leading to the Gestapo escort until he was in the cell by the door. There was one other Royal Air Force officer left in the gaol, Flight Lieutenant Ellis. He had, by coincidence, escaped on the same night as the seventy-six, but not from the north compound of Stalag Luft III; he was not therefore on the Gestapo's sheaf of index cards, and he was subsequently returned to his camp, and made his report after the war. These two officers used to lend each other the solitary comb they had, using a slave-labourer in the gaol as messenger. On 13th April 1944 Cookie Long was not there to lend his comb. An urn bearing his name, but with no date, was delivered much later at Sagan with the inscription that cremation had taken place at Breslau.

Numbers 3 and 4 out of the tunnel, following Marshall and Valenta, had been Squadron Leader Roger Bushell and Lieutenant Bernard Scheidhauer. Though they were not very communicative about their plans, it was known that they intended to take a train to Breslau and probably lie up there for some time before moving across to France, where Scheidhauer's contacts were. Because they got out before the air raid they were able to catch their train to Breslau almost as soon as they got to Sagan station. They were later seen on Breslau station by Bob Van der Stok. But after this sighting they were never seen again by any of their companions, nor could their ashes subsequently be identified, except by elimination. The French flight lieutenant Van Wymeersch had, after some circuitous train journeys, boldly bought a ticket straight to Paris, Gare de l'Est, but was arrested on the train at Metz. The Gestapo officers who arrested him were chatty enough to tell him that owing to a change of form of which his forgery department could not be expected to be aware there was a defect in his papers, and two other officers with the same fault in their papers had been arrested on 26th March 1944 in Saarbrücken (that is, 45 miles east of Metz and some 550 miles from Breslau). Van Wymeersch was eventually sent to two prisons in Berlin, from which he escaped, and then to the concentration camp at Sachsenhausen. He survived, and was able to file this information. It helped to identify two urns. Two caskets of ashes, hearing no names or dates, but marked 'Saarbrücken', were sent to Stalag Luft III, and it was concluded that they contained the remains of Roger Bushell and Bernard Scheidhauer.

The pair following them out of the tunnel had been the South African lieutenants Johannes Gouws and Rupert Stevens. It was understood that they were going to Switzerland via Breslau. They had not caught the train they intended to, but saw it steaming out of Sagan station. Because of the delayed start, only Bushell and Scheidhauer were on this train. The platform began to fill up with other impatient officers, mainly dressed in business suits made from dyed blankets with herringbone and other bourgeois designs carefully inked in. 'Wings' Day, who had had to pull the fat out of the fire after the air raid, asked Rupert Stevens why he was still here. Stevens said he supposed the air raid had delayed the service. Eventually a train for Breslau came in at about one o'clock, and most of the officers boarded it, including Bob Van der Stok, who was to arrive in England four months later. He saw Gouws and Stevens in the booking hall at Breslau at four in the morning, with Bernard Scheidhauer near them but not acknowledging them. No other sighting was made of them. Lieutenant Alexander D. Neely, Royal Navy, who after a hair-raising trip to Berlin and Stettin came back to Berlin and took a train to Munich, was arrested on that journey because his papers were not in order. He was taken off the train at Munich and interrogated there. He was told on 30th March 1944 that two officers had been caught on the frontier the previous day. Munich is about 360 miles from Breslau, and 100 miles from the Swiss border at the Bodensee (Lake Constance), for which the South Africans said they would be heading. Two urns bearing their names were sent to Sagan with the date of death given as 29th March 1944, and the place of cremation Munich.

'Wings' Day and Pawel Tobolski, who had chatted briefly to Gouws and Stevens on Sagan station, had not taken the one o'clock train to Breslau, but the following train, which was going to Berlin. They left the Silesian station there separately, but met again outside, and made a successful contact at an address in Berlin which had been supplied by IS9. Next morning they went separately to the Stettiner station and travelled to Stettin, the port at the mouth of the Oder from which Muller and Bergsland had already sailed, carefully screened by Swedish sailors. Tobolski had notes of helping hands to be found here, but the contacts failed—brothel raided. After an uncomfortable thirty-hour session of feeling very nakedly on the run, the two officers fraternized with some French prisoners of war whom they ran across at midnight. These prisoners, who had a sort of freedom as slave labour, took them back to a disused factory where their working party was housed. They assured Day and Tobolski that the French would not give them away. However, when all the French but a couple of observers had gone to work next morning the door was thrown open by two plain-clothed Gestapo officials levelling revolvers, and the Germans asked for 'the two Tommies'. Day and Tobolski were marched through the streets to the Gestapo headquarters in Stettin with their hands above their heads. 'Wings' Day confirmed from a Gestapo interrogator that they had been given away by one of the Frenchmen, and observed that it was a dirty trick.

'Agreed', said the interrogator suavely. 'You'll be glad to know that when we have no further use for an informer we make sure to get his identity known to his comrades. Then they can dispose of him. And it saves us the trouble.'

After five days in prison Day and Tobolski were taken by train to Berlin. Day was interrogated at the Kripo headquarters by General Nebe, and eventually sent to Sachsenhausen/Oranienburg. He never saw Tobolski again, after 2nd April 1944. An urn bearing Tobolski's name was brought to Sagan with no date of death but a stamp indicating cremation at Breslau, 180 miles from Berlin.

Two of the officers whom Wing Commander Day noticed on Sagan railway station were Squadron Leader Tom Kirby-Green, who had been Big S during the months leading up to the escape, with Flying Officer Gordon Kidder, a Canadian with whom he was travelling. Their companions had watched with alarm when they saw a woman security officer from the Stalag question them—to which they replied only in imitation Spanish, since their role was of imported Spanish labourers—after which she asked a captain of the German Military Police, who was on duty at the station, to examine their papers. The forgery department had worked well enough on this set, because the two officers had their papers returned, and took the train to Breslau. But they were never seen again. It was thought that they were making for Hungary by way of Czechoslovakia, in order to contact friends of Kirby-Green. Two urns, unnamed but bearing the stamp '29 March 1944, Mährisch', were thought to contain their ashes. Mährisch Ostrau is the German form of the name of the Czechoslovakian town Moravská Ostrava (now just Ostrava).

Tim Walenn, the gentle artist who had headed the forgery department, had observed the drama on the platform at Sagan station with the greatest satisfaction. Flight Lieutenant Walenn, who had nobly shaved off his P/O Prune moustache for purposes of disguise, was travelling to Danzig with Flight Lieutenant Romas Marcinkus, the many-talented Lithuanian. Urns bearing their names and the location Danzig were eventually sent in. But two other urns with similar information as to name and place arrived with them. The names on the second pair were of two other forgery experts, Brettell and Picard.

Henri Picard, who was travelling with Gordon Brettell, had been assumed to have been making for Belgium, his native country, and the reason for his arriving at Danzig was never clarified. But that fact was accepted beyond dispute. The Swiss Protecting Power, moving about the country with less control than the German High Command approved, had reported privately to the British Government that, unknown to any German officials, Brettell, Marcinkus, Picard and Walenn had passed the night of 26th–27th March at Willenberg and the night of 27th–28th March in Danzig with work detachments from the British prisoner-of-war camp Stalag XXB. A further probe into the personalities of Stalag XXB had, in the summer of 1945, produced a statement from Company Sergeant-Major J. Fulton of the 2nd Seaforth Highlanders, who had been British Man of Confidence—senior ranking man—at this camp, that he had returned to the camp on an evening at the end of March 1944, and had heard that four RAF officers, who had been put into sharp arrest on the previous night, had been taken away. A sergeant-major of the Wiltshires had rekitted them by giving them British battledress in exchange for their rough-tailored disguises, and had had the foresight, or quartermaster's caution, to ask them to sign for their new uniforms. This enabled him to pass their names on to the Protecting Power when it was later widely rumoured that they had been shot. Sergeant-Major Fulton remembered one of the signatures without reference to the lost files of communication with Switzerland. It was Brettell.

Henri Picard had come fairly late out of the tunnel, because he had stayed to do a stint of hauling the ropes on the inter-station trolleys which were drawing the escapers along through Piccadilly Circus and Leicester Square. The man he had relieved was Flight Lieutenant Sydney Dowse. Dowse, another veteran escaper, had decided to travel alone, take a train to Berlin, lie up for a fortnight with a contact whose address he had, and then move on to Danzig and take his opportunities from there. By the time that he left the tunnel, however, the time-table was already retarded by hours, and the last straw for him was that the air-raid siren sounded. He had enough experience to realize that the train schedule would be distorted as severely as the planned timing of the exits from Stalag Luft III. He joined Flying Officer Stanislaw ('Danny') Krol, who had been awaiting him in the wood beyond the wire and was to make the first part of the journey with him. They went into a whispered conference. 'There is a balls-up because of the wrong location of the tunnel exit', said Dowse. 'It will very soon be discovered by the sentries, and there will be a bloody ambush on Sagan station. The train is out. I think we should hoof it.' 'Which way?' asked Danny Krol. 'East. At least it's towards Poland. Have you got any friends there still?'

They marched east for twelve nights, passed Liegnitz, passed Breslau, were heading well. They reached Oels, and came within two miles of the old Polish border. On the thirteenth day of their trek they were seen by a member of the Hitler Youth, who called the Home Guard and saw them conducted back to the civil police station at Oels. Out came the Gestapo from Breslau. After lengthy interrogation Dowse was told that, with his record of four previous escapes, he would have to go for further interrogation in Berlin.

'What about my friend?' Dowse asked. 'Will he be shot?'

'God in Heaven, no,' said the Gestapo. 'He is being sent back to Sagan. We can promise you that.'

'Then can I go and see him?'

'Sorry, that's against orders.'

'When do we leave for Berlin?'

'Tomorrow morning.'

At six o'clock the next morning Dowse sent a message to Danny Krol through the French barber in the gaol, saying he himself was off to Berlin, but Danny should not worry because he was going to Sagan. When the Gestapo came for Dowse he slipped out of his cell and ran round the corner to Krol, and said goodbye, repeating the message. Dowse went on to Berlin and Sachsenhausen. Krol never emerged. The last meeting had been on 12th April 1944. His urn showed that he had been cremated at Breslau, on a date unspecified.

Flying Officer Dennis Cochran was a loner. He was a fluent German-speaker, and he had made a good break once before, in the uniform of a Luftwaffe private with an artistically carved wooden rifle over his shoulders. There was one positive sighting of him. Van Wymeersch, taking a breather between trains at Frankfurt am Main on the way to France, had seen Cochran sweeping the streets there with some French workers on the Sunday after the escape, 26th March 1944. Cochran's disguise, an adaptation of the cast-off uniforms worn by transported labour all over Europe, eminently fitted him for this role, and he seemed to be getting on very well. Van Wymeersch deliberately did not speak to him, for the sake of the security of both. Since he knew that Cochran was heading for Freiburg, in preparation for the descent into Switzerland around the Rhine at Basle which was the ambition of many escapers, this meant that Dennis had accomplished some two-thirds of his 550-mile journey. But nothing more was known of Dennis Cochran except that, five days later, on 31st March 1944 according to the plate on his urn, he was cremated at Natzweiler, a concentration camp near Strasbourg where the SS Captain Josef Kramer, later to achieve notoriety as the 'Beast of Belsen' for his activities as commandant there, had been operating an experimental gas-chamber.

Two officers who had been allocated early places in the escape were the Norwegian lieutenants Hallada ('Harold') Espelid and Nils Fuglesang. They were out of the tunnel by half-past ten. 'Wings' Day later recalled that he believed that they were taking a train and eventually making for the Danish border, but no positive sighting of them was ever reported. The urns came back to Sagan bearing only their names, without an indication of the date of their death or the place of their cremation.

Flying Officer Arnold Christensen was also assumed to have been making for the Danish border. His parents had come from Denmark, and he had specialized within the escape organization on intelligence regarding this area. He was travelling with the Australian Squadron Leader James Catanach, and they were seen by Lieutenant Neely, RN, on a train going from Sagan to Berlin. They left this train at half-past seven in the morning after the escape, and nothing more was known of them. Urns carrying only their names, with no record of when or where they died and were cremated, ultimately reached Sagan.

The last of the count of fifty was Flight Lieutenant Anthony Hayter, of Newbury in Berkshire. It was believed that he was planning to travel alone to Mulhouse. Nothing more was known of his fate. An urn with no identification marks at all was subsequently brought to Sagan, and it had to be assumed that it contained Tony Hayter's ashes.

This patchy record of information, based on the observations of some of the survivors and the bare evidence bluntly stamped into the iron plates on some cremation urns, was all that was known of the fate of the victims of the Stalag Luft III murders sixteen months after the crime.

McKenna spent a long time digesting it and analysing it.

The evidence of Westhoff indicated an intention to kill emanating from the very centre of the German Reich and radiating through Hitler's subordinates who executed his orders: what the Nuremberg Indictment called a general conspiracy. The statement of Wielen indicated some massive butchery based on Görlitz gaol, but scattered to distances scores of miles from it. The evidence of the cremation plates suggested that murders had been committed at places as widely separated as Czechoslovakia and the French border.

A vainglorious man had given an angry order which had been slavishly carried out, and he had dodged answering for it by putting a pistol in his mouth. That was the normal irresponsibility of a man elevated beyond his capacity. What impressed McKenna was that there were a dozen crimes, not one, and that they had not been done in passion or the heat of battle, but meanly in cold blood.

None of these factors made the case easier to solve.

McKenna read the rest of the file. The summary prepared by the Judge Advocate General's department appended a few fresh facts and conclusions which had been added to the file as the information came in. There was an early assessment of Colonel von Lindeiner-Wildau based on an MI9 interrogation of a German prisoner of war captured before D-Day. This man had served on the staff of Stalag Luft III. He said the Commandant was pro-English, and he punished members of the camp staff who behaved incorrectly towards the prisoners. He told the prison staff that the prisoners were not barbaric Russians, but Englishmen, who were a different proposition entirely—an interesting echo of the almost official German attitude to the Russian prisoners of war, whose masters had not signed the Geneva Convention (and therefore, of course, did not necessarily apply it, and certainly would not brook the presence of representatives of a Protecting Power).

There was an MI6 report reflecting unease among the German officer caste aroused by the Sagan murders, and expressed shortly after Mr Eden's speech to the House of Commons. A German official in a neutral country—clearly trying to get his message through to London—was quoted as saying that the German High Command, particularly its Luftwaffe element, were seriously concerned by the killings, realized that there would be damaging repercussions on the British attitude towards the German Army and Air Force *after the war*, and made no attempt to deny that the Royal Air Force officers were murdered rather than justifiably shot according to the German version. Finally, in a passage of direct pleading to London, the official said that the German High Command was anxious to convey to the British Government that the victims had been handed over to the SS on instructions from 'the highest quarters'—which was the normal euphemism to indicate Hitler, working either through Keitel militarily or Himmler concerning security, and in this case working through both.

A detailed United States intelligence report on American prisoners of war inside Germany devoted some stress to the morale maintained at Stalag Luft III, where the American flyers, after first sharing a compound with the British and Allied (and, indeed, helping to dig the first tunnel) had been shifted into another compound. The appreciation noted that the outstanding example set by the British in the camp, and the excellent briefing by Royal Air Force officers on escape and evasion, had combined to make Stalag Luft III the best-organized American camp. It was expected that the recent murders of the fifty RAF men would result in a temporary cessation of escape activity.

A long Military Intelligence summary of the work done in the first four months after the news of the killings came through virtually acquitted the Luftwaffe of complicity in the crime, *unless the Commandant had been ordered directly by Göring to hand over the prisoners to the Gestapo*, 'which would be strange, as Göring and Himmler were not on good terms at that time'—an accurate enough mid-war assessment, as was later proved at the Nuremberg Trials. The summary pinpointed certain German personalities who should be considered as implicated in the shooting, and should be interrogated after the war. They included Dr Scharpwinkel, an SS Sturmbannführer and Chief of the Breslau Gestapo; Colonel Seetzen, inspector of security police in the Breslau defence area; and General Ernst Heinrich Schmauser, the senior SS and police leader in that area. Later, when Colonel von Lindeiner himself became a prisoner of war after the German capitulation, the former commandant added to the list the names of Kaltenbrunner, Wielen and Absalon.

The last documents in the parcel of papers which McKenna had been told to study gave an overall assessment of the prospects of the investigation.

It was not an optimistic appraisal. There was little chance of getting any further positive evidence from Allied sources. The Germans connected with the case must be traced and interrogated. This was a highly difficult operation, since not even the identities had been verified for vast numbers of Germans now held in prisoner-of-war and internment cages. The registers both of the wanted men and of men in custody were incomplete. Moreover, since the Allies were unwilling to feed the hundreds of thousands of unproductive manpower in the prison camps all through the winter, they were instituting a speedy interrogation system with the object of getting rid of able-bodied prisoners after asking not too many questions, rather than of concentrating on the possible war crimes they might have committed.

The organization for making an active search *outside the cages* for the many men now on the Wanted List for the Sagan crimes was, said the assessment, too small to cope amid the abnormal conditions of Germany in 1945; and Silesia, which was the root of the crime and the scene of many of the murders, was banned to British investigators because it was now in the Russian zone of occupation. As soon as Sagan had been overrun by the Russians, in March 1945, the British Ambassador in Moscow had given the Soviet Foreign Minister full details of the case, had asked for inquiries to be made on the spot, and had handed over a list of men wanted at that date for interrogation. Mr Vishinsky had replied that the information had been conveyed to the competent Soviet authorities, but the details were insufficient, and would make identification very difficult. He promised to pass on any information resulting from the Soviet investigation. And that five-months-old letter was, in August 1945, the last letter in this particular file.

A request to the Czech Government for aid had met with a warmer response. But there seemed an urgent need for specialist men working in the field concerned only with the Stalag Luft III case, which at the moment, as far as War Crimes Investigation Units were affected, was everybody's affair, and therefore nobody's. The report concluded:

> In view of these difficulties it would appear that the best way of increasing the speed and efficiency of the investigations might be to set up temporarily a small unit to make investigations in Germany. There can be little doubt that the employment of a small group of officers with police experience and a knowledge of German would be well justified having regard to the facts:
>
> (1) that it is one of the worst of the war crimes committed against British nationals in general and the RAF in particular;
> (2) that it involves the major war criminals;
> (3) that a large number of victims are involved; and
> (4) that it has aroused considerable public interest.

Before his allocated week was up, Flight Lieutenant McKenna took the files back to Group Captain Nicholas at SIB HQ.

'What has all this got to do with me, sir?' he asked.

Nicholas waited, then said, 'I want you to go to Germany to start the ball rolling to implement this promise of Anthony Eden's that those responsible for this crime will be brought to justice.'

McKenna said, 'You've picked the wrong man. I can't speak more than two words of German.'

'No problem', said Nicholas. 'We can provide you with all the interpreters you want.'

'I still think it's impossible to do this job', McKenna persisted. 'At this time, three months after the surrender, when all the people have gone to ground with false identities! We can't even go to the scene of the crime for a start.'

'There are plenty of crimes, plenty of scenes,' said Nicholas. 'You've had far less to work on with other cases. Go for a fortnight and report back on the prospects. I'll attach you to SIB BAFO.[1]'

McKenna looked pained but dutiful. He saluted and left.

'Per ardua ad astra', said Nicholas cheerfully.

'Ad astra per Anthony Eden', McKenna commented to the closing door.

[1]Special Investigation Branch, British Air Forces of Occupation.

Flight Lieutenant McKenna was haunted by a nightmare, which became a waking dream, a formalized vision of the deaths of these men which he was to requite, and a scene which, he was eventually to know, never actually occurred in the cases he was pursuing. The customary Gestapo method of liquidation was a revolver-shot at close quarters through the nape of the neck, and McKenna could not expunge the memory of information he had once been given that a man's teeth could sometimes be blown out by such a shot. Against his will he had to follow the sequence of this mental image of the victim standing with hands fastened behind his back, watching his killer draw a pistol and go behind him, rest it against his neck for a few seconds, and then explode the shot through the spinal cord into the head.

Less of a chimera was McKenna's constant preoccupation with the tailored ease with which the Gestapo had gone underground. A statement by a Gestapo man captured soon after VE-Day illustrated the relevance of his disquiet on this subject. The man, Fritz Barnekow, said:

> *On 2nd May 1945 I met in Kiel Kriminaldirektor Schäffer, who told me that the entire local Gestapo and SD (Security Service) were going to Flensburg and I could join them. I agreed, as I had heard that at Hannover the Gestapo had been lynched by the local population after the arrival of the Allied troops. On 3rd May 1945 I burnt my Dienstpass and, not wishing to confide in my wife, told her that I was going to hide at Schierensee until the first rumpus had died down. I set off on my bicycle and, after spending an hour in Schierensee, got a lift to Flensburg and went to the Gestapo Dienstelle. I was told that Fritz Schmidt, Erwin Müller, Johannes Post and two others were in Niebüll with a waggon-load of supplies, and they intended to disappear from the public eye. Schmidt, Müller and Post arrived and called a meeting where Sturmführer Dr Venediger announced that 137 members of the Sipo (Security Police) were now assembled in the Landesmuseum at Flensburg, and he was going to issue them with documents to enable them to submerge as members of the regular Forces. Navy paybooks were issued to all those at the meeting. Schmidt and Müller said they intended to hide in a dug-out, and when things had quietened down they meant to find work as discharged sailors. With Post and the other two they intended to go into hiding on the west coast of Schleswig near Tönning, Heide or Meldorf. For this purpose they said they would split up and leave the ration lorry hidden in a central location from where they could draw food daily by bicycle. On 4th May 1945 Schmidt, Müller, Post, myself and three others went to Niebüll, where the last four of us were given new uniforms and identity cards of the Frontier Police by Oberführer Oberst Sohmann. I then burnt my Navy paybook. We were given a movement order for Süderlügum and went off, leaving Schmidt, Müller and Post behind. I heard later that Schmidt acquired the uniform of a naval captain, but afterwards discarded it. We went from Süderlügum to Aventoft, where we were put on a frontier post and given the job of checking identity cards. On 11th May 1945 an order appeared that the identity cards issued by RSHA Berlin to the Frontier Police were no longer valid, so I was sent to get new ones through official channels. I was asked by a British officer why I wanted them. I was arrested and, after interrogation, admitted that I had been a member of the Gestapo.*

This statement, taken three months before the SIB was officially pursuing the Stalag Luft III case, was misfiled and only tardily recovered. Three of the Gestapo officers named in it, Post, Venediger and Schmidt, were subsequently hunted by McKenna. It took two years to arrest one of them, and twelve and twenty-three years respectively before the others were sentenced.

3 Cyanide and old rope

On 3rd September 1945, the sixth anniversary of Great Britain's declaration of war on Germany, Flight Lieutenant McKenna flew from Northolt in an RAF Dakota to begin the investigations in Europe, seventeen months after the crime. He took with him Flight Sergeant H. J. Williams, a well-built, bluff and occasionally tough man with a friendly manner and a reputation for hard slogging, whom he had noted in the SIB headquarters in Princes Gate Court. McKenna registered him as 'the typical old stamp of policeman': Williams had served in the Portsmouth constabulary before joining the Royal Air Force.

They had a three-hour flight to reach Bückeburg, an airfield near Minden, 30 miles west of Hannover.

'So there are just the two of us, sir,' observed Williams.

'We're starting the ball rolling', said McKenna. 'Are you ready for a briefing?

'We have 106 names on the Wanted List. They have all been circulated to CROWCASS[1] and to British and American registers in Europe, and copies have been sent to the Czechs and the Russians. Let's intensify that general search. But let us make a special concentration on the pyramid between Berlin and Breslau.

'Breslau is 180 miles south-east of Berlin and about 80 miles south-east of Sagan. It was the centre of German Military District VIII, which controlled Sagan. The Gestapo regional office at Breslau controlled Liegnitz and had sub-offices at Hirschberg and Görlitz, which all lie to the west, on the way to Sagan. Thirty-five of the escaping officers who were picked up east of Sagan were eventually imprisoned at Görlitz and interrogated by the Gestapo. From there, twelve officers were returned to Sagan, and twenty-two were shot in batches of from six to ten in various unknown places.

[1]The Central Register of War Criminals and Security Suspects, located in Paris.

Germany, boundaries at 1st September 1939

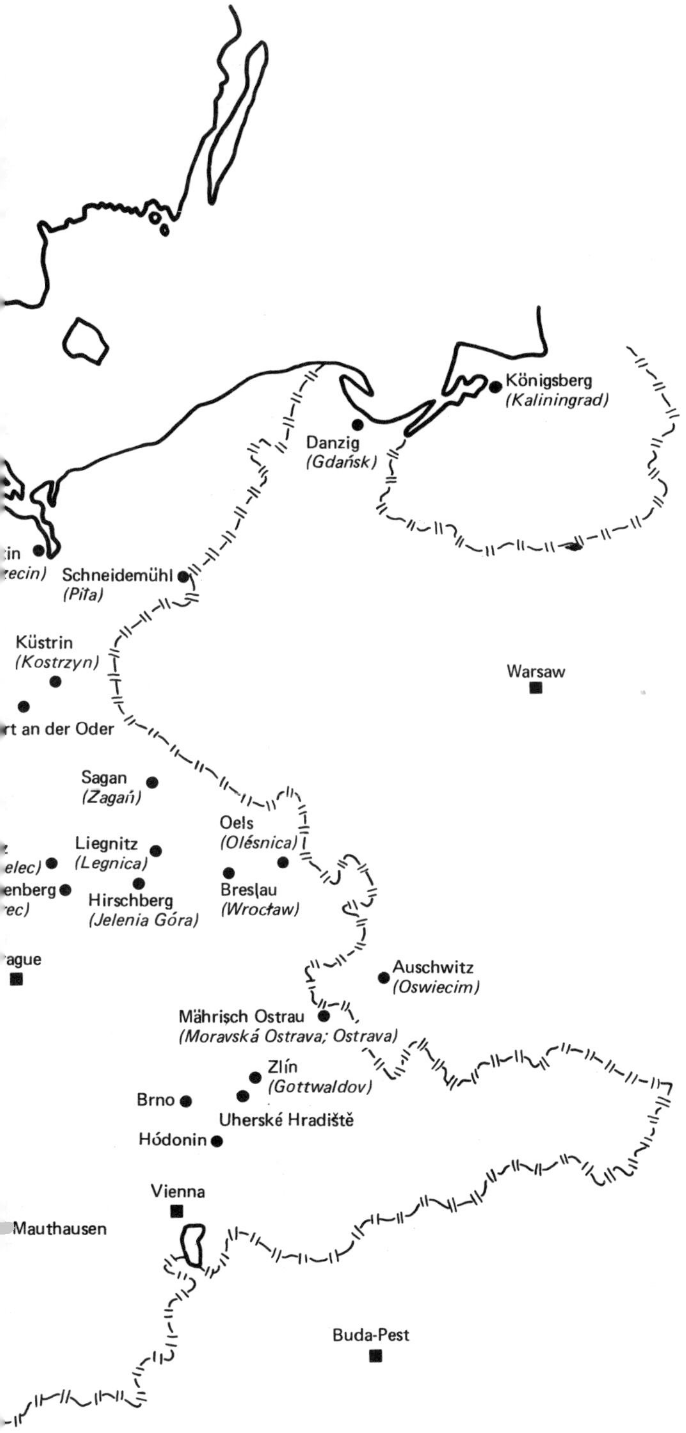
Königsberg
(Kaliningrad)
Danzig
(Gdańsk)
Schneidemühl
(Piła)
Küstrin
(Kostrzyn)
Warsaw
Sagan
(Żagań)
Oels
(Oleśnica)
Liegnitz
(Legnica)
Breslau
(Wrocław)
Hirschberg
(Jelenia Góra)
Auschwitz
(Oswiecim)
Mährisch Ostrau
(Moravská Ostrava; Ostrava)
Zlín
(Gottwaldov)
Brno
Uherské Hradiště
Hódonin
Vienna
Mauthausen
Buda-Pest

The twenty-third was Flight Lieutenant Long, and they kept him for some three weeks before they shot him. One day we must go into that: Cookie Long was one of the most active of all the tunnellers; he personally dealt with two tunnel collapses on the night of the escape, when there were still half of the men who eventually escaped, trapped on the wrong side of the fall. Why did they keep him so long? Did they hope to torture him for information, or were they getting their numbers right from Berlin, and reserving him for Number 50, as announced?

'However: twenty-three men taken out of Görlitz and shot. Their urns show that they were cremated at Görlitz, Breslau and Liegnitz, and we gather that they were always burned at the nearest crematorium to the place where they were murdered. Liegnitz is where Edgar Humphreys went down.'

'Someone you knew?' asked Williams.

'I knew two of them. While I was in the civil police at Blackpool I was liaison officer with the OC, RAF, Squires Gate, Wing Commander Styles. I got to know some of the general reconnaissance aircrew there. One of them was a Hawker Henley pilot, young Edgar Humphreys. We became great friends, I often used to go and have a drink with him in the mess. He would show me round the Henleys. He was posted to an operational squadron, and was shot down in a raid on the Channel ports. Finished up in Stalag Luft III along with another man I knew, Bob Stewart. Stewart and Humphreys were together in the party of ten that were taken out and shot somewhere near Liegnitz.'

'Strange that you should come on to a case involving your friends.'

'They're all our friends, really,' said McKenna. 'Now, twenty-three officers shot from Görlitz, controlled by Breslau Gestapo. In addition, four officers were captured at Hirschberg and imprisoned there: Flight Lieutenant Wernham, a Canadian; Flight Lieutenant Kiewnarski, a Pole; Flying Officer Pawluk, another Pole; and Flying Officer Skanzikas, a Greek. In the pattern of the killings they were almost bound to die, because only four Dominions officers out of nineteen survived, and all fifteen officers of Continental origin were shot: the Gestapo just kept the three Czechs for prolonged interrogation about the Czech Resistance. Except, perhaps through a merciful chance, a flight lieutenant called Ernst Valenta. He was one of the liveliest, and possibly—from the German point of view—the most dangerous man in the camp. His speciality was intelligence on German affairs, and counter-propaganda against German morale. Any German guard who spoke to him in Sagan was soon convinced that the Reich had already lost the war. Ernie Valenta had before the war completed an intelligence course at the Staff College in Prague. Fortunately, very few knew about that, even among the British officers. If the Germans had known I can well believe that it was better for him that he died at Liegnitz. With Humphreys and Stewart.

'Well, the four at Hirschberg were doomed to death, and die they did. The four urns give a date of death, but no place of cremation. But they were imprisoned at Hirschberg, and therefore they died under the authority of the Breslau Gestapo. That makes twenty-seven dead. And in further addition, there were two isolated cremations at Breslau. They were both Poles. Danny Krol, a flying officer, walked through the snow for twelve days with Sydney Dowse, and they were eventually captured at Oels, which is 18 miles the other side of Breslau. Dowse was sent to Sachsenhausen, Krol was eventually shot. And Pawel Tobolski, another flying officer—I suppose he was the cheekiest of the lot. He wore the uniform of a German *Unteroffizier*, took a train to Berlin, and got his forged pass stamped by the RTO to get another train to Stettin. He was travelling with Wings Day, and they were caught at Stettin. Harry Day went to Sachsenhausen. But the Gestapo took Tobolski 200 miles south to Breslau before they shot him, and his urn shows cremation at Breslau.

'Twenty-nine deaths out of fifty, done within the area of the Breslau Gestapo. There *must* have been some central authority. Get the men who ordered those deaths—they could have used a mobile execution squad to do it—get them, and get the men who did the shooting, and we've wiped out over fifty per cent of the Wanteds.

'Right. What's the connection between Breslau and Berlin? This is one of the few hard facts we know, because we've got our hands on the Kripo Chief in Breslau. He was captured a fortnight before the capitulation. He's still under Army interrogation, but he has made one statement that interests me, and he'll make more. His name is Max Wielen. He's over sixty, he's a professional policeman, and he's a wily old bird.

'As head of the Criminal Police, Wielen had responsibility for action against prisoners of war after an escape. One of Himmler's men had separate responsibility for counter-measures to prevent escapes. Wielen sounded the general alarm, the *Grossfahndung*—national hue-and-cry—when he got the news of the seventy-six, and he went to Stalag Luft III for a swift recce the same day. After the week-end he was summoned to Berlin. He was told by his boss there that Hitler had gone round the bend at news of the escape, and had ordered that over half the recaptured prisoners had to be shot. Many of the officers were held in his area. He *says* he was told that when the officers who had to be shot had been selected he was to hand them over to the Gestapo Chief in Breslau, a man called Dr Scharpwinkel—his brother-officer, if you like, though they hated each other's guts.

'We don't know whether that last statement is the truth or whether Wielen was told to do the shooting himself, because we haven't got Scharpwinkel, we haven't got Wielen's boss in Berlin, and we haven't got Scharpwinkel's boss in Berlin, though we can account for the people above them in the chain of command. But there is a probability that Wielen's story is correct, and that it was the Gestapo and not the Kripo who did the shooting—because the Kripo did not have the staff or experience to do this sort of thing, and the Gestapo did.

'In that case I would look for a compact execution squad under Scharpwinkel's orders. Say twenty men at the most; it could be fewer. The maximum number they took out into the country and shot at any one time was ten. So I see relatively few men shooting all the twenty-nine.

'If *I* had been Scharpwinkel and I had an extermination mob handy, that's what I would have done: I'd have said, "We've got a nice little squad together, operating from Breslau. We'll go to Görlitz today and take six from there and get them seen off, and then tomorrow we'll go to Hirschberg or Liegnitz and so on and so on. But we'll keep the same team together on the need-to-know basis—the fewer in the know, the better the security. So the Gestapo in the sub-offices have not become involved, and they can't talk if the time ever comes."

'We can only get at the truth by finding the missing men and closely interrogating the ones we have got. That's something to concentrate on.'

McKenna took out a notebook and began to draw a chain of command.

'Hitler gave the order to shoot the fifty: Supreme Commander.

'Keitel took it: Chief of the High Command.

'Göring accepted it: Reich Marshal and jack-of-all-trades, but what's relevant here is that he was Air Minister and Commander-in-Chief of the Luftwaffe.

'Himmler snatched the execution of it: Reich Führer SS.'

McKenna wrote:

HITLER
KEITEL
GÖRING HIMMLER

'Now, let's forget the military side—Directorate of Prisoners of War, Luftwaffe Inspector, and all that—for a moment, but not for ever: we shall want them too. On the security side, Himmler has grabbed the order as Head of Security Services. He passes it for implementation to Kaltenbrunner, boss of RSHA.[1] The RSHA in Berlin had seven departments, called *Ämter*, of which I suppose the most experienced butchers were Amt III, which claimed to have exterminated two million people through its *Einsatzgruppen*, Special Action Groups—and it could be that they passed some of their zeal across to their comrades. Amt IV in Berlin controlled the Gestapo, Secret State Police. Its chief was Heinrich Müller, and he

[1]Reichssicherheitshauptampt: Central Security Headquarters.

was Scharpwinkel's boss and the boss of all the other regional Gestapo heads who carried out the twenty-one Sagan murders away from the Breslau area. Amt V controlled the Kripo, the Criminal Police. Its chief was General Artur Nebe, and he was the boss of Wielen and many others. Nebe ordered the Kripo, in whatever areas Sagan prisoners were caught, to hand them over to the Gestapo. And this was then an unprecedented action.

'When Wielen was summoned to Berlin after the Stalag Luft III escape it was Nebe who—on the most favourable interpretation of Wielen—gave him his orders to surrender the officers to the Gestapo. Wielen says Nebe showed him an order, signed by Kaltenbrunner and deriving from Himmler, stating that Scharpwinkel should get his precise instructions from Müller. Scharpwinkel later confirmed to Wielen that he had received these orders.'

McKenna drew another pyramid. 'So we have:

HITLER
HIMMLER
KALTENBRUNNER

MÜLLER	NEBE
SCHARPWINKEL	WIELEN

'Now, there are just a couple of side-swipes to make it difficult. Apart from High Command and Luftwaffe control, Himmler and Kaltenbrunner had a special security department for the prevention of escapes by prisoners of war. They worked alongside the Kripo but reported direct to Berlin. In the Breslau Military District the security officer was a Kriminaldircktor (say, Chief Inspector in the police and Major in the SS) called Erich Brünner. His deputy was a Kriminalkommissar (say, Detective Inspector in the police and Captain in the SS) called Dr Günther Absalon. Brünner made an inspection of Stalag Luft III before the break-out, and (but I'm only putting this forward as a possibility) might have deliberately failed to uncover the tunnelling and other escape preparations because Berlin wanted that escape to take place, so that an occasion would be offered for deterrent slaughter. Absalon arrived at Sagan eight hours after the escape, and was nosing around for weeks afterwards.

'Trust the RAF. The lads in the camp called him "My son, my son".

'The dismissed and court-martialled Commandant of Stalag Luft III, whom we have in the London Cage, thinks that Absalon is one who knows all about it. I have his description with me, but you might like to know that he is summed up as "Good German type with polished manners; the perfect drawing-room criminal".

'The counter-escape men are only the first complication. The second is that the Kripo and the Gestapo had an organization in which they worked together, and in this case they were known as the Sipo.[1] The Sipo head in the Breslau area was General Ernst Schmauser, and his deputy was Colonel Seetzen. An MI9 appreciation of the Sagan crime made over a year ago tends to go for Schmauser and Seetzen as the key personalities of the crime. That was before we heard what Wielen had to say. But they could certainly give useful information.

'Now let's cross a few of them off. Hitler, suicide. Keitel, awaiting trial at Nuremberg. Göring, Nuremberg. Himmler, suicide. Kaltenbrunner, Nuremberg. Wielen, in custody. There you are, it leaves us only seven to find.'

~~HITLER~~
~~KEITEL~~
~~GÖRING~~ ~~HIMMLER~~
~~KALTENBRUNNER~~

BRÜNNER	SCHMAUSER	MÜLLER	NEBE
ABSALON	SEETZEN	SCHARPWINKEL	~~WIELEN~~

'Some of them are probably dead. The rest are on the run. Seven men who know all about it. Two—Müller and Nebe—who supervised the fifty murders. The rest concerned with at least twenty-nine. And in spite of what MI9 say, the man I'd most like to get my hands on is Scharpwinkel. He did it. He was there.'

McKenna put his notebook back in his pocket.

'Right?'

McKenna was a fluent and lucid speaker. But it could hardly be claimed that he had given his assistant the fullest opportunity to absorb his case.

'Right', said Flight Sergeant Williams loyally.

'And remember there are only ninety-nine others on the list', said McKenna. He pulled a German phrase book from his pocket and buried his nose in it. After an interval a mutter escaped from behind the book.

'Ein Bier bitte', said McKenna exploratively.

It was a completely clear day, and McKenna waited to ascertain that the sea was no longer beneath them. He had rarely flown over Germany in his Lancaster at less than 15 000 feet, and he was interested to see the country without the encumbrance of flak or fighters. They landed at Bückeburg on a wire-lattice runway, and clouds of dust rose in the sky. After passing the immigration procedures, McKenna and Williams were driven to the Special Investigation Branch headquarters building in Rinteln. The most obvious sign of devastation in the town was that the bridge over the Weser had been blown by the retreating Germans, and a ferry was in operation. The two men found their quarters and settled in. Group Captain Nicholas had flown over to ease them into SIB BAFO, to which they

[1]Sicherheitspolizei: Security Police.

were only attached, with formal reporting responsibility to London, and to discuss the lines of investigation.

The first two days were taken up with conferences and suggestions. McKenna had an outline of the operations and scope of the military record centres he would soon be visiting, but he immediately expanded the enterprise. He proposed that personal visits should be made to the prisoner-of-war cages in the British, American and French occupied zones, since the Central Registry might not have up-to-date information. He did not at that time realize how great an operation he was suggesting—it eventually demanded a year's work—but he proceeded to extend even that. Most of the wanted men had a security police background, and they were possibly in Civilian Internment Centres if they had been picked up under their own name, or had been later denounced. These CICs would also need to be combed. McKenna further proposed a descent on Berlin to seek former members of the RSHA, and to examine records if any were left. He suggested that the same procedure should be directed to all the Kripo and Gestapo offices controlling the locations where cremations were known to have taken place. And with a last abandoned throw proposed that a similar foray should be made on the former Gestapo headquarters now in the Russian zone. In the meantime, he urged that a large number of copies of the Wanted List should be printed, so that he could leave the particulars at every police unit he visited.

McKenna was taken on a tour to be given the necessary introductions to the heads of the existing agencies. Group Captain Somerhough, commanding the North Western Europe War Crimes Investigation Unit, from whose activities the Stalag Luft III inquiry had been hived off, pleasantly and optimistically offered him as much accommodation as he would require in the unit's holding gaol at Minden.

Then McKenna and Williams began to reconnoitre the state of the records in the complex of military headquarters around Rinteln. At Bad Oeynhausen, some twenty miles away, he saw the war crimes files held by 21 Army Group, and the War Crimes Commission's files held by the Judge Advocate General's Military Department.

Checking card indexes and files of arrested persons, they were encouraged to discover that two on the Wanted List had been traced and pulled in: Behrens and von Massow. Von Massow had been the Censor at Stalag Luft III, and had been deposed and court-martialled with the Commandant after the escape. He was wanted only for questioning, with no thought of a subsequent charge. It was thought that he might have had previous knowledge of illegal Gestapo action planned against escaping prisoners of war which was at least vaguely known to some of the camp staff before the escape. Behrens was an SS Gruppenführer, a lieutenant-general of police, who was thought to have been working in RSHA Berlin at the time when the

Sagan murders were ordered and executed. But when Behrens was brought over to London for a full interrogation it was discovered that he was the wrong man—a Behrens who had not worked in Berlin. This sort of error was common enough in the initial stages, when the pressure to get men into the bag was strong, and the screening personnel virtually non-existent.

McKenna and Williams began a sweep of the war crimes record offices and RAF police units in a quarter-circle to the north of them, as far as Schleswig, near the Danish border, 260 miles away by road. They met the liaison officers of the United States Army who were to sanction their permits to enter the American zones. They combed card indexes to copy down all information obtainable, including hearsay reports from others already in custody, about the whereabouts or reputed fate of persons on the Stalag Luft III wanted list. Wherever they went they circulated and recirculated the names and descriptions of Scharpwinkel, Absalon, Seetzen and their four superiors on whom McKenna had decided to concentrate.

Moving about the country as they were now, the investigating officers began to take some fleeting account of the toll of war. In town and countryside they saw the destruction, the roadside graves, the armoured vehicle graveyards that marked the land battle for Germany. On the way to Schleswig, McKenna had to pass through Kiel, the scene of his first bombing operation on 23rd July 1944, and found the experience altogether depressing. The docks were non-existent, and in the centre of the town he saw one large concrete shelter which had taken a direct hit from a 20 000-lb high-explosive bomb, trapping five hundred people inside. On another day he had to make a duty call at Belsen Camp seeking former Gestapo members on his Wanted List who might later have been transferred to Belsen camp staff, and consequently were for the most part still in custody there.

The overpowering impression at Belsen was the smell, although all the prisoners' hutments, which had crowded sometimes a thousand dead and dying into a space allocated for twenty-eight people, had been burnt to the ground four months previously as some measure of disinfection. The smell lingered from the last thirteen thousand corpses which the Germans, though working in full panic, had not had time to bury before the British arrived to liberate the camp; and from the dripping excreta of thirteen thousand others, prostrate with typhus and starvation, infected through contact with and cannibalism of the dead against whom they leaned, who died in the next few weeks because they were too feeble to respond to the emergency medical aid channelled into the camp.

McKenna saw piles of bones still stacked in sheds, and wide graves marked with numbers of the order of 350 and 450, which he took to be grave registration numbers until he was told that they recorded the totals of corpses recently bulldozed into each grave. In some horror, he asked an agricultural worker in the field outside the camp whether he had known that all these terrible things were going on in Belsen. 'Oh, no,' said the man, 'we thought it was just a detention camp.' 'But you must have smelt it all', persisted McKenna. 'You must have seen the smoke from the crematorium chimney?' 'Never', said the farm-worker, and then he contradicted himself with a remarkable declaration of local virtue.

'We're good people around here', he claimed. 'Not like in other parts of Germany. We never frighten our children by threatening to put them up the chimney as they did in other places.'

'What do you mean, "up the chimney"?' asked McKenna.

'Well', came the answer, 'the chimney of the crematorium, you see. In other places, when children were naughty, the parents used to say "If you're not good, we'll burn you up the chimney". We are not like that here.'[1]

Days of travel—arduous enough amid the prevailing state of the roads and the inadequate condition of what grace-and-favour vehicle they could twist out of the transport section at this early time—alternated with days of routine work spent in tabulating and classifying the information they were accumulating from the scattered card indexes. Against the names on the wanted list they were entering the exact jobs formerly held, the places at which the men had served, their precise activities in March and April 1944, the location of their families, the likelihood of a decision to rejoin wives or mistresses when they all went underground with false identity papers at the time of the capitulation—all the grandly named 'intelligence' which was largely derived from the gossip of other interrogated prisoners. When they had registered what sparse information they had collected during their first ten days they made

[1]Belsen was not established as an extermination camp, as Auschwitz was. But the transfer from Auschwitz to Belsen of Josef Kramer, Irma Grese, Juana Bormann, Elisabeth Volkenrath and other SS officials confirmed a policy of the extermination—by starvation, shooting and even savaging by hounds—of all sick persons, pregnant women and other prisoners unfit to work. Prosecuting at the Belsen trial, September–November 1945, Colonel T. M. Backhouse refuted Kramer's claim that the appalling state of the camp was due to a breakdown in organization caused by the advance of the British Army. He said, 'In the Wehrmacht camp, about a mile up the road, where the food for Belsen came from . . . there was a fully staffed bakery, with a grain supply sufficient to produce 60 000 loaves a day, which it did immediately afterwards and does today with the same staff and the same stock of grain. There were medical supplies which are not exhausted yet.' There were large stocks of unused medical supplies in Belsen camp itself. Kramer's (British) counsel said, in mitigation, that the concentration camps contained undesirable elements from 'the dregs of the ghettoes of Central Europe'. He later apologized for this statement, saying, 'I have been acting only as the mouth-piece for the accused'. British prisoners of war were among those murdered at Belsen.

a few forays to knock off comparatively easy targets on their Wanted List.

McKenna and Williams had now been joined by Sergeant Willem Smit, a Dutchman who was the first of a long line of interpreters seconded to the SIB by a Liaison Corps from the Netherlands Air Force. They blooded Smit with a short run to Osnabrück to trace a minor character on their list, Leutnant Heinrich Wilhelm Willman, on whom they had a partial report. They traced Willman's parents to a peasant home on a castle estate at Hünnefelde. The old couple were perturbed at the visit, although McKenna gave them no indication that it was concerned with a war crime. Their son Heinrich, they said, was an Army doctor. He had been wounded before the end of the war, and was now in a prisoner-of-war hospital near Duisberg. They submitted with anxiety to a search of the cottage, and produced a packet of letters from their son. McKenna leafed through them and asked Smit for a translation of one dated 21st March 1944. It was written from Kassel, far removed from Sagan, where their Willman had been serving, and McKenna was fairly certain that they had come on a fool's errand. But he took the address of Willman's present hospital, and said that, since he was bound to see their son eventually, he would pass on any message the parents would like to send. The old couple gratefully composed a few affectionate words.

They drove back to Rinteln. 'A wasted day', said Sergeant Smit. 'Not at all', replied McKenna. 'Negative information is still information. See to your rations. Because our next port of call is Düsseldorf.'

Ten days after his arrival, McKenna had sized up the situation. There were months—he did not then estimate years—of work, but the job could be done. He reported to London that the prospects were fair, but added that the first priority was a detailed combing of internment camps within the whole of Germany, and that, in his rank of flight lieutenant, he had insufficient status with the Allied forces with whom close liaison was necessary. The French in particular were granting him little notice, and he felt that the investigation would go faster if an officer of higher rank were appointed. He had made extremely slight impact on the Russians, but attributed that to political attitudes rather than any question of rank. London therefore sent out Squadron Leader W. P. Thomas, with Sergeant Hicks of the SIB, on short assignment since Thomas was already near his release from the Service.

Two days were spent on the induction of the new members of the team. 'We have very few particulars', Squadron Leader Thomas observed with gloom. 'The only channels of information are the camps and internment centres. There are scores of these camps, and millions of Germans to be dealt with by elimination. The records are uncertain, and rarely disclose the real identity of the internees. It will be many months before we can possibly cover the ground.'

'All routine work takes time, sir,' said McKenna. 'But getting your hands on just one man will often lead to another. I still suggest, however, that we keep our eyes on a few of the priority wanted, and go for them outside the slow comb-out of the camps.' And he got Thomas's agreement to an exploratory raid on the domicile of one of his most wanted men, Dr Günther Absalon.

McKenna, Williams and Smit drew their food and blankets, and set off in a Hillman for Düsseldorf. At that time the autobahn held until they had bypassed Kamen, the scene of McKenna's first daylight bombing operation. Then they had to divert through the overwhelming devastation of Dortmund, Bochum and Essen, which had all been targets for McKenna. In Essen they pulled up in the street to eat their corned beef sandwiches. A small boy, with only a ragged jersey on his back, pressed his nose against the car window and watched them. It was raining, and his cap was too big, so that the peak was pushed back by the side of the car and the rain fell on his forehead. McKenna wound down the window. '*Ich habe nichts zu essen*', the boy said: 'I have nothing to eat'. '*Wie lange*, how long?' asked McKenna in the German he was beginning to acquire. The boy gave no answer. 'Would you like these sandwiches?' McKenna offered, abandoning the language, but easily understandable from the vigour with which he swept everybody's sandwiches into a pile. He passed them to the boy, who shoved them inside the front of his rough jersey and ran fast down the street to the rear of the car before anyone could change his mind.

The three airmen drove on through a succession of the ruined towns of the Ruhr to Duisberg, and rejoined an autobahn for Düsseldorf. The town major here could offer them no accommodation in the city, and they drove ten miles south to a staging-post barracks.

On the next morning the military Public Security Officer introduced the team to the Düsseldorf Criminal Police, who directed them to the addresses they were seeking, logged from the information they had acquired from their card indexes. They crossed to the left bank of the Rhine, drove into Neuss and on to Heerdt, where they located what they had been given as the address of Absalon's parents.

Both the father and the mother, Paul and Martha Absalon, were in. Smit introduced McKenna and Williams. 'May we come in? We are here', he said, on McKenna's instructions, 'to see if we can possibly get in touch with your son, Dr Günther Absalon, who may be able to help one of his friends who is defending himself against a serious charge.' ('What is the point', McKenna had said when briefing Smit, 'of saying: "We're trying to hang your son. Can you tell us where he is?" ')

The Absalons were very sorry, but they had had no news of their son for about a year. They feared that he had been killed by the Russians in the defence of Breslau. They would permit—how could they not?—a search of their house. 'Attic to cellar', said McKenna to

Williams, and they conducted a rigorous search. They found one letter from Dr Absalon, dated 26th September 1944, which corroborated the statement of the parents, and one photograph of a family group. Frau Absalon, who was clearly one of the subjects of the photograph, identified her son Günther on it, and gave permission for McKenna to keep the print. The party sat down in the living room, and McKenna emphasized how important it was to the fate of Absalon's friend that the doctor should be found. Frau Absalon cogitated, and volunteered the information that her son had been very friendly with a woman in Heidelberg, Dr Hildegarde Deutsch, and perhaps if she were interviewed she might have later news of Günther. She lived at 4 Peter Schnellbachstrasse, at Neckergemundt, just outside Heidelberg. McKenna took the name and address and thanked her.

The three investigators then drove to another address, where they found Absalon's wife. Gerda, who was living with her mother. She was a good-looking woman of about thirty, and was comparatively voluble about her husband, who she said was a doctor of law and three years older than she was: she also provided a photograph. She confided that she had had an unhappy time with her husband because neither she nor her family had been members of the Nazi Party, and if she could find him she would petition for a divorce. If they were looking for other people who might know of his whereabouts, she thought it her duty to say that he had a great friend called Frau Deutsch, who was living at the house of a Dr Zuccamaglio at an address in Heidelberg: 22 Peter Schnellbachstrasse. McKenna gravely thanked her for the information and asked permission to keep a photograph of her husband which they had come across. When he asked what she thought had become of her husband Frau Gerda Absalon said she thought he had been killed by the Russians, or else had committed suicide when he realized that Germany was defeated. The last letter she had received from him, which was in the Herr Hauptmann's hands at that moment, was dated 7th February 1945. This was just before the siege of Breslau. Previously he had written to her once a week.

McKenna left Frau Absalon, made a routine visit to the Düsseldorf Labour Exchange to check that Absalon was not working locally under his own name at anything from lawyer's clerk to male nurse, and drove south to his bare barrack quarters. Next day the party drove through Duisberg to the prisoner-of-war camp at Lintorf. McKenna saw the security officer there and received permission to interview a number of men whom he had noted from the available records. As he had expected, they gave him no information, but only the satisfaction of crossing chores off his list. He then asked to see Leutnant Heinrich Wilhelm Willman in the camp hospital.

They were taken to the bed of a young man, a German army doctor whose hand had been shattered in battle towards the end of the war. McKenna asked him some kindly put but shrewdly framed questions, and was soon satisfied that this man was not the Willman on his list. 'I have been to see your parents', he told him, 'and they asked me to give you their love and pass on these messages.' He turned to Smit, who relayed the news from Hünnefelde. Willman was deeply moved and thanked them. They left him sitting in silence with his eyes shining.

It was not an uninterrupted drive back. McKenna, in his attempt to recruit all agencies into supporting the short-staffed SIB investigation, had enlisted—at least by circularization—sections of the Missing Research Enquiry Unit, and he wanted to call on one of these detachments. The MREU were concerned with locating the graves of Royal Air Force aircrew who had crashed in Germany, identifying the dead and arranging for their reinterment. They used isolated teams of one or two officers with NCOs and local German assistants. 'How you can help me', McKenna told the senior officer of the detachment he visited, 'is, I suppose, merely to keep your ears open and ask one or two additional questions. What is the attitude of the resident population towards you?'

'As long as they didn't butcher our men on landing,' said the officer, 'which is rare enough and generally recognizable by their reaction, they work very freely with us. They are wary at first because they think we think they pilfered the bodies of the dead. When they realize that we accept that they probably did do that, they talk very openly with us.'

'They have less inclination to talk openly to us', said McKenna. 'Since at the moment we have no precise idea where a single one of our officers was shot, I'd be obliged if you could work the subject of isolated Gestapo shootings into your conversation in supplementary questions. The location of the crime means everything to us. Once that is established, we can begin to sieve the personnel who may be responsible.'

Once they were back at Rinteln, Williams flew to London to collect some papers under secret cover which were at SIB headquarters. McKenna wrestled with the problem of the Scharpwinkel pyramid between Breslau and Berlin. 'I must find Scharpwinkel', he told his interpreter, Bill Smit. 'No replies have come in from any of the units we have circularized. The Russian liaison teams are giving no response at all, and we must go to Berlin as soon as possible. We have to travel to see the civil police in Hannover in the middle of the week. In the meantime we have to do some civil police thinking ourselves. Did you never want to be a detective?

'Scharpwinkel and Absalon were serving in Breslau. Breslau was strongly menaced by the Russian advance at the beginning of this year. The Germans declared it a fortress, and fought it to the last. The siege proper began on 14th February, about a week after Absalon's last letter to his wife. It lasted for eighty-two days, and the city finally surrendered on VE Day. Now what became of Absalon and Scharpwinkel?

'*Somebody* knows about them. Where do *we* find somebody?

'When you make a town a fortress you clear out the non-combatants. Or they slip out without being told. And, just before a surrender, the combatants pile out too and try to rejoin their families. Now, where were the citizens of Breslau evacuated to? We'll ask the nearest civil servant. In Germany the bureaucracy always knows. Come down with me, and we'll see the local boss.'

The Bürgermeister of Rinteln was delighted to answer so simple a question. 'The people from Breslau were all evacuated here', he said.

'Here? Rinteln?'

'Rinteln, a few in Minden, with an overspill in the little towns around.'

'Do you have records of your local people who took in evacuees?'

'Of course.'

The German enthusiasm for documentation came to McKenna's rescue, as it was to help the investigating team so often during the inquiry. The Bürgermeister turned his staff loose on the records, and within a few hours they produced the names and addresses of local people who had accepted the Breslau evacuees.

'There is only you and me to do it', McKenna told Smit. 'We are going on the knocker, as from now.'

McKenna had already acquired enough German to make basic inquiries, so he separated from Smit on the understanding that he would call him in if a promising lead required detailed interpretation. It was hard, foot-slogging work in dirty weather. At the end of the second day he came to a long street, at the extremity of which was one house on his list where nobody had answered the door on the three occasions when he had already called.

It was raining hard. He was tired and hungry and wet, and longed for a return to the central heating of his mess and a stiff hot drink. The house seemed such a long distance up the road, and he was depressed at the waste of time it entailed. 'But no', he told himself, 'you'll do it. What were you trained for?'

He knocked at the door. A woman answered. He checked her name. 'Do you have anybody here from Breslau?' 'Yes.' 'Man or woman?' 'Man.' 'What's his name?' 'Klaus Lonsky.' 'Where is he?' 'He's not in at the moment, but I'm expecting him any time.' 'Do you mind if I wait?' 'No, come in, sit down and rest.'

An hour passed. Klaus Lonsky came in, a young man in his middle twenties. McKenna introduced himself and said, 'I'm looking for a man called Scharpwinkel. Do you know him?'

'I did know him, by sight', said Lonsky. 'I've seen him often.'

'Do you speak English?'

'Yes.'

'Thank God', said McKenna. 'It's the end of the day.'

'Can you describe Scharpwinkel?' he continued in English.

'Dr Scharpwinkel was head of the Gestapo in Breslau. Age about forty, height about one metre seventy-five, perhaps more, because he stooped forward as he walked. Very slim build, thin fair hair, scars on his right cheek.'

'That's the man', said McKenna. 'Where is he?'

'He's dead.'

'Dead?'

'Yes, killed by the Russians. He must have been.'

'What were you doing in Breslau? Did you have any contact with Scharpwinkel?'

Lonsky explained that, having a Polish father and a German mother, he had avoided political and military affiliation, but he had been conscripted into the Wehrmacht in 1939. By 1943 he had been posted as a lieutenant in the Military Police in Breslau. He had not had personal contact with Scharpwinkel, but knew him well, and a number of others in the Breslau Gestapo.

McKenna fished into his wallet for a photograph and passed it across. 'Who is that?' he said.

'Dr Absalon,' said Lonsky without hesitation. 'I knew him, and his boss Dr Schumacher. . . .'

'Not Brünner?' interjected McKenna.

'There was a Brünner, Kriminalrat Brünner, responsible for prisoner-of-war escapes. I thought Dr Absalon's boss was Dr Hans Schumacher in the Kripo.'

'Thank you', said McKenna, noting the name. 'Who else did you know in Breslau?'

'Dr Kah.'

'Kah? Was he important?'

'Dr Kah was an Obersturmbannführer and head of the SD.'[1]

'You certainly go in for doctors. Who else do you know?'

Lonsky mentioned Wielen, Seetzen, and a new name which McKenna carefully noted: an SS officer called Wieczorek who, he said, was Scharpwinkel's deputy in Breslau.

McKenna closed his book and looked very steadily at Lonsky.

'And now, what has become of all these men?' he asked. 'Scharpwinkel, Seetzen, Absalon and the others?'

'They're dead. Or else they have been captured by the Russians, which amounts to the same thing.'

'How are you so sure of that?'

Lonsky began to talk about the siege of Breslau. When the city was declared a fortress all ancillary military formations were dissolved, and their personnel flung into active defence. He himself was transferred from the Military Police and sent to the 'front line'. At first this consisted of trenches dug in the suburbs, but gradually they were given up and the defenders fought from house-block to house-block. Scharpwinkel formed a fighting body of Gestapo officers, Criminal Police and Volkssturm (Home Guard) and threw them into the front within a few streets of the Gestapo offices.

[1]Sicherheitsdienst: SS Security Service.

He gave this force his own name, the Scharpwinkel Unit. McKenna got the impression from Lonsky that Scharpwinkel was almost recklessly determined that these men should die—and thinking it over later he hazarded the notion that perhaps this unit included Scharpwinkel's death squad, already denounced by Eden, and their leader was intent on destroying the evidence which survivors might yield on interrogation. The losses of the Scharpwinkel Unit were immense. Lonsky believed that they had been wiped out to a man. And everyone else who had served in Breslau thought so too. Scharpwinkel had died with them.

'But you don't know for sure, do you?' asked McKenna. 'You never saw his body?'

'No. But he must be dead.'

McKenna considered for a minute, then rose and thanked Lonsky. As he said goodnight, he asked, 'You don't know anyone else round here who served in Breslau?'

'No.' And then Lonsky stumbled in his speech. 'Well, there might be one other.'

'Who?'

'I was friendly in Breslau with an infantry lieutenant called Hubertus Zembrodt. I heard that he had made his way to this area after the capitulation. He's not in Rinteln, because if he were I should know. I think he may be in one of the towns and villages outside.'

'Thank you very much', said McKenna.

'Zembrodt', he reported to Squadron Leader Thomas next morning. 'Hubertus Zembrodt. I have an appointment in Hannover today. Can you get a sergeant to go through the local records after this man?'

McKenna and Smit drove to Hannover in a jeep. McKenna had decided to make discreet liaison with the German civil police. Such a step did not then have the wholehearted approval of the Judge Advocate General's office in London, but McKenna had already noted that, where comparatively untainted officers had been restored to positions in the civil police—still under the control of the Military Government—their professionalism responded to his own, and there seemed a genuine wish among some of them to play a perhaps penitential part in a renewed pursuit of justice against branded criminals. McKenna got the approval of the Public Security Officer in Hannover, and then made contact with the two senior officers of police. With Smit he called on a number of other British units, and after a long day turned for home in the evening light. After some forty miles they turned off the autobahn for the home stretch. They were in forest country, and there was mist in the gathering dusk.

McKenna uttered an exclamation and sharply braked his jeep. Then he coasted very slowly forward and stopped. In front of the jeep, at neck height, an old metal hawser with some of its strands parted under tension was tightly stretched across the road, lashed to trees on either side.

'Thirty miles an hour would have been fast enough to cut our heads off', he observed to Smit, as he went to his toolbox and prised the wire rope off the trees with a spanner. They coiled the hawser, put it in the back of the car, and drove on reflectively.

McKenna learned from Squadron Leader Thomas next morning that there had been no success so far in finding Hubertus Zembrodt. 'I'll carry on with it today, sir', he said. 'If you agree, I should also like to circulate one more name in my Breslau pyramid and re-circulate another. Lonsky has given me the name of a Hans Schumacher who was Absalon's superior officer at Breslau: he is not the same as the General Karl Schumacher who is Number 77 on our list. There is also yet another high-ranker, who sticks out about a mile higher than before, after I have been thinking about him. He's Dr Ernst Kah, head of the SD in Breslau. Even assuming that Scharpwinkel was playing his murders very close to his chest on the need-to-know security basis, I fancy Kah must have known something. The SD made it their business to know most things: they even listed the names of the people who had voted NO in Hitler's referendum, and that was a very classy piece of detection.[1] Kah is already on the list, Number 12. But, with your permission, I'll put the circulations through before I go off after Zembrodt. There is some urgency. He's worth recirculating. I'd rather like to get my hands on Kah.'

At that moment Dr Ernst Kah was newly smarting under arrest and interrogation effected through the routines of vigilance already observed by Group Captain Somerhough's North Western Europe War Crimes Investigation Unit. He had been taken the previous evening, at almost the exact time when McKenna had been wryly examining the wire rope lashed across the road to kill him.

An informer had passed the word to the Royal Air Force Police Unit in Hamburg that morning that there was an SS Obersturmbannführer named Ernest Mercier in hiding at the Swedish Mission hostel in Hamburg. An SIB man, Sergeant Taylor, went there and asked the secretary if she had any confirmation of this. The secretary looked through the files and said that a man called Ernest Mercier had left the hostel about a week before, and had given the forwarding address of 23 Gurlittstrasse. Taylor followed the trail, and found that the address given was a boarding-house.

The landlady said Mercier had left three days previously, but it was possible that he might call back for correspondence. Taylor asked her to telephone his police office immediately if Mercier returned. At seven in the evening the landlady telephoned to say that Mercier had arrived. Taylor drove furiously to the boarding-house and arrested the man. He produced the identity papers of a

[1]Himmler used the Sicherheitsdienst for security control of internal political affairs.

displaced person in the name of Ernest Mercier, of French nationality, and he also possessed a supplementary ration card with a Military Government stamp. Taylor brought him to the unit office. He refused to make any answer to questions, and Taylor consigned him to the civil police lock-up for overnight detention. An hour later the police telephoned and said they had nabbed Mercier in the middle of an attempted escape. Taylor sent two NCOs to the police station immediately with orders to question the prisoner strongly. He then admitted that he held the rank of Obersturmbannführer in the SD. Next day, under interrogation by Taylor, he admitted that he was Ernst Kah, ex-Breslau and ex-Görlitz. He had obtained false papers as a displaced French native, and had bought on the black market the supplementary ration card he was found with. Since this was a genuine card, correctly rubber-stamped, Hamburg security coincidentally began a comb-out of Military Government offices to find who was passing these cards for profitable and illegal sale. On the strength of these documents Kah held a genuine permit signed by a British officer which gave him carte blanche to travel through Germany buying wines for the officers' messes of various British authorities.

It would be difficult to conceive a more useful document to give to a Gestapo man on the run.

Under further interrogation, Kah admitted that he knew of the whereabouts of another SS officer on the run in Hamburg. As McKenna had remarked, you had only to catch the first and others followed. This man was none other than Standartenführer Seetzen, the Security Police colonel who was one of McKenna's seven most wanted men.

'Tonight we will take you for a drive', said Sergeant Taylor to Dr Kah.

At an hour after midnight two official cars drew up outside a house in a Hamburg suburb. Kah was under escort in the second car. Officers from the first car went into the house and brought out a man. He was placed in the headlights of the second car, and Kah mutely indicated that this was Seetzen. Seetzen was put in the first car and driven towards the police unit. On the journey his escort heard a crunching in his mouth, and the man suddenly stiffened. His heels ground forward towards the front seat, and his body arched. The car was immediately diverted to a hospital. But on arrival Seetzen was found to be dead from cyanide poisoning, after crunching a capsule locked into the bridgework of his teeth.

McKenna had had two depressingly unrewarding days in search of Scharpwinkel through the hoped-for tracing of Hubertus Zembrodt. He battled through rain and a howling gale to reach his billet after a full day on the knocker. As he shook out his greatcoat, the telephone rang.

'Hamburg here. Bad news for you, I'm afraid. We've got your man Seetzen—'

'Bad news! You couldn't have given me better. When can I—?'

'He's dead. Since early this morning. Suicide. Cyanide. The same trick as Himmler.' And the circumstances were explained to McKenna. 'We didn't let you know before. We had to established identification. We only had a sighting when we picked him up. His papers were in the name of Gollwitzer. But there seems little doubt now that it's Seetzen.'

'Did he say anything? About Scharpwinkel?'

'Sorry. Not a word. I suppose he was making up his mind to bite that capsule. We'll put in a full report. Sorry about this. Still, it's one crossed off your list.'

Curiously, the officer in Hamburg made no mention of Kah.

McKenna took the blow as philosophically as possible. One off the list. But no progress towards Scharpwinkel. Where the hell was Zembrodt?

On the next day McKenna calculated that he had covered every location in the direct vicinity of Rinteln, without finding a lead to Zembrodt. There remained only the small town of Barntrup, eighteen miles away. McKenna bundled Smit into a light railcar, and at the end of a rackety journey they went to the Bürgermeister's office.

Smit made an immediate impression with the Bürgermeister's secretary. He was chattering and flattering for so long in a German too advanced for McKenna's understanding that the officer began to get restive. Smit applied himself more directly to the task: Looking for a retired infantry officer from Breslau called Zembrodt; any hope of their holding the relevant file?

The town-hall staff were, under the exhortations of the Bürgermeister's jolly secretary, delighted to help. The local police were anxious not to be left out of active co-operation. Between them they produced registers of every sort. 'Silly me!' said the secretary. 'We have a separate file of former members of the armed forces living in the town.' Her polished finger-nail slipped daintily into the meagre Zs. 'Zembrodt, Hubertus,' she said. 'Alverdiessennerstrasse 20. The police officer would like to show you where it is.'

'Show' was exactly what the police officer did. He had a reluctance, understandable in a country area, to escorting two officers of the army of occupation all the way to an ex-officer's front door. McKenna told Smit to stay out of sight round the corner in any case. This was not so much to avoid embarrassment to their unsuspecting host as an old policeman's interest in knowing if anyone dashed out of the back door when a uniformed man came to the front.

The place was a tiny cottage. The time was early Saturday afternoon. McKenna knocked, and a pleasant man of about thirty came to the door, poorly dressed but smartly turned out where the man could conquer the material.

'Herr Zembrodt?' McKenna asked.

'Yes.'

'A friend of yours has sent his greetings. Klaus Lonsky.'

'Oh, how is he? Come in, come in.' McKenna went in and sat down.

'I'm looking for a man called Scharpwinkel', he began.

'You won't find him.'

'Why?'

'He's dead. Killed by the Russians.'

'How do you know?'

'My wife will tell you.' He went to call his wife. She was very young, just over eighteen. When Zembrodt spoke to her she began to tell McKenna a story. But she was speaking fast, and in some excitement, and McKenna could not understand it. He excused himself and brought in Smit. Frau Gerda Zembrodt's narrative was slowly pieced together.

She had met her husband in Breslau, which was her home. He had served in France and Russia, and after convalescence from a wound had been sent to Breslau as an Oberleutnant of the infantry at the end of January 1945, a fortnight before the siege began. Six weeks later, on his twenty-ninth birthday, they had been married. He was seriously wounded again on 24th April, and was sent to Breslau's No. 6 Hospital in the Priester Seminar. A fortnight later, on the night of the capitulation, Gerda Zembrodt had taken a job as an assistant nurse in the same hospital. Wounded men were still being brought into the hospital, and she particularly remembered a tall and extremely surly man who had been carried in on a stretcher and was put in a ward opposite her husband's. He was listed as Leutnant Hagamann. About four days after the surrender—that is, on 10th or 11th May 1945—at 10.30 in the morning, two Russian officers came into the hospital with the German Dr Mehling, who was in charge of all the hospitals in Breslau. Gerda Zembrodt rushed straight into her husband's ward, but the Russians went into the ward opposite. With them was a Russian woman in civilian clothes, but carrying a pistol in her hand, and she seemed the dominant personage in the Russian trio. Frau Zembrodt did not see what happened in the opposite ward, but she was told of it immediately afterwards by another nurse, Charlotte Färber, and she did see something of the sequel.

The Russians strode into the ward. The woman shouted in German, 'Which is Hagamann?' There was a silence, and then the wounded lieutenant in the corner raised his arm and said, 'I am Hagamann'.

The Russian woman marched to the bed and screamed at the man, 'You are not Hagamann. You are Scharpwinkel.' She stripped the bedclothes off him with her free hand and ordered, 'Get out!' The man pointed to his wounded leg. 'Get out!' she said, and he hobbled into the centre of the ward.

After stormy shouting between the beds the man admitted that he was Scharpwinkel, head of the Breslau Gestapo. He was told that he was to accompany the Russians as he was. A nurse put a greatcoat over his shoulders. The Russians told Dr Mehling that, as he was in charge of the hospital, and had admitted a man under a false identity, he too was under arrest. The group of five went out, and Gerda Zembrodt saw them go.

As the party disappeared into the hospital yard there was a burst of gunfire. A shocked silence fell on the hospital. Nobody moved for some time, until they heard a car drive away.

'I saw them go into the yard at the back', said Frau Zembrodt. 'That's where it happened. That's where Scharpwinkel was killed.'

'Did you see the body?' asked McKenna.

'No. I dare not go out.'

'Did you see any bloodstains?'

'No. They took the body away in the car.'

McKenna decided to leave the young German couple in peace after his visit, and accordingly took formal evidence from them on the spot. All statements take disproportionately more time to write than they do to read, and Smit, writing in German and not legally trained, had necessarily to consult McKenna about phrasing and take his instructions about what was admissible. Consequently it was dusk when they left the cottage and trudged to the rail-stop.

'So Scharpwinkel is dead too', said Smit with disappointment.

'Not yet.'

'What do you mean, sir?'

'I'm not satisfied.'

'No, sir, you will be very unhappy', said Smit, mistranslating him.

'I'm not satisfied, because I'm a policeman. Where is the body? What is the evidence of death? A burst of gunfire? In a city that had been taken by storm four days previously! It was a wild town. There was rape and loot and summary justice going on. Why do you think this young girl Gerda Zembrodt became a nurse at the capitulation? If she had wanted to be near her husband she could have gone in when he was wounded in April. She went in on 7th May because she thought it was the only course she could take to save her body, and I have no doubt her husband agreed. It was a wild town. At the mercy of the victors. I haven't a doubt that the nurses heard a burst of gunfire. It could even have been done to put the fear of God into Scharpwinkel. But we hear nothing of a body, nothing of any blood—nothing, incidentally, of that Dr Mehling who was arrested at the same time.

'There's still a solid chance that Scharpwinkel is with the Russians. 'We've had no joy from Russian liaison officers here at Bad Salzuflen and the other places, no joy at all. Very well. We'll go to where we hope the real liaison is done. We'll go and see the Russians in Berlin. Dear comrades, have you got our Scharpwinkel? Someone has hit him for six and please may we have our ball back?'

'Berlin', said Smit in his singing Dutch–English. 'I have always been wanting to see Berlin.'

In London Wing Commander Bowes took out his list of fifty officers who, according to German official sources, had, by provocatively getting shot whilst trying to escape, necessitated a register of strength decrease through death in Stalag Luft III. Against the twenty-nine names of those who had died within the Breslau Military District, beginning with Henry J. Birkland of Calgary and ending with John F. Williams of London, he wrote in column 16: 'SS Standartenführer Seetzen; suicide 28.9.1945. Max Wielen in British custody.' He was careful to write this twenty-nine times.

From Rinteln, Flight Lieutenant McKenna set out for Berlin. As he recorded the incidents of that journey:

> *I set off rather late in the day in a Ford V8 four-by-four, with my Dutch interpreter and all my papers. Leaving the British Zone at the checkpoint at Helmstedt, 110 miles from Berlin centre, one of our people said, 'You're cutting it a bit fine to get in before dark'. I went through the Russian checkpoint. The light faded. Three-quarters of an hour later, near Magdeburg, the engine raced, the car slowed, and I knew that a half-shaft had gone. I drove on to the centre reservation. I thought, 'This is a hell of a mess. Nobody will come through now.'' But we heard a roar up the road, and along came a jeep with two Americans. I stopped them, and said: 'I have papers here which I don't want to get into anybody else's hands'. The papers were the lists of our wanted people, my own personal notebook, and my travel passes from the French and the Americans. If I had lost these I might have had difficulty in getting replacements, and the French and the Americans would have taken a very dim view if our authorized travel papers had fallen into Russian hands. I asked the Americans: 'Would you be kind enough to take my sergeant to Berlin, and I'll sit and wait for the Aid Department to come out. Please tell them exactly where I am.' They went off, and I saw their tail light disappear. Suddenly everything went silent. It was the quiet part of the day when not even the birds can be heard. I'm sitting in the car, flaming cold, but I think 'I've got a good overcoat and blankets', and I wrap myself up. I reckoned I had some four hours to wait. Then it started to snow, really hard, and the countryside was quieter then ever as the snow muffled the sounds in the air. I started the engine once or twice to warm it a little. Eventually I dozed off. I awoke to the sound of a metallic rattle coming up on the right-hand side like a lorry with solid tyres and chains round them. It stopped, and I could see several people moving around with oil lamps. I listened, but I couldn't make out what they were saying. Eventually some characters came up and knocked on the window. I opened the door, and they started talking in Russian. I tried to answer in English and what bit of German I knew, but I was getting nowhere. Then one said a word like* papirosi, papirosi, *and I recognized the Russian for* cigarettes. *I said 'No papirosi'. They wouldn't accept that, and showed that they meant to look for themselves. They were all carrying firearms and I had to get out. They made me stand in the weather while they climbed in the car and searched it. They came out empty-handed and stood around, and eventually one of them came up and shook hands with me, and they got into their truck and drove away. I went fast asleep again. About midnight a car drove up from the Berlin direction. Squadron Leader Berry, an RAF DAPM from Berlin, got out and ticked me off soundly for getting caught out there in the middle of the night. I asked what I should have done. 'You should have abandoned the car, what does it matter? We can't tow this thing*

away with a broken axle, we'll have to get out a Heavy Aid Detachment in the morning.' I asked him: 'Have you seen my sergeant interpreter?' He said 'Yes, we've got all the papers in Berlin.' 'Well, that's all that matters,' I said, and I was driven back to Berlin, a hot bath and bed. Next morning I borrowed a car and went straight down the autobahn to see what had happened to my Ford. There was no trace of it. It had vanished in the night. You could see where it had been from the tyre marks on the grass reservation, but there was no trace of the car and we never saw it again. I telephoned Group Captain Brown and he said: 'Don't worry. Are you sure there were no papers in it? Right, then forget it. We'll write it off.'

4 The man who lied for Germany

'But Scharpwinkel is bloody dead', said Wing Commander Bowes. 'It stands to reason. We'll write him off. We won't waste any more time on him.'

'I don't agree, sir,' said Squadron Leader McKenna. 'I think we should press this until we get some response. The Russians have got to say something sooner or later.'

'You didn't get much change out of them in Berlin', Bowes commented.

'There's a very good letter to Stalin in the post', said McKenna. 'I wrote it myself.'

'Flannel!' said Bowes.

It was ten weeks after the Zembrodt statements. Wing Commander Bowes had arrived in Rinteln as Officer Commanding the Special Investigation Branch in the British Air Forces of Occupation, which included responsibility for all criminal investigation within the British occupied zone of Germany—but Bowes had his own priorities. McKenna had been promoted to acting Squadron Leader. The tiny investigation team had scored modest successes, through patient routine work. Some half-dozen names had been eased off the Wanted List. They were all of essential witnesses rather than potential accused, but the information obtained through their interrogation had been instructive.

McKenna had made his visit to Berlin—the first of many. He had not, as Bowes had hinted, been accorded a triumphal entry by the Russians, but he was not dissatisfied. The senior British officers dealing with Russian liaison there had strongly encouraged him to follow his inclination and fish for Scharpwinkel, if he was in Russia, through high-level channels of the Judge Advocate General's office in the British Army of Occupation. Making concentrated inquiries about others in his pyramid, he heard a widely believed but unconfirmed story that Müller, the Gestapo chief who was one of his top seven, had been seen in Berlin in the last stage of the land-battle, on the veranda of his office, wearing his best white uniform, while Russian tanks were penetrating the street outside. He had apparently been determined to go down in style; but McKenna did not cross him off his list.

He heard in Berlin that Kah was in custody near Hamburg, and drove back to interview him. On his arrival at Rinteln he found a new member seconded to the team, Pilot Officer Stephen Courtney. Courtney had reported in with a huge German shepherd dog which he had acquired during his progress through Germany before the surrender. The animal was called Fritz, and slept in Courtney's room. McKenna looked doubtfully at it. 'Is he safe?' he asked. 'He frightens *me* sometimes', said Courtney cheerfully.

McKenna took Courtney to interview Kah, but could not see the prisoner, since the Army were reserving him for fourteen days' interrogation. When they did at last see the former chief of the Breslau security police, he confirmed the responsibility in the chain of command of the dead Seetzen and the others, and added one name to their Wanted List: Fritz Panzinger, who had been adjutant to Heinrich Müller at RSHA Berlin. The only immediate response to a quick circularization of Panzinger was the news from Berlin that his wife, who was Müller's sister, had committed suicide by poisoning a few days before the capitulation. Kah was completely co-operative. 'Germany has lost the war', he said, 'and will not recover again. England is the only country which can lead Europe and establish Europe again. I do not say that as a joke.' But McKenna concluded that Kah was not a likely contender for any guilty complicity in the Sagan murders, and he sent him to the London Cage for full interrogation without bothering to take an immediate formal statement.

McKenna completed a number of other inquiries which it was convenient to expunge from his notebook. He saw Anton Kaindl, the former commandant of Sachsenhausen concentration camp, who was held in internment at Paderborn. Though multiple charges were being prepared against Kaindl, McKenna was himself interested only in checking the administration through which Wing Commander Day and four others who had escaped from Stalag Luft III had been consigned to Sachsenhausen, thus confirming Gestapo responsibility for the operation. One macabre answer stayed in his mind following a query from a war crimes investigator who was sharing the interrogation with a different purpose. Question: How long did it take to burn the bodies of 140 men in the crematorium? Answer: 48 hours. But McKenna was later to remember Kaindl, who had innumerable deaths on his head, as a possible pawn to offer in the battle for Scharpwinkel.

He was gratified to learn that Brünner, whom he had listed as Absalon's chief at Breslau, had been traced in a prison camp of the American forces. He forwarded the news to his superiors in London. They had more time and opportunity than he to extract Brünner from the Americans and interrogate him in London. He noted that Josef Kramer, during his trial at Lüneburg for atrocities at Belsen, had admitted pushing internees into the gas chamber at Natzweiler, where Kramer had previously served. Natzweiler had been marked as the location of the cremation of Flying Officer Dennis Cochran. He made a memorandum to start inquiries in the French zone regarding any record of the delivery of Dennis Cochran's body to that camp. He received reports from the interrogation of prisoners who retailed gossip—or originated it—about the fate of General Nebe, the Kripo Chief at RSHA Berlin who, in McKenna's reconstruction, had passed to Müller the names of the officers who were to be shot.

Nebe, three months after the Sagan murders, had been a conspirator in the bomb plot against Hitler. It had been suggested by some sympathizers that he had unwillingly consented to involvement in the Stalag Luft III crime because he dared not show his hand as an opponent of Hitler at that stage, when the lives of fifty officers were weighed against the extinction of the Führer. Certainly he had been pursued after the failure of the plot. He disappeared, and simulated suicide, leaving his suitcase on the bank of the Wannsee, the lake to the west of Berlin. He was later arrested, and confined in the Gestapo headquarters in Berlin. He was seen there at the end of November 1944, and was credibly said to have seriously attempted suicide soon afterwards. The weight of evidence made it likely that he was executed in February 1945.

Müller, Brünner, Nebe . . . McKenna's short list was diminishing, but not through the informative confrontation he would have liked. He set his small force to a renewed attack on combing the internment camps before the winter set in. Now that he had Pilot Officer Courtney as an addition to his strength, he reallocated the areas. He himself took the camps in the British zone of occupation. Courtney was given the American zone. It was intended that Flight Sergeant Williams should take the French zone. But the French were disorganized, and said it would be many weeks before they could receive regular inquisitors, but they would accept the occasional single inquiry. Williams therefore worked with Courtney, either interrogating in parallel to double the speed of action at any one camp, or interrogating alone at a nearby camp. The American zone was a very wide area with an awesome number of prisoner-of-war cages and internment camps. Courtney computed that there were over 150 000 prisoners of war in the United States 3rd Army zone alone, apart from those in the civilian enclosures.

There were the first formalities of getting from the Americans the necessary passes to go into the zone and the detailed introductions to the commandants of the camps. 'The drill is complicated, but precise,' McKenna told Courtney, driving him to the United States War Crimes Liaison office in Bad Oeynhausen to introduce him. 'Colonel King and Captain Ivy here will issue your travel authority once you've got a movement order. You have tell them the towns you mean to visit, the purpose and length of stay. Take a copy of these papers to our own accounts section in Bad Eilsen and get an issue of dollar scrip there. Always take sufficient currency. Take ample petrol and oil too. Be sure you have the addresses of British Liaison officers in the American zone who will issue more petrol and oil coupons. But fuel is an extremely doubtful proposition in the French zone, so if you go there load up with your own jerricans. Driving down to the US zone you'll find it convenient to night-stop at Wiesbaden. Get accommodation from the USFET[1] billeting officer in each town. If you find a war criminal in one of the camps and want to extradite him, get in touch with Lieutenant Colonel Boyd-Maunsell, our liaison officer at the War Crimes Centre in Munich.'

And Courtney started. The additional drill was still 'complicated but precise'. Arrive at a camp with interpreter; see the commandant; explain he was searching for Gestapo, Kripo and Sipo members; be taken by escort to camp administrative officer; thence to the documentations team; go through the register of inmates; make out a list of likely men; ask for them to be sent separately at twenty-minute intervals into the interrogation room.

The routine started: name, place and date of birth, occupation in Germany; which rank held in the police; what places had the man served at, and at what time; if there seemed to be any evasiveness over the period March/April 1944, come round to the question with a different approach—who was his commanding officer at that time, and who were other senior officers? After a short time an interrogator knew the regional hierarchy of the Gestapo and the dates of appointment better than any prisoner who was trying some impromptu deceit. The questioning was intended to culminate in a disclosure of the particular man's activities at the time of the Sagan escape, and the activities of anyone else in the Gestapo or Kripo that he was acquainted with. It was a coarse screening process. Any man thought of sufficient interest to justify lengthier interrogation would be arrested and cleared for transfer to the London District Cage—the Kensington Palace Gardens headquarters of the War Crimes Investigation Unit.

It was a coarse screening process, but it was also positively productive, if generally on a minute scale and at a snail's pace. It gave the SIB team its first chance to add to the information already received from the Judge Advocate General, and the accumulation of knowledge enabled them to crack down much more sharply on lies and evasions as they grew experienced.

It was also a soul-destroying job. The autumn was well advanced, and the weather was breaking. The internment camps were in the main former German concentration camps, and if there was no

[1]United States Forces, European Theatre.

longer the smoke of death in the air, there was all too often its abiding smell. The camps were vast areas with tight enclosures, barbed wire and high observation posts everywhere, squalid huts standing in lakes of shallow water and connected by duckboard paths. The atmosphere of depression and desolation which both McKenna and Courtney absorbed in these camps had to be broken by far more spirited, purposeful expeditions in search of topically needed evidence or raids for a wanted man. McKenna spent some time in November 1945 making forays for Leutnant Werner Awe, formerly adjutant to Stalag Luft III, who was not found for six months and then gave the London District Cage important evidence that the camp staff knew in advance, more clearly than the Commandant had conceded, that British and American prisoners would be 'stood up against the wall' when recaptured after escape.

Courtney, at his end of the country, welcomed the diversion of going to Nuremburg, where the principal trial was beginning, to interrogate Baron Gustav von Steengracht, Number 59 on the JAG's Wanted List. Steengracht, who as an ex-official had suffered automatic arrest since the German surrender, was held in custody in the cells adjoining the court room at Nuremberg, where he had been summoned as a material witness. He had been an under-secretary at the German Foreign Office during the war, having previously served under Ribbentrop at the German Embassy in London. His duties included the co-ordination of International Red Cross and Swiss Government activities regarding prisoners of war. He had heard of the death of the fifty officers from Stalag Luft III, he declared, only as a rumour in the German Foreign Office. When he had made inquiries he had been officially assured by the military and the SS that the gossip was untrue. 'Who do you think carried out the killing?' Courtney asked. 'The SS, acting on Hitler's orders,' was Steengracht's prompt response.

Courtney went on to Munich for a long stint on the index cards held by the Americans, and on rewarding stocks of records which had been stored in Munich by the Germans and not destroyed before the surrender. As a result of his work here, he decided that he would have to go to Dachau. It was just a few miles away, and he discussed the atrocities committed at this notorious concentration camp with the City Hall officials in Munich who were supplying him with the local records. They said that they had not known anything about Dachau at the time. They were aware that there had been heavy traffic on that side of the city. They said that they had assumed that Dachau was a light industrial complex.

Courtney arrived there, at half-past four on a winter afternoon. The sky was blackening. The camp was an enormous site, of the order of a thousand acres, partitioned into compounds by wire. In the middle was a heavily wired stockade on a hill. Courtney made his introduction and was admitted. The Americans courteously showed him the gas chamber. All around the camp, in waste areas, there were still high piles of human ash, like the tips from a coal-mine.

Courtney said he had to go to the star compound where the SS prisoners were kept. This was the stockade on the hill in the centre of the camp. An American in the guardroom said:

'You'd better not go up there this time of night, mister. You may not come out again.'

'It can't be as bad as that', said Courtney. 'After all, they're disarmed.'

'They're funny people', said the guard.

'I've come a long way', said Courtney, 'and I propose to go up there.'

'It's up to you. But you must leave your gun and your dog.'

'Why?'

'Because they'll take the pistol and shoot the dog, and the next move is up to them. They are tough nuts in the SS compound.'

Courtney went up with his interpreter. It was a long march up the hill in the darkening winter night. Courtney felt he was ascending Calvary. They were admitted, and they explained their mission to the officer in charge. They saw the men they wanted to interview. No one made any statement under interrogation incriminating himself or anyone else in the compound. But they were more generous in their information about higher officers who had not been caught. Courtney came away with strong leads as to the whereabouts of three men on his wanted list. Clumping down that hill in the dark, away from the sinister men in the compound, he saw again the shapes of the hills of ashes. This was indeed Golgotha, the place of a skull.

He passed his information back to McKenna, who followed up the information and arrested Colonel Richard Wälde and his superior officer in the Luftwaffe administration of Stalag Luft III, Lieutenant-General Walther Grosch, with another man on the list, General Rudolf Hoffman. These three were, in McKenna's term, not bloodstained. But the information they gave under interrogation in the London Cage did show that Wälde and Grosch were informed in advance of the decision to shoot the prisoners, though Grosch said he had cited the Geneva Convention and protested. They were in law accessories before the fact, but their evidence was considered as of more use to confirm the role of Müller and Nebe as the agents of Himmler and Kaltenbrunner, rather than as self-incrimination.

McKenna, amid all his routine interrogations and the diversionary raids which were usefully shortening the Wanted List, had not forgotten Scharpwinkel. Every man who had had any connection with Breslau had been closely questioned. Accumulated information was woven into the known story. McKenna had received a hint that Absalon, besides his disciplinary action against the German camp staff after the escape, had participated in at least one of the shootings organized from Breslau. McKenna promoted Absalon from a key witness to a potential accused.

He had also received details of the fate of General Schmauser, Seetzen's superior as head of the Breslau Sipo. He utilized the information. As the result of his continuing pressure, the Major-General Chief of Staff of the British Army of the Rhine, the United Kingdom occupying force in Germany, sent, on 17th December 1945, a letter to Colonel-General Serov, Chief of the Department of Internal Affairs and Army Group, Russian Occupation Forces, Berlin, with a copy to Squadron Leader McKenna:

> With reference to my letter dated 13.11.1945 I am now able to add a further description of Dr Scharpwinkel and of Ernst Heinrich Schmauser, who was in a motor car which collided with a Russian tank in February 1945, when he was injured and taken prisoner eight miles south of Breslau. [The descriptions followed of Scharpwinkel, Schmauser, Absalon and others, all wanted for trial and interrogation in connection with the Stalag Luft III murders.]
>
> I request that I may be informed whether these men are in Russian hands and whether you are prepared to hand them over to the British. Should you be prepared to do so, I request to be informed of the place at which the handover may take place.

At this point Wing Commander Bowes arrived at Rinteln, a lion in winter, charged with taking over Special Investigation Branch affairs in Germany.

Briskly—after formally ridiculing McKenna for his persistence over Scharpwinkel—he swung in twelve extra sergeant investigators with their essential transport, drawing them from the RAF Police detachment in Brussels. He squeezed three extra cars out of BAFO headquarters. He commandeered another dozen interpreters. He set teams of NCOs and interpreters under Courtney to comb the complex of camps in the American zone, and put six men with interpreters on the task of checking all records in the prisoner-of-war and civilian internment camps in the British zone. He stopped the dangerous gap in the investigation occasioned by an unwillingness of the French to have the disorganized state of the records in their zone exposed by zealous on-the-spot inquiries, and handed over this diplomatically difficult job to Squadron Leader McKenna. 'Extra measures may bring this inquiry to a speedier conclusion', he reported to Group Captain Nicholas in London. 'This investigation is being given priority No. 1 over all other inquiries.'

Bowes had a nature which expressed itself in activity. He was a fighting commander who had to be in the field himself. A report came in from the RAF Police Unit in Berlin that a prisoner in a civil gaol had informed on another prisoner who had shared his cell with him. The second prisoner had confided that he was a former member of the SS who had fooled the English 'because they were too stupid to prove anything against him', and that he 'knew a little about this case of the fifty RAF officers'. Bowes dashed to Berlin, interrogated the man concerned, and eliminated him as a loud-mouth on the subject of the Sagan murders—but slammed charges against him for signing documents denying any previous connection with the Nazi Party, which he had completed to obtain favoured employment with the British. Soon afterwards another informant told the RAF in Berlin that a criminal whose photograph had been published in the newspapers was in reality Dr Günther Absalon. Bowes went to Berlin again, took the man into custody, brought him back to Rinteln, shaved off his beard and—without explanation—shoved him in front of Klaus Lonsky, whose proficiency in the English language, so acceptable to an exhausted McKenna hunting Breslau evacuees three months previously, had earned him a job in the Military Government District Food Department. Lonsky talked to the man as requested, and was asked if he had seen him before. Lonsky said he had not. He was told that the man was suspected of being Absalon. 'Absalon is much taller, has lighter hair, more hair, and a different voice', maintained Lonsky. Bowes double-checked by sending a photograph of the man to Absalon's wife in Düsseldorf, who was waiting to divorce him, and she denied his identity. The man was sent back to Berlin to face his original charges of swindling and possessing two firearms.

Patient parallel investigation by the reinforced inquiry teams was yielding valuable leads about the Danzig murders of Brettell, Marcinkus, Picard and Walenn; about the Munich murders of Gouws and Stevens; and about the cremations at Saarbrücken which were presumed to have been ordered for Bushell and Scheidhauer. These leads were all being keenly followed.

But, if success seems to come magnetically to the energetic, it certainly came to Bowes. In early February he was handed the opportunity of the big breakthrough which was to herald the long line of arrests that transformed the investigation.

Both the Soviet Government and the Czechoslovak Government which had been restored after the German surrender had been asked for aid in the Stalag Luft III investigation with the greatest possible urgency. The Czechs had a full dossier of war crimes to handle, as barbarous as, even if more diffused than, the appalling massacre at Lidice. But seven of the Sagan murders could be assumed to have been done on their own soil. The urns of four men known to have been imprisoned at Reichenberg—Bull, Mondschein, Kierath and Squadron Leader Williams—had been marked Brüx, and a fifth man, Stower, who had been last seen at Reichenberg but whose urn was unmarked, must have died on Czech territory; the urns of Kidder and Kirby-Green were marked Mährisch Ostrau[1].

[1]The German names of Reichenberg, Brüx and Mährisch Ostrau

The Czechs, who had suffered their own loss after the Stalag Luft III escape, did not ignore the British plea. They included its content in the pursuit of their own investigations. In the autumn of 1945 they picked up a driver called Friedrich Kiowsky who had worked for the Gestapo. They invited to his interrogation a Czech lawyer with a personal interest in the Sagan case.

In early December 1945 this man, Dr F. V. van der Bijl, wrote to the British Ambassador in Prague:

Hotel Esplanade,
PRAHA II.
December 2nd, 1945.

Sir,

Squadron Leader T. G. KIRBY-GREEN: deceased.

Detailed information has just come into my possession regarding the alleged murder of two Royal Air Force officers on March 28th, 1944. I have personally questioned a former Gestapo man who was an eye-witness of the murder. I have every reason to believe the complete accuracy of the report which I submit to Your Excellency, although more than this I cannot certify.

Thomas Graham KIRBY-GREEN. British. Born in Nyasaland on 28th February, 1918. Gave his rank as "Major" of the Royal Air Force; i.e., Squadron Leader. I think there is little doubt this was Squadron Leader KIRBY-GREEN who was formerly Officer i/c of the Training Flight of 311 Czechoslovak Squadron RAF whilst stationed at RAF East Wretham, Norfolk. . . .

Dr van der Bijl narrated in some detail the escape of Kirby-Green from Sagan with a Canadian flight lieutenant whose name was unknown to him. They had been arrested in Zlín, Moravia, and were taken in two cars towards Breslau by way of Moravská Ostrava. The drivers of these cars were named Kiowsky and Schwartzer. Kiowsky was in custody, and van der Bijl had recently interrogated him.

Kiowsky had had Kirby-Green in his car with a Gestapo officer Erich Zacharias. At a spot ten kilometres before Moravská Ostrava the cars were stopped to allow the prisoners to relieve themselves. They were still handcuffed. While he was relieving himself Squadron Leader Kirby-Green was shot twice by Zacharias. A Gestapo man who had travelled with the Canadian in the other car shot his prisoner also. Zacharias then removed the handcuffs while he waited for uniformed German police to take away the bodies.

The murders, said van der Bijl, were ordered by Hans Ziegler, Chief of the Gestapo in Zlín, who forbade any discussion of them for fear of later International Red Cross investigation. To foil any

---

were rejected after the war, and the towns reverted to their Czech names of Liberec, Most and Moravská Ostrava, which will be used henceforth.

future inquiry, Zacharias, Kiowsky, Schwartzer and the unidentified second murderer were later sent to the scene of the crime with a lawyer, the chief criminal counsel from the Brno Gestapo named Koslowsky. He had a large-scale plan of the place in his hand. He reconstructed a false account of the killings and coached the others in contrived circumstantial evidence alleging an attempted escape by the prisoners which resulted in their being shot at a range of twenty-five metres.

The man Erich Zacharias had three other murders alleged against him in Zlín. His age and other particulars were given. He was said to be now living in the British Military Zone of Germany, having received from the British authorities a certificate saying that he was a 'harmless person'.

Dr van der Bijl concluded by urging an immediate inquiry into these murders and a search for Zacharias.

'I would add', he said, 'that I am deeply interested in the fate of Squadron Leader Kirby-Green, who was a gallant and distinguished officer with whom I had the honour to serve in the Royal Air Force.'

This letter, which suffered lamentably normal delays of diplomatic priority, screening, intelligence appreciation and interdepartmental ricochets, did not reach SIB Headquarters until January 1946. It contained the first summary of an eye-witness account of any of the Sagan murders, and its descriptive detail was to be a sadly standard form for the narratives of many of the other shootings.

Clearly it demanded urgent action. Bowes asked for immediate facilities to interrogate the man Kiowsky in Czechoslovakia. These diplomatic permissions came through while Bowes was in Berlin investigating the false sighting of Dr Absalon. He flew immediately to London as the quickest means of getting to Prague. (From Berlin to Prague is roughly 200 miles direct. But, amid the delicate post-war diplomatic niceties, the route Berlin–London–Prague was the orthodox way in 1946.)

During the previous month Flight Lieutenant A. R. Lyon, of the Air Directorate of Intelligence, had had to deliver to their homes in Germany three senior aeronautical scientists whom he had been interrogating in England. Bad weather delayed his flight back from Frankfurt. After two days he invited himself aboard an American freighter which was announced on the airfield Tannoy as bound for Bovingdon. The aeroplane, a Dakota, was defective and had to force-land at Brussels. That evening, in a Brussels transit hotel, Lyon met Major Pancheff, a smart, precise, energetic and enthusiastic officer who was deputy to Lieutenant-Colonel A. P. Scotland, commanding the London District Cage of the War Crimes Investigation Unit. Pancheff, when he became aware of Lyon's experience of interrogation in the German language, virtually recruited him on the spot to join the Stalag Luft III investigation. He arranged an interview with Scotland, who passed him on to Group Captain Nicholas of the SIB. Nicholas managed Lyon's posting from ADI (K) and told him that he should spend some days briefing himself from the case files available. Lyon heard at Princes Gate Court that Wing Commander Bowes was shortly going to Czechoslovakia, and he went to Group Captain Nicholas to ask if he would consider that he might accompany Bowes. As he made his request he noticed an officer regarding him dourly from the near side of the desk.

The group captain asked Lyon to wait outside for a moment. The other officer was Wing Commander Bowes, and the ensuing identity-check was freely reported by Bowes to Lyon later. As the door closed Bowes turned to Nicholas, and inquired:

'Who the hell is that?' and added a biased description of Lyon.

This was the opening salute in a remarkable relationship between two not obviously compatible men.

They flew to Prague, where the Air Attaché, Group Captain G. C. Wyatt, DFC, conducted them to a conference with members of the Defence Staff. A clockwise tour of relevant prisons and police offices in the country was arranged, from Prague to Brno, Uherské Hradiště, Zlín[1] and Liberec. The SIB officers were allocated a Czech liaison officer and travelled by train to Brno. Czech Army Intelligence there arranged for the interrogation of over two hundred former Gestapo staff held in Brno central prison.

The prison was a grim place, dark, cold and damp. The prisoners spoke freely, and one provided information of great value. The Czechs were so intent on providing exhaustive facilities that they conducted Bowes and Lyon to the prison hospital. There were four or five men there, all at the end of their time. It was a gloomy room with some ten plank beds along each wall. 'It was not only the smell of pus, urine and excreta that was so overpowering', Lyon recalled. 'The smell of death was there too.' This is a phrase which occurs with striking consistency in the accounts of the investigating officers journeying through post-war Europe, and it may be questioned. Lyon said, 'This is no melodramatic phrase. I cannot describe what I call the smell of death, but believe me, once you have got it in your nostrils you know what it is.'

The hospital examinations yielded nothing. It was doubtful if the sick men there were capable even of understanding the questions. The main interrogations were in an office inside the prison. Either Lyon, speaking German, or the Czech officer, Captain Brück, speaking his own language, put the same short series of questions to prisoner after prisoner. For the most part they had no useful information—the great majority of these thin, miserable and hopeless men had been Gestapo clerks, transport mechanics and even office

[1]Zlín, where Kirby-Green and Kidder were imprisoned, is now called Gottwaldov. Liberec, as has been stated, is the German Reichenberg.

cleaners: they had collaborated in sowing the wind, and they were reaping the whirlwind.

The one voluble man was a 33-year-old SS Hauptsturmführer, Franz Schauschütz, with a police rank equivalent to detective inspector. (By an equalization decree, SS officers were given a police rank, and vice versa: a few policemen managed to evade this.) He had been the immediate subordinate of Kriminalrat Hugo Römer, a departmental head in the Brno Gestapo whose Chief was Regierungsrat (Chief Inspector) Wilhelm Nölle. The Czechs privately described Schauschütz as *ein Gauner*, a scoundrel, and he was awaiting trial on a number of counts. Lyon formed the opinion that his eagerness to give all the information he could dredge up was based on the hope that his testimony might qualify him to be transferred to British custody as a relevant witness, and thus escape the death sentence that almost certainly awaited him after a trial in Czechoslovakia. This ambition was not fulfilled.

On the day of the dawn murder of Kirby-Green and Kidder—which Schauschütz said he then knew nothing about—Schauschütz was sent by Römer to take over the police office at Zlín and allow the officer in charge to go on leave. This officer was Hans Ziegler, and although he was on leave he came into the office occasionally to tidy up previous work which he did not wish to delegate to Schauschütz. Ziegler was a name which already registered in the memory of Bowes and Lyon as the man who, according to van der Bijl, had ordered the killing of the two Royal Air Force officers.

About a fortnight after the murders, on 13th April 1944, Römer arrived in Zlín from Brno. Later that night a senior Gestapo NCO, Adolf Knippelberg, also arrived from Brno, having been sent by Nölle to bring Römer a secret teleprinter-message which it had not been possible to retransmit to Zlín, because Zlín did not have a teleprinter machine capable of taking Top Secret messages under the precautions in force.

Römer told Schauschütz that there was a little Top Secret faking matter he wished him to carry out. Two English pilots had recently been shot on orders from RSHA Berlin, and Berlin was now requiring a formal report on this incident on lines already indicated—that the officers had been shot whilst trying to escape after making a pretext that they wanted to relieve themselves. Knippelberg would help with the preparation of this false report wherever Schauschütz might be in doubt, said Römer. Knippelberg would get it right, for he had shot one of the officers himself, and had already delivered one faked report to Berlin.

Knippelberg confirmed this to Schauschütz, and tut-tutted a little at the rather offensive wording of the secret teleprint message from Berlin, which he said he had just brought to Römer. It was a multiple-address Top Secret message to a number of Gestapo stations reprimanding them for the clumsiness of their previous false reports on the circumstances in which their English aircrew officers had been shot, and laying down a formula on which a substitute false report was to be submitted, using the date, serial number and register number of the former, rejected report.

Knippelberg said that such censure could not possibly apply to Brno. Knippelberg had personally delivered this false report to SS Obergruppenführer Müller at RSHA Berlin, and Müller himself had congratulated Knippelberg on the 'outstandingly well-faked report' which the Brno Gestapo had concocted. In the anteroom of Müller's office there had been couriers from other Gestapo stations, who had been shooting English flyers and delivering falsified reports. They had to stay in the anteroom until Müller had read their reports. 'But none of them got a personal commendation for lying as well as we did', said Knippelberg proudly. 'So this new report is going to be no trouble. It is just that Berlin expects an international inquiry, and this top secret teleprint says the reports must be able to stand scrutiny from any foreign commission without any fear of the consequences.'

Schauschütz, a murderer himself but a clerkly man with a talent for cooking the books, sat down and, amid occasional nudges from Knippelberg, compiled the report for Berlin, which Römer accepted without alteration. It was given to Knippelberg to send from the teleprinter at Brno with its capacity for top secrecy, and Schauschütz reminded Knippelberg to observe that it was antedated and to ensure that it was given an old serial number and the antedated entry of the original in the register.

This was the story Schauschütz told in the prison interrogation room in Brno. In his ingratiating eagerness to be of enough service to the British to merit extradition, he spoke for several hours, with Lyon translating his revelations, point by point, to Bowes. Bowes needed time to study even the notes of what he had understood before any real interrogation could take place. Schauschütz was sent away to write a full statement. Bowes and Lyon summarized what they had discovered.

They had the name Knippelberg as a murderer. They had a number of accessories before the fact. They had a very circumstantial account of central control by the Gestapo at Berlin of actual murders ordered by Top Secret teleprint, covered up by reports dispatched by courier to Berlin, with the accounts later rewritten to an ordered pattern in fear of international investigation.

After pondering on these matters at the end of the day, the SIB officers courteously assented to the pressure of their Czech officer hosts to accept some of the extremely lavish hospitality which they were determined to accord to investigators hunting down the Gestapo. After the wining and dining, Bowes and Lyon were taken to a bar which had been a favourite drinking haunt of the Brno Gestapo during the occupation. An artist had decorated the walls with erotic paintings of satyrs carrying off naked girls, said to be secretaries at the Gestapo offices, whose imminent experiences were in no doubt at all. The heads of the satyrs were well-executed portraits of Gestapo officers. Bowes stared hard at one. 'That's Schauschütz', he said. 'And this is Knippelberg', said a Czech officer. 'Can I have that painting photographed?' asked Bowes. 'This is the first mug-shot of a murderer I have got my hands on in this case.'

They interrogated Schauschütz next day, and he was comparatively unshakeable. In their re-examination they were mainly concerned with confirmation of the names of the persons involved in the shooting—which they now knew to have taken place at Hrabuvka, west of Moravská Ostrava—of Squadron Leader Kirby-Green and Flying Officer Kidder. Schauschütz implicated, in order of rank, Kaltenbrunner; Müller; Nölle, who would have received the orders from Berlin; Römer, who had been told to carry them out; and Knippelberg, one of the men who had done the actual shooting.

Under questioning, Schauschütz said he was not aware that Zacharias of Zlín was involved, but it was possible—Schauschütz did not know him well enough to sum him up as 'suitable for an exceptional duty, and one who, above all, would remain silent': a concise and realistic expression of the Gestapo criteria. He named the five Gestapo drivers available in Zlín, including Kiowsky, but expressed no opinion on Kiowsky's suitability for a secret job. But if the Brno driver Schwartzer had been the other driver employed, Schauschütz would have expected this. Schwartzer was Römer's personal driver, and could keep his mouth shut. These responses to interrogation, when Schauschütz was being given leads about men already in Bowes's book, but which he answered objectively without hastening to damn anybody already obviously suspected, conveyed an impression of candour in the man which gave more credibility to his other, as yet untested, statements.

Bowes and Lyon went on eastward to Uherské Hradiště, where the driver Kiowsky, whose interrogation by Dr van der Bijl had triggered this sequence of the investigation, was in custody. The party now included another Czech officer, Captain Vaca, who had been loaned to them because of his exceptional knowledge of the Gestapo in the Zlín area. With the ready liaison which the SIB officers were now getting used to, they were met at Uherské Hradiště by Judge Molowsky, an active justice in the local People's Court, and taken to his office.

Kiowsky was brought in, pale, thin and frightened. Lyon conducted the interrogation in German, consulting Bowes as he went along, and occasionally accepting an interjection from the enthusiastic Judge Molowsky, The answers were taken down in statement form in German by a typist in the room.

The interrogation lasted many hours. Halfway through the judge introduced flagons of beer and an outsize bottle of slivovitz to relieve the pressure. Kiowsky's narrative was not entirely continuous or straightforward, because he was over-anxious to conceal any implication in the murder which he might be suspected of having.

He was forty years old, and had served as a Gestapo driver in Zlín since 1939. He said that on a night in March 1944 he had been ordered by Ziegler, his boss, to prepare his car for a journey to Breslau. He met at the police office the driver Schwartzer from Brno, who said he was going too. At 9 p.m. Kiowsky was summoned to Ziegler's office, where he saw Ziegler, Zacharias and a Gestapo official from Brno whose name he did not know.

Bowes, who had acquired a sheaf of photographs of Gestapo members in Czechoslovakia, in addition to the portraits in the bar in Brno, pushed them towards Kiowsky and asked if he recognized the man. Kiowsky identified Knippelberg as the fourth man in the office. Ziegler said that Kiowsky must drive non-stop to Breslau with two English flyers, and the trip must not be discussed on any account within the Gestapo office or anywhere else. Zacharias then told him that, before he prepared his car, he was to fetch an interpreter for the interrogation of the prisoners, and then bring the prisoners from the civil police station, in Zlín. He did this. He was able to describe to Bowes the appearance, clothing and apparent age of the prisoners, who were handcuffed, bare-headed and wearing sports jackets. When Ziegler went in to interrogate them there was some difficulty about removing the handcuffs from the wrists of one of the officers, and they were torn away. The officer protested at this, and at wearing handcuffs at all. Ziegler told the interpreter to tell the officer that when tramps were picked up in the street they would be treated like tramps.

Kiowsky then described the journey of the prisoners, one in each car, in the direction of Breslau. The start was made about midnight. Twenty kilometres short of Moravská Ostrava the cars were stopped and the officers were told that they could relieve themselves by the roadside. The handcuffs were removed. As they stood on the verge first one of the officers and then the other leapt over the ditch and made a dash for freedom. Zacharias and Knippelberg fired at them as they were running, and they were killed.

'This is where we stop', said Bowes.

Lyon looked at him.

'I want to hear all about this attempted escape, all over again, in very great detail', said Bowes.

Lyon questioned Kiowsky closely. The man repeated a circumstantial account of the alleged breakaway by the officers. He was made to go over it more than once.

It was a crucial point. If there had been a genuine attempt to escape there was justification in shooting.

'Tell us about it again', said Lyon.

Kiowsky repeated his story.

'Did they run fast?' asked Lyon.

'Yes.'

'Like a sprinter?'

'Yes.'

'Arms going up in the air?'

'Yes'.

'What happened to the handcuffs?'

Kiowsky thought for a moment.

'They had no handcuffs. They had been taken off. I said that.'

'Had they been handcuffed in the front or behind?'

'In the front.'

'Then why were the handcuffs taken off?'

'I don't understand.'

'You don't need to have handcuffs removed from the front if you want to relieve yourself.'

Kiowsky was uneasy.

'Ask him', said Bowes very quietly, 'ask him how much petrol he had in the car.'

The question was put. Kiowsky said he had had a full tank.

'Ask him,' said Bowes, 'how far that would get him. What was the range of the car on a full tank?'

'Three hundred kilometres.'

'In that hill country? In ice and snow? What time were the officers shot?'

'Four a.m.'

Bowes was bypassing Lyon now and yelling directly at Kiowsky in English. Lyon interjected the translations, speaking as strongly as Bowes.

'You'd been going for four hours already. You hadn't yet reached Moravská Ostrava. You weren't a quarter of the way to Breslau. Where did you mean to fill up?'

'Where did you mean to refuel?' repeated Lyon.

Kiowsky was suddenly very grey in the face.

'You say you'd been told to go non-stop to Breslau', shouted Bowes. 'You hadn't a chance of reaching Breslau without filling up. That would be the first thing any driver would think of. *You knew you weren't going to Breslau.* You knew those officers were going to be shot before Breslau. You were driving them to be murdered, and you are as guilty of the murder as Zacharias and Knippelberg.'

'No!' said Kiowsky. His forehead was extruding clear sweat, and he could not hold himself up in his chair any more.

'Give him a stiff drink', said Bowes.

Lyon glanced at Judge Molowsky, and poured a full glass of slivovitz for Kiowsky.

'Now . . .' said Lyon.

'They were still handcuffed. They did not try to escape,' said Kiowsky. 'But I was still in the car when they were shot. I had nothing to do with it.'

'We'll start again', said Bowes.

Kiowsky recommenced his narrative. The typist took it down.

It ran roughly as before, until the point where the handcuffed officers entered the cars at midnight. Kiowsky transported the younger officer—Flying Officer Gordon Kidder—who could speak some German.

'I wish to add', said Kiowsky, 'that I asked Ziegler before our departure what we would do about petrol, as I did not have sufficient to get to Breslau. Ziegler replied, "You will not have to drive to Breslau". Although I said nothing to Ziegler, I got the impression that the two flyers would not reach Breslau alive.

'As I was driving, I asked Zacharias what was going to happen to them, forgetting that the officer behind could speak German. Zacharias sat beside me, and said nothing, but turned his thumb downward. Then I knew for the first time that the two were going to be shot.'

He described the shooting, which he said had occurred before he could get out of his car, when he was giving a cigarette to the driver Schwartzer, who had come up to his window to ask for one: 'At the precise moment when we were lighting the cigarettes, two shots were fired almost simultaneously, one by my car and the other by the second car. I saw the officer collapsing on to the roadside, to the left and slightly in front of Zacharias. At the same moment Zacharias fired a second shot. This officer was handcuffed with his hands in front of him. He fell into the ditch. I immediately got out of the car and saw that the second officer was also lying in the ditch. I heard two shots in the vicinity of the second car also. The Brno official came to Zacharias and told him to take the handcuffs off the officers, so that no one would see that they were manacled. I saw nothing that gave me the impression that the officers had wished to escape or attempted to. I stood by the ditch and saw the two bodies lying there. There was a lot of blood on the snow. . . .'

It was decided not to press Kiowsky beyond that point on that day. In the morning he described the discovery of the bodies by uniformed police, and Zacharias's explanation that he belonged to the Gestapo and would handle the whole affair. The bodies were taken away in a van. Kiowsky drove Zacharias back to Zlín and heard him report to Ziegler, 'Herr Kriminalrat, everything has passed off smoothly. The bodies have been taken to the crematorium in Moravská Ostrava, and a doctor will be there to make an examination.' Ziegler warned that the occurrence must never be discussed. A month later Koslowsky met all the participants at the scene of the crime, reconstructed a fictitious escape, and coached all four in the story they were to offer if questioned by the International Red Cross. Kiowsky's statement coincided with Dr van der Bijl's summary of his previous interrogation in every respect, except that van der Bijl had confused the roles of Zacharias and Knippelberg, then unnamed, to the extent that it was Knippelberg who had shot Kirby-Green: and the murders took place, not on 28th March 1944, but at dawn on the following day.

Judge Molowsky and Captain Vaca bustled about, arranging for interviews with any Czech official or Gestapo prisoner who could throw more light on the murders. Bowes and Lyon were taken to see the interpreter whom Kiowsky had brought in for the interrogation in Zlín. He was an auxiliary clerk in the Gestapo, now confined to prison. He gave corroborative identification details of the two officers. They said they had been captured at Hódonin, in southern Moravia. Flying Officer Kidder said he had studied languages at Quebec University, and had improved his knowledge of German during his captivity. Squadron Leader Kirby-Green had told the interpreter that he was married and had one child. He had seen these officers put into 'the small cells at the end of the corridor'. Bowes had seen these cells. They were mere cupboards in the wall.

Bowes interviewed a policeman who had brought in the bodies for cremation, and who could give a description of the wounds. Bowes and Lyon went to the crematorium at Moravská Ostrava, and checked this description of the wounds with the private record of the attendant who had burned the bodies; knowing whose body had been burned first enabled them to identify the separate urns by their serial numbers—for the urns bore the stamp 'Mährisch Ostrau' but no names.

The crematorium attendant remembered the incident well, and before cremating the bodies had made sketches of the locations of the wounds. He had noticed that the clothes worn by the dead officers were unusual—they had, of course, been fabricated in Stalag Luft III's amateur tailoring department. He said something characteristic of many humble people in conquered territory, revealing a reaction which tyrants might more readily remember. 'I always knew that a day would come when my evidence would be wanted. I have seen enough horror in my duties. The Gestapo used to bring me for cremation bodies that had been so badly burned with their hot-iron tortures that sometimes it was difficult for me to decide whether they were men or women. And I knew there was something strange about the situation of these two men they brought in shot. There was no way I could establish the identity of the bodies, so I did the best I could by sketching the wounds. I reported everything I recorded to our own people when the end of the war came, because I was sure that some day there would be inquiries.'

With the encouragement of Judge Molowsky, the SIB officers took Kiowsky out to the scene of the crime and made him reconstruct the shooting and simulate, with the policeman who had been sent out with the crematorium van, the position of the bodies in the ditch, which Bowes photographed. They got valuable evidence from a Gestapo sergeant in custody who had been on duty in Moravská Ostrava on 29th March 1944 when Knippelberg drove in, at between 4 and 5 a.m., and asked for an ambulance to convey two dead bodies. This man knew Knippelberg, and re-identified him from Bowes's photograph. He remembered that Knippelberg had telephoned

Brno Gestapo from the Moravská Ostrava office and had spoken to his chief, Römer, who had been awaiting the call even at that time of day. Knippelberg said, 'Herr Kriminalrat, I am bringing the two dead men to the crematorium'. Then he hung up immediately. Bowes now had witnesses who would be sufficient in a court of law to incriminate Römer and Ziegler as the instigators of the crime—the evidence against Nölle was not yet irrefutable—and against Knippelberg and Zacharias as the executants, with the drivers and Koslowsky as accessories.

The problem was to find the criminals. There was a strong rumour that Ziegler had committed suicide at the end of the war, but that was a rumour that many a Nazi on the run liked to encourage. Against that, there was a very circumstantial report by one serving policeman that both Ziegler and Koslowsky, the Gestapo lawyer who had arranged the false cover-story, had recently been seen at a hotel in Zell am See, in Austria, which they had frequently visited during the war. Römer and Knippelberg were known to have been briefly in American hands immediately after the surrender, but in the subsequent power-sharing the Americans withdrew from Czechoslovakia in favour of the Russians, and Römer and Knippelberg had been transferred to Red Army Camp 33, near Brno; but that camp had been disbanded in September 1945, and the subsequent movements of Römer and Knippelberg were unknown.

As for Zacharias, a Gestapo man who had been at liberty until September 1945 said that both he and Ziegler had been given papers by the Americans (not by the English, as Dr van der Bijl had reported) saying that they were former Customs officials, harmless persons with no Nazi record. Using this identity, Zacharias had worked for a farmer in Mittenwald, Bavaria, which was in fact his birthplace. But he was now said to be working at a port in north-west Germany in the British zone. The Gestapo man even had two addresses at Wesermünde at which he might be found—those of his parents and one of his brothers. This lead was confirmed after a surprising disclosure by Judge Molowsky that Zacharias's wife was still living in Zlín. Lyon rushed to see her, and found her seething with resentment against her husband, and only too willing to talk. She was a good-looking Czech girl of about twenty-five. She had evidently led an appalling life with Zacharias during her marriage to him. She confirmed that he was in north-west Germany, and wished Lyon every success in tracing him.

The information supplied by Frau Zacharias seemed so important that, with the assent of Judge Molowsky, she was confined under guard in comfortable quarters for ten days in case she had a change of heart and decided to let Zacharias know that the Royal Air Force were after him. Bowes made up his mind that he must go immediately for Ziegler and Koslowsky in Zell am See, and Zacharias on the coast. The investigation into the Reichenberg/Liberec murders in Czechoslovakia would have to be postponed.

Bowes and Lyon therefore motored back to Brno and took the train to Prague.

Telephone communication in Czechoslovakia was then unreliable, and they had been unable to warn the Air Attaché that they were coming. When they arrived they sent a signal to SIB Headquarters in Rinteln summoning McKenna—who was believed to be on investigation in the American zone— and some SIB sergeants to meet them in Wiesbaden. Then they tried to arrange air transport to Wiesbaden for themselves. But the bad winter weather had closed in, and all flights were grounded. They waited in Prague for two days, with nothing to do except write up their notes and prepare instructions for the teams which were to meet them—for Bowes was actively preparing a grand descent on Zell am See.

All air transport remained cancelled. Finally they learned from the American Embassy in Prague that a truck was pushing out to Frankfurt the following day. They hitched a lift in this canvas-covered 15 cwt, and drove west in the intense cold. In the driving snow the driver went straight through the Czech–German frontier post, only realizing his error when bullets came whistling past. They made Schweinfurt that night, and went on to Frankfurt in the back of a lorry, sitting in straw bales. They finally got to Wiesbaden, frozen and filthy, and fell gratefully into warm baths at the luxury Schwartzerbock Hotel. McKenna, very spruce by comparison, had come in from Paris, not the American zone as they had thought, to meet them. He introduced them to good champagne being sold in the bar at five marks a bottle—then about the price of one cigarette on the black market—and the exhausted new arrivals thawed into amity.

Bowes stayed only to brief McKenna on Zacharias's reputed whereabouts in the north, and to hand over photographs and documents. He set off by road for Zell am See with Lyon and two sergeants whom he had ordered to meet him with transport at Wiesbaden. It was a long journey in hard conditions into the Austrian mountains to a point east of the Kitzbühel area, some 25 miles south-west of Hitler's Berchtesgaden. They night-stopped at a small German pub where there were beds but no food, and the officers and sergeants clustered round a Primus stove and a kettle in Bowes's bedroom, brewed tea and shared out the rations. In Zell am See they contacted the Americans in charge there, and prepared a post-midnight raid on the hotel, named Landhaus Brichta. The Americans had recently arrested the proprietor, Brichta, for black market activities, but his wife was in residence.

The inn was a small Austrian timber building at the top of a steep snow-covered hill, with a narrow road winding up to it. The Americans loaned a dozen men, and they split into three parties. At one in the morning of 9th March 1946 an American officer led his party up the precipitous slopes at the back of the hill. Bowes led the frontal attack, and Lyon led the raiding party taking the eastern ascent. All men were armed. There was no moon, but orders had been agreed not to use torches on the way up. In the freezing air they slithered up the rocks, often two steps forward and one step back, and finally met at the top. Men were placed to cover all doors and window-exits, and an American officer hammered at the door. It was opened by an alarmed Frau Brichta in a thick nightgown. The officers demanded the guest-book. No recognizable name was entered, and the party brought in sergeants to man the corridors and began a massive search, interviewing the occupants one by one, examining their identity documents, and comparing the photographs with the holders and with the sheaf Bowes held from Czechoslovakia. They found no trace of Ziegler or Koslowsky. The occupants seemed mainly middle-class Austrians on the run from the Russian occupation in the east, living on the sale of jewellery which they had brought with them.

They interviewed Brichta in gaol next day. He said he did remember being visited by officers of a Gestapo unit in Czechoslovakia during the war, but his guest-book had been destroyed—he did not say by whom.

'I do remember Ziegler and Koslowsky', he said, 'but I have not seen them for a year. Nor do I want to. They bled me white, never paid a bill, commandeered not only my food and drink but also my money—for which they offered me nothing in return except immunity from arrest. And look where that safe-conduct has got me', he added, gazing angrily round the gaol. The SIB officers were not entirely satisfied with his answers, as Brichta probably gathered from Freddie Bowes's consistent refrain to Lyon's translated answers: 'Tell him he's an effing liar'. But nothing could be proved. The raid had to be written off as a failure. Any immediate arrest as an outcome of the Czech operation had to come from McKenna.

The news was awaiting them at Rinteln. Zacharias had been arrested, and had escaped.

When he was called to Wiesbaden McKenna had abandoned a progression of inquiries in which he had met both disappointment and promise. Working in the French zone, principally on the Saarbrücken murders, he found that a principal witness of whom he had been informed was now untraceable in the French lists, and might have been prematurely released. He crossed to meet Courtney in the American zone, and there saw a Gestapo man in custody near Nuremberg who admitted his connection with the Saarbrücken case, and had actually interrogated Bushell and Scheidhauer after their arrest. This man could not yet be released from American interrogation, and McKenna took Courtney to Paris for a quick check on the CROWCASS files. He then received Bowes's signal to rendevous at Wiesbaden, and sent Courtney back to the American zone, where he sprinted into action which resulted in two arrests.

At Wiesbaden Bowes briefed McKenna that Zacharias was thought to be in the Hamburg, Bremen, Wesermünde area.

McKenna knew this manor well, and had good liaison with the Americans, who controlled a coast enclave in this nominally British zone. He took a Dutch interpreter, Lieutenant Vreugdenheel, and dashed to the nearest port, Bremen. He got in touch with the United States Army local investigations unit and checked the movements of German civilians and the registers of German and other nationals employed by the American military and civil administrations in the vast port area.

There was no record of Zacharias—McKenna was relying on the presumption that he had not changed his name because he had copies of the papers issued to him as a 'harmless person'. On the same day McKenna pressed on to Wesermünde. He saw the United States Army commander, Colonel Rich, who took him to his civil administration officer, Captain Leather. Leather, a tall Texan, was flat out to help, and hung a small shroud over the office clock. 'If we've got anybody here of the name of Zacharias', he said, 'we'll find him.' They worked well into the night. 'Zacharias!' said Leather, with his finger in a file. 'Erich Hermann August Zacharias, came to Wesermünde September 1945, now working as a clerk in 283 Refrigeration Plant in the docks.

'We've even got his address', he added. 'Shall we go?'

'No', said McKenna. 'The address is old, and it may have changed. If we go round and he's not there—even if he's still living there, he may be away for a couple of days—someone may give him the wire that we have been around. Leave well alone. I've come here in total darkness. No one except you knows that I'm here in the town. Far better to make a call on him at work tomorrow.'

Leather agreed, but ruefully. 'That means I shan't be in on it', he said. 'You'd better meet Lieutenant Freshour.'

Next morning McKenna joined Lieutenant Freshour, who had brought an escort of military police. They guarded the exits as Freshour and McKenna and Vreugdenheel walked into a long basement office. McKenna had his photograph of Zacharias. They walked between long rows of desks illuminated by green-shaded lights.

'That looks like him, right at the far end', said McKenna, and walked up to a clerk behind a desk. He tapped him on the shoulder.

'Are you Zacharias?'

'Yes.'

'May I see your identity card?'

The man produced it.

'I am a British officer in the Royal Air Force investigating the Stalag Luft III murders. I have reason to believe that you were involved in the murders of Squadron Leader Kirby-Green and Flying Officer Kidder, and I am taking you into custody.'

'I understand.'

'I shall have to search you.'

They searched him for arms, and found nothing. Zacharias was handcuffed and taken outside, then driven to the local Civilian Internment Camp. Here he was stripped and searched for poison. He was a fair, spare, thin-nostrilled man of thirty-four with outstanding muscular development.

In Captain Leather's presence, McKenna questioned him. Zacharias seemed more resigned than frightened. He admitted that he had personally shot and killed Flying Officer Kidder on the orders of Ziegler, who had cited orders from a higher source. He gave details of the two deaths. He said he had had no qualms about the assignment, because he thought the airmen might have been responsible for many German deaths by bombing, and in any case he had no option but to obey higher orders.

He signed this interim statement, though later, when he had girded himself to go on the offensive, he contested almost every sentence in it. McKenna turned to Captain Leather and asked, 'Can we go home now?'

'Where's home?'

'British base. Minden.'

'Hell, no, he's ours.'

'I found him.'

'We had him. You can see Colonel Rich if you like.'

Colonel Rich explained that there was a United States Army instruction that no prisoner could be handed over to another Power without prior clearance from their own War Crimes Investigation Unit at Frankfurt am Main.

'But you've got nothing on him,' protested McKenna, 'except perhaps for false papers. We've got him for murder, and there are another twenty-five murders that the Czechs want him for.' This was indeed the figure, possibly exaggerated, that the Czechs had mentioned, and they had given Bowes the details of three. They had made him promise that if by any chance a case could not be substantiated against Zacharias Bowes would hand him back to the Czechs.

'Sorry, son,' said Colonel Rich. 'We've got to go through the routine.'

'How long will it take?'

'Day or two. Maybe a week.'

'What happens to him in the meantime?'

'You've no worries at all. We'll put him in our local prison, which is supervised by us.'

'How is it staffed?'

Colonel Rich had to concede that the prison was staffed entirely by German gaolers.

'You make me very worried', said McKenna. 'Well, sir, if that's your ruling, fair enough. Would you object to my speaking personally to Frankfurt on your telephone?'

'Help yourself.'

McKenna rang an acquaintance in the American unit at Frankfurt who promised to push through the clearance as fast as possible. He also telephoned the British Liaison Officer in Wiesbaden, who agreed to increase the pressure. Next morning, when the clearance had not come through, McKenna decided to carry out a short interrogation of Zacharias regarding Gestapo personalities in Czechoslovakia, and the prisoner was brought to the American offices for interview through Vreugdenheel's translation. At noon the news came that the clearance was through. McKenna sent the prisoner back to the gaol to get some lunch before they set out for base. When McKenna returned to the Public Safety Office at one o'clock he was met by a rueful Captain Leather.

'Bad news. Zacharias has escaped.'

As the prison van was being driven slowly through the main gates to pick him up Zacharias had broken away from his escorts and sprinted between the van and the gate. An armed warder chased him and was about to fire when a woman came out of a house between them. Zacharias disappeared across the remains of a bombed building.

A general alarm was raised, and road blocks mounted, but he had got away before the immediate hunt could be mounted. McKenna got to the telephone and made a general circularization for the wanted man. He called a conference of the American forces and organized a general search of all Zacharias's known haunts and the addresses of all his friends in Wesermünde. The Americans called in the local police and enlisted the Post Office to intercept mail directed to all these addresses. There was nothing else for McKenna to do but wait. He went back to base. Bowes was extremely affable to him, and said they must resign themselves to the outcome of the American operation. McKenna went out again on the long trail round Germany in search of other suspects.

On the nineteenth day McKenna was in Berlin and made a routine call to base. 'They've got Zacharias', said Bowes, bubbling with cheer. 'Get back to Wesermünde, Mac, and drag him back from the Americans. And, Mac—'

'Yes?'

'Hang on to him!'

'Joke over', said McKenna.

The Americans had intercepted, through their mail check, a letter to a friend of Zacharias in Wesermünde from someone in Fallersleben, a town north of Brunswick, almost on the border of the Russian zone. In the letter was the sentence 'Erich has been ill but is improving, and will soon be on his way'. The Americans promptly raided the house at Fallersleben, and found Zacharias fully dressed in a bedroom, preparing to go out into the night. He had been caught by a margin of minutes before slipping out into the Russian zone.

Captain Leather told McKenna in Wesermünde, 'You know, it was a good thing he escaped. In the round-up we caught a hell of a lot of other people we wanted to lay our hands on.'

Colonel Rich said, 'You'll be on your toes to keep him. But you have only your interpreter and yourself in that car. What gun do you use?'

'I don't carry a gun', said McKenna. The Americans looked at him incredulously. 'You've got to have a gun', said Rich. 'Here you are, take this.'

And for the first time in his investigatory career, McKenna escorted a prisoner into the holding prison at Minden carrying a long Biretta machine-pistol with twenty-eight 9-millimetre bullets in the magazine. He was acutely embarrassed by the burden.

McKenna made immediate arrangements to fly Zacharias back to the London Cage, and in the meantime took a fuller statement from him. Zacharias, having had time to plan, was already vastly changing his story from the original simple confession. He now said that his original orders had been to take out and shoot two British agents who had been dropped by parachute into Czechoslovakia to foment sabotage and resistance, and these agents were always executed after capture. But in any case, the officers had made an attempt to escape, and had been shot at extreme range. McKenna listened, and noted, and left it to Colonel Scotland in London to sort it out.

Zacharias had been very depressed on recapture. But when he learned that he was being sent to London he became much brighter. 'Now I shall see it for myself', he told McKenna in his cell. 'Technically, England has won the war. But London has been reduced by the Luftwaffe bombing to the level of a rat-infested ruin. The population has been evacuated to Scotland, and the Government had to go to Canada. I shall be very pleased to see London now.'

'But that's just not true', said McKenna.

'We know it is true all right. The Führer said so. Goebbels and Göring told us so.'

Their aircraft landed at Croydon, and they were met by an RAF driver with a Hillman saloon. 'This man wants to see the bad state of London', said McKenna. 'I don't think we can do anything more spectacular than the usual route: Thornton Heath, Streatham, Clapham, Chelsea, Earl's Court, Kensington.' They got into the car, and McKenna settled himself to watch Zacharias. He was looking keenly all round, almost begging to see something that justified Hitler's statements. The further they went the more depressed he got. Eventually he slumped in his seat, only occasionally looking out of the window from the side of his eye.

'I saw a lot of people', said McKenna, as he delivered him to Kensington Palace Gardens. 'Did you see any rats?'

Zacharias said nothing.

'You've seen for yourself now', said McKenna, 'that your Führer's propaganda is a lot of lies.'

Handing over Zacharias to Colonel Scotland, McKenna mentioned that he had made a troublesome escape, and suggested extra precautions. 'It won't happen here', the colonel assured him benevolently. 'He'll be in an escape-proof compound at Kempton Park, and we have the Scots Guards to look after us.' Forty-eight hours after his return to Germany McKenna received a signal from Colonel Scotland asking for all available photographs of Zacharias to be sent by the next aircraft, as he had escaped again. He had in fact cut his way through a very strong door with a primitive instrument made from a light tin plate, got over a number of fences and swanned away into the dark with a stock of rations he had saved from his meals. But he had lost a shoe in the exercise, lamed himself, and was recovered while lying up in some bushes.

Zacharias had now perfected his story that Ziegler had ordered him to take out and shoot, by superior orders from Berlin, two 'supposedly British officers' who were among the many constantly being dropped over Moravia and Bohemia to carry out sabotage and espionage. Zacharias had been convinced that the 'superior orders' came from Hitler. Ziegler had reinforced the solemnity of the occasion by making all the participants take the SS pledge of secrecy through a formal semi-Masonic handshake, implying that the penalty for breaking the secret was death. The high point of the secrecy was to be the false account that the men were shot trying to escape. The normal sentence on prisoners of this category was death, and 'I had no reason whatsoever to doubt that these parachute agents had forfeited their lives. I thought the sentence had been passed in the proper way. Nevertheless, I asked Ziegler to relieve me of this order because I did not feel capable of shooting a man in the back.' However, the issue was most fortunately resolved for his conscience, because the prisoners did, in fact, attempt an escape. They jumped, and were shot as they landed on the other side of the ditch. 'The whole story seems rather incredible,' Zacharias conceded, 'because if you first get an order to shoot somebody while he is allegedly trying to escape, and afterwards in fact he does try to escape, then it is very hard to make people believe this story.'

Zacharias candidly declared that he recognized this serious difficulty. There were also a few loose ends which he had forgotten to weave in from former stories: in his very first confession made to McKenna at Wesermünde within a short time of his arrest he had mentioned that he had had no qualms about the assignment because the terror-flyers he was dealing with had probably killed many Germans by bombing: in his last statement he was not aware that they were aircrew officers, but was told that they were parachute agents. Zacharias, however, manfully did his best to get his most polished story accepted during seven days' interrogation at the London Cage. He had also resisted any suggestion that he had been involved in other murders which the Czechs had mentioned: two of these, as summarized in Zlín, included the rape of girls before their murder. On 11th April 1946 Colonel Scotland was about to conduct a further interrogation of Zacharias when Group Captain Nicholas brought into his office at Kensington Palace Gardens Flight Lieutenant Lyon, who had flown from Germany with the original statement made by the driver Friedrich Kiowsky in Judge Molowsky's office in Uherské Hradiště, and with the long screed from Schauschütz.

Lyon asked permission to interrogate Zacharias on Kiowsky's statement. Scotland agreed, unwillingly, as he later admitted at the subsequent trial: he said then that he had not been so interested in getting Zacharias's confession to the murder of Flying Officer Kidder as in getting from him information on Gestapo hot-iron methods of torture in Czechoslovakia—which was not, of course, ever the subject of an SIB-investigated charge against Zacharias.[1]

Lyon was embarrassed to find that Zacharias was made to kneel with his tunic and shirt off, which Scotland said—but Lyon could not confirm—was the normal position for a Gestapo interrogation. This 'Gestapo stance' was not said to have been used for any other interrogation in the London Cage. Under Scotland's impatient gaze, Lyon was short and sharp with Zacharias.

'I have Kiowsky's statement here', he said. 'Kiowsky has firmly said that you knew you were going out to shoot the officers, because when he asked you what was to happen to them you answered by turning your thumb down. Kiowsky says the officers made no attempt to escape. Kiowsky says the officers were shot dead at very short range. We also have the evidence of someone you never thought of, the attendant at the crematorium, who also testifies that the wounds were inflicted at very short range. I may add that the Czechs have given me details of other murders they allege against you, including the rape and murder of a girl from your office who overheard a telephone conversation in which you compromised yourself. And the Czechs will be highly delighted if you can get off the present charge against you of the murder of Flying Officer Kidder. Because they have an option on your body, and they will get you back for trial on a number of murder charges, and they will undoubtedly hang you.'

Zacharias rose from his knees.

'I can only die once', he said. 'I will tell you the truth. The officers were murdered. I am sorry. They were handcuffed. They did not try to escape. The officers were killed under Ziegler's orders.'

Colonel Scotland made an exclamation of disgust.

'Get him out', he said.

[1]*From the trial transcript:*

COLONEL SCOTLAND: I did not want Lyon to be successful.

FRAU DR OEHLERT (*Counsel for Zacharias*): Why not?

COLONEL SCOTLAND: I thought that the torture story was a very much more important one from Zacharias than a confession of shooting guilt. If I had a confession of shooting I could not get a confession of torture.

A hut in Stalag Luft III before the escape. Flight Lieutenant Edgar Humphreys, who was shot with nine brother officers and cremated at Liegnitz, is in the left foreground, in airman's uniform.
The Commandant at Sagan, Colonel Lindeiner, suspecting a trap set by Gestapo provocation, warned the Senior British Officer against mass escapes.

The roll of honour which Group Captain Massey mounted to commemorate the dead Fifty. The photographs, identified by numbered names, read horizontally.

26. Langford, P.W.
27. Leigh, T.B.
28. Long, J.L.
29. Mc Garr, C.A.
30. Mc Gill, G.E.
31. Marcinkus, R.
32. Milford, H.J.
33. Mondschein, J.T.
34. Pawłuk, K.
35. Picard, H.A.
36. Pohe, P.P.
37. Scheidhauer, B.W.
38. Skantzikas, S.
39. Swain, C.D.
40. Stevens, R.
41. Stewart, R.C.
42. Stower, J.G.
43. Street, D.O.
44. Tobolski, P.
45. Valenta, E.
46. Walenn, G.W.
47. Wernham, J.C.
48. Wiley, G.W.
49. Williams, J.E.
50. Williams, J.F.

The fresco on the beer-cellar wall in Brno. Schauschütz and Knippelberg are caricatured below the fat sow. 'Can I have that painting photographed?' asked Bowes. 'This is the first mug-shot of a murderer I have got my hands on in this case.'

Friedrich Kiowsky, handcuffed, was taken to the scene of the crime after confessing to participation in the murder of Squadron Leader Kirby-Green and Flying Officer Kidder. Below, with a policeman he reconstructs the position of the bodies.

Ausweis.

Inhaber dieses Lichtbildausweises ist

der/die Erich Zacharias, Zollbeamter

geb. am 16.12.1911 in Wartjenstedt Bez. Hildesheim

wohnhaft in Mühldorf Mittenwald Straße/Platz

Mühldorf am Inn, den 17.5.45

Der Bürgermeister der Stadt Mühldorf am Inn

Stadt Mühldorf am Inn

I. A.

Geb. RM 1.20

G.R.Nr. 1763/45

The Gestapo connections of Erich Zacharias, the murderer of Flying Officer Kidder, got him false identity papers, describing him as a Customs clerk, nine days after the German unconditional surrender. Arrested ten months later, he escaped but was reclaimed by Squadron Leader McKenna (carrying Biretta machine-pistol) and Flying Officer Vreugdenheel of the Netherlands Military Liaison Mission.

Royal Air Force Special Investigation Branch officers. Wing Commander Bowes doffs his hat for a small girl in Breslau, where pipe-smoking Flight Lieutenant Lyon questions an inhabitant. Near Munich, Flight Lieutenant Courtney stands by the telegraph pole deliberately shot up by Geith and Weil as part of their cover story for the murder of Lieutenants Gouws and Stevens. After the breakthrough at Kiel Flight Lieutenants Lyon (left) and Harrison survey the field where the Gestapo shot four officers.

12 britische Offiziere

Staatsangehörigkeit 1	Nr. der Erkennungsmarke 2	Name 3	Vorname 4	Geburtstag 5	Geburtsort 6	Vorname des Vaters 7	Familienname der Mutter 8	Name und Anschri[ft] der zu benachrichtigend[en] Person 9
Kanada	689 St.L.1	Birkland	Henry	16.8. 1917	Winnipeg	Christian	Jonanson	334 3 rd A W,Calgary, Alberta,K.
Brite	760 St.L.3	Brettell	Edward Gordon	19.3. 1919	verweigert	.-	-.-	Mr.V.Brett The Grange Chertsey,
Brite	667 St.L.1	Bull	Leslie	7.11 1916	London	Leslie	Comlosy	Bontside, Dansfold G Survey.
Südafrika	621 St.L.1	Bushell	Roger Joyce	30.8. 1910	Springs Transv.	Benjamin	Wingate White	Mrs.B.D.Bu Broadme.st Hermanus, Cape Prov.
Brite	55 Oflag. XXI B	Casey	Michel John	19.2. 1918	Allahabad Indien	Michel Lewis	O'brien	Mrs. .T.Ca 3 Front St Tynemouth,
Australien	702 St.L.3	Catanach	James	28.11 1921	Melbourne	-.-	-.-	Mr.W.M.Cat 373 Glenfe Malvern, S Melbourne.
Neuseeland	676 St.L.3	Christensen	Arnold George	8.4. 1922	Neuseeld.	-.-	-.-	Mrs.L.Chri 813 Duffer Neuseeland
Brite	727 St.L.3	Cochran	Dennis Herbert	13.8 1921	Clapton London	-.-	-.-	Mrs.Herber 144 Essex Leyton E 1 England.
Brite	189 Oflag. XXI B.	Cross	Jan Kinston Pembroke	4.4. 1918	Coshan Hants.	Pembrok	Boyd	Mrs.Pembro Fastoke Lo Hayling Is
Brite	643 St.L.3	Espelid	Harold	6.10 1920	Bergen	-.-	-.-	Miss Pyne, 11 Huddles T.P.London
Brite	456 St.L.1	Evans	Brian Herbert	14.2 1920	Shelton, Devon	herbert	Fletcher	Mrs,H.Eva r Higgate Cyncoed, C.
Norwegen	1264 St.L.3	Fuglesang	Nils	verweigert		-.-	-.-	Fuglesang, Floro, Nor

The first sheet of the register of 'Dec
Flight Lieutenant Courtney in Mun
burial: Sagan. Shot whilst trying to

Abgang durch Tod .

Dienstgrad	Truppenteil (m. Kp. usw.)	Matrikel-Nr.	Ort und Tag der Gefangennahme	Verwundungen, Verletzungen, Tod (Beerdigungsplatz)	Bemerkungen (z. B. Zugänge von anderen Lagern, bei Fluchtversuch oder Meuterei erschossen)
10	11	12	13	14	15
F/lt.	RAF.	35233	6. 11.41.	[illegible]	Flucht-versuch erschossen.
F/Lt.	"	61053	26. 3.42.	"	"
F/Lt.	"	43932	5. 11.41.	"	"
S/Ldr. .	"	90120	23. 5.40.	"	"
F/Lt. rld.	RAF	39024	16.10.39.	"	"
S/Ldr.	RAAF.	Aus - 400364	5. 9. 42.	"	"
F/O	RNZAF.	NZ-413380	20.8. 42.	"	"
Cochran, F/O	RAF.	122441	9 11. 42.	"	"
S/Ldr. e.	RAF.	39305	12. 2.42.	"	"
P/O	"	110378	27,8. 42.	"	"
e Rd. F/Lt.	"	42745	7. 12.40.	"	"
P/O	RNAF.	742	2. 5. 43.	"	"

4g. Sagan

ength through Death' found by
st two columns read: 'Place of
e columns of dots indicate *ditto*.

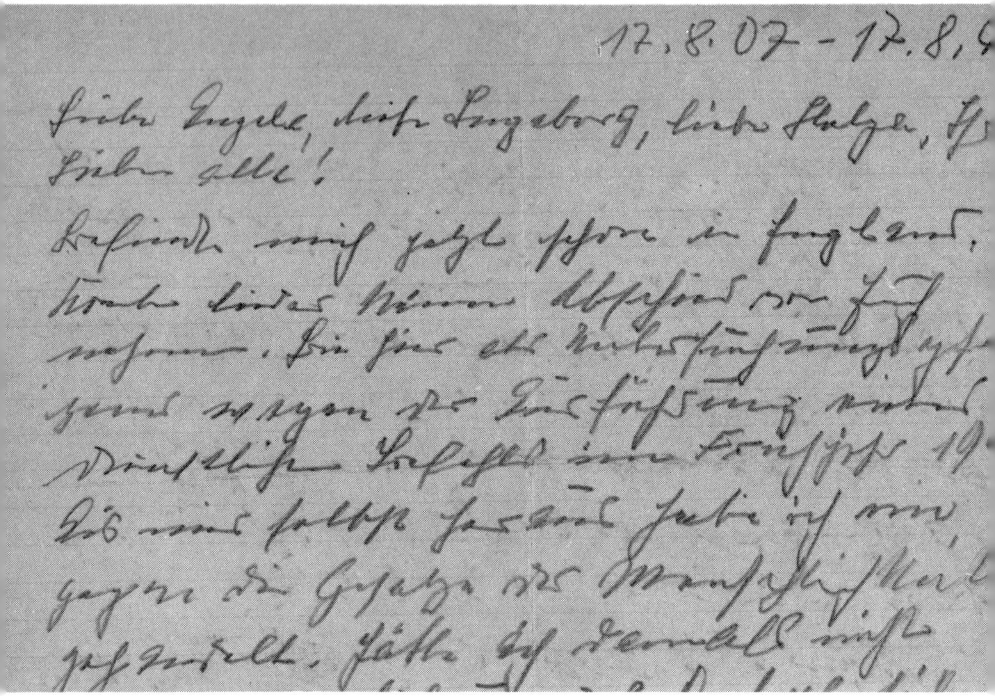

17.8.07 – 17.8.4

Liebe Angela, liebe Ingeborg, liebe Helga, Ihr Lieben alle!

Befinde mich jetzt schon in England.

Arrested for the murder of Squadron Leader Bushell, Emil Schulz was flown to England. The aircraft force-landed at Manston and Squadron Leader McKenna had to take his prisoner to the Cage by a trippers' train from Margate. Sitting on the floor of the corridor, Schulz wrote his birthday letter to 'Dear Angela, dear Ingeborg, dear Helga . . .' (See page 164.) In the dock at Hamburg Schulz, centre, consults his German barrister.

The picture of Johannes Post, murderer of the four officers at Kiel, skiing with his mistress, Marianne Heidt, was constantly carried by Squadron Leader McKenna, and was finally the means of identifying Post. Dr Alfred Schimmel, the man who would not kill on Good Friday, is seen in (non-combatant) war panoply, left, and in captivity with Post, right.

Rogues' Gallery:
Ziegler (Brno/Zlín), suicide in London Cage 1948.
Absalon (Breslau/Sagan), died in Russia 1948.
Fritz Schmidt (Kiel), sentenced to two years' gaol 1968.
Hilker (Strasbourg), case dismissed 1966.
Koslowsky (Brno/Zlín), executed by Czechs 1947.
Knippelberg (Brno/Zlín) prematurely released by Russians 1945.
Has successfully evaded recapture.
Müller (RSHA Berlin), reported as a suicide 1946.

This picture was 'acquired' from the German records at Stalag Luft III by Flight Lieutenant William Hancock when the prison camp was evacuated on the approach of the Russians in 1945. A note captioning the photograph said that it represented the shooting of two of the Fifty who escaped from the North Compound in March 1944. This caption is almost certainly incorrect, although the scene illustrates the popular view—held apparently also in Germany—of what happened. Although the exact circumstances of a small number of the murders are uncertain, it is highly unlikely that any *pair* of officers were shot in a prison compound. The typical action is that they were gunned down by the side of the road, as in the sketch over the page.

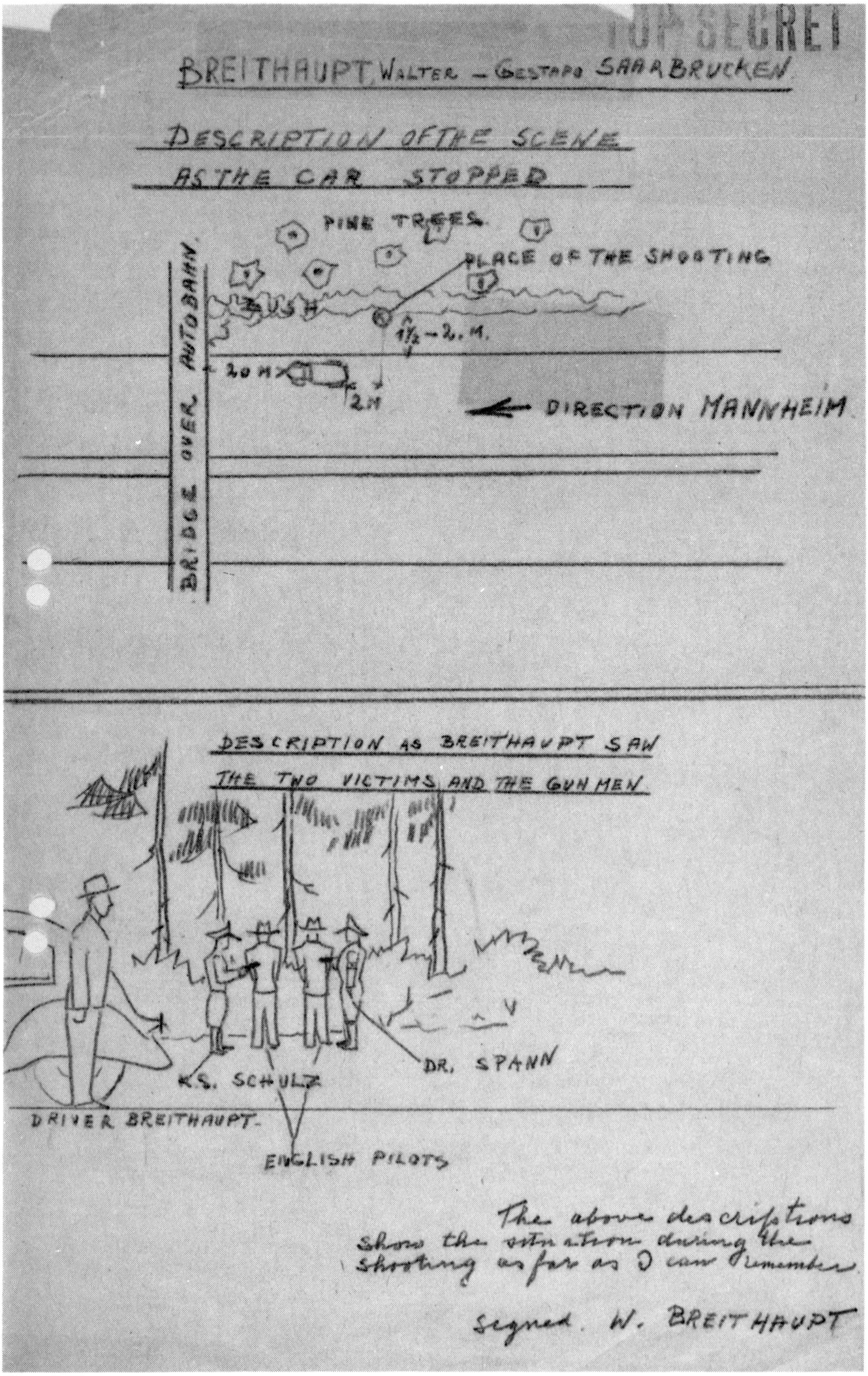

Carbon copy of a sketch by Walter Breithaupt (the English translations entered by a Dutch interpreter) incriminating Dr Leopold Spann and Kriminalsekretär Emil Schulz in the murder of Squadron Leader Bushell and Lieutenant Scheidhauer. (See page 158.)

To all Prisoners of War!

The escape from prison camps is no longer a sport!

Germany has always kept to the Hague Convention and only punished recaptured prisoners of war with minor disciplinary punishment.

Germany will still maintain these principles of international law.

But England has besides fighting at the front in an honest manner instituted an illegal warfare in non combat zones in the form of gangster commandos, terror bandits and sabotage troops even up to the frontiers of Germany.

They say in a captured secret and confidential English military pamphlet,

THE HANDBOOK OF MODERN IRREGULAR WARFARE:

". . . the days when we could practise the rules of sportsmanship are over. For the time being, every soldier must be a potential gangster and must be prepared to adopt their methods whenever necessary."

"The sphere of operations should always include the enemy's own country, any occupied territory, and in certain circumstances, such neutral countries as he is using as a source of supply."

England has with these instructions opened up a non military form of gangster war!

Germany is determined to safeguard her homeland, and especially her war industry and provisional centres for the fighting fronts. Therefore it has become necessary to create strictly forbidden zones, called death zones, in which all unauthorised trespassers will be immediately shot on sight.

Escaping prisoners of war, entering such death zones, will certainly lose their lives. They are therefore in constant danger of being mistaken for enemy agents or sabotage groups.

Urgent warning is given against making future escapes!

In plain English: Stay in the camp where you will be safe! Breaking out of it is now a damned dangerous act.

The chances of preserving your life are almost nil!

All police and military guards have been given the most strict orders to shoot on sight all suspected persons.

Escaping from prison camps has ceased to be a sport!

'The escape from prison camps is no longer a sport', the notice that incriminated the German High Command.

The Memorial to the Fifty, built by brother officers at Stalag Luft III to contain their urns, as Wing Commander Bowes and Flight Lieutenant Lyon saw it in May 1946.

Zacharias was taken away. Captain Cornish, an officer on Scotland's staff, took a full confession from him. When it was signed Cornish asked if he had any other deaths on his conscience. Zacharias gave details of the murder of one Czech girl whom he had arranged for another man to shoot while Zacharias was having sexual intercourse with her in a wood.

At Zacharias's trial he refuted all these confessions, including the highly circumstantial account he had given immediately after Lyon's short interrogation, which was probably his most accurate. He said in the courtroom that this statement had been made under torture from an electric machine thrust into his body in Scotland's office. Scotland was forced to impugn the Government maintenance services by giving evidence that he had no electric probe for the orifices of Zacharias or anyone else, and it would not have worked if he had had it, because there was only one electric socket in his office, and the wall-plug of that was defective.

McKenna and Lyon were in the courtroom as Zacharias's defence re-examination came to its climax. The question had been asked: Why, amid all the contradictory statements and confessions which Zacharias had made—and in view of his final choice to stick to the second statement made to McKenna in Minden (saying he thought the Royal Air Force officers were subversive agents, but he was helped off the hook by the fact that they did actually and incredibly try to escape)—why had Zacharias not mentioned to McKenna in extenuation that he understood that the order for the officers' deaths came from Hitler, and was therefore so much the more difficult to oppose?

Zacharias replied that he had lied for the sake of Germany.

'I did not make this statement upon oath', he said, 'so I did not regard it as too important. I left quite important facts out, of which the most important was the Sagan Order, the fact that the killing had to take place on higher orders, which I assumed to be Hitler. I felt that this statement was not on oath, was not a sworn statement. Secondly, I felt that because of the interests of my own colleagues and because of the reputation of the whole German people, I really could not make such a damaging revelation as this reference to Hitler's orders to kill the fifty.'

Frau Dr Oehlert, counsel for Zacharias, very carefully framed her next words, which were to be her client's:

'Do you want to say that the whole reputation of the German people would have suffered severely if you told the truth about the Sagan Order, and did you think at that time when you made this statement that the existence of the Sagan Order was not known?'

'That is what I wanted to say', said Zacharias gratefully.

McKenna and Lyon, experienced policemen who were familiar with the whole gamut of defensive ploy as exercised from the dock, looked at each other, not so much in incredulity as in tortured admiration.

At his headquarters office in Germany, Wing Commander Bowes made entries against the names of Squadron Leader Tom Kirby-Green and Flying Officer Gordon Kidder:

Erich Zacharias in British custody, 1.4.1946.
Friedrich Kiowsky in Czech custody.
Friedrich Schwartzer, possibly in Czech custody but not seen. [The fact that Schwartzer was held by the Czechs was later confirmed by the news that they had executed him with Kiowsky.]
Otto Koslowsky reported burnt to death tied to a Czech lamp-post. [This was untrue. Koslowsky was eventually arrested by the Czechs and executed with the others for crimes inside Czechoslovakia.]
Franz Schauschütz in Czech custody, death sentence likely. [This forecast was true.]
Hans Ziegler, Adolf Knippelberg, Hugo Römer, Wilhelm Nölle: WANTED.

Against the names of the twenty-nine who died in the Breslau Military District, Bowes entered:

Wilhelm Scharpwinkel ?dead?
Ernst Schmauser in Russian custody.
Erich Brünner in American custody.
Günther Absalon ?in Russian custody?

At the end of his list of victims Bowes boxed entries concerning the high German officials now formally accepted as members of the general conspiracy against the officers from Stalag Luft III:

Adolf Hitler suicide 30.4.1945.
Heinrich Himmler suicide 23.5.1945.
Hermann Göring on trial at Nuremberg.
Wilhelm Keitel on trial at Nuremberg.
Ernst Kaltenbrunner on trial at Nuremberg.
Artur Nebe executed by Gestapo February 1945.
Heinrich Müller: WANTED.

5 Debit deceased with cost of coffin

Flight Lieutenant Steve Courtney—he had now been promoted—had learned, after some months on the Stalag Luft III investigation not to go out at night in Wiesbaden. Wiesbaden was a base town which he had to use often for liaison in the American zone, where Courtney was mainly working. But the Royal Air Force uniform was extremely unpopular there. Courtney was chased through the streets and stoned in the dark, and found his car overturned in the street in the morning. The motor-car was very easily identified from its RAF roundel on the bonnet, and Wiesbaden was highly indignant with the RAF. Bomber Command forces had dropped a thousand tons on the Hessen capital one night, mistaking it for Frankfurt, 25 miles away. 'I can understand your resentment', said Courtney, a Westcountryman, to a citizen in the bar who was trying to explain the situation. 'It's like bombing Bath instead of Bristol. But at least it was a mistake. When Hitler gave the direct order for his Baedeker raids, which he plainly called terror attacks[1] and invented the phrase, the intended targets were Bath and Exeter. Your aeroplanes came in at six hundred feet to blow holes in Bath, which was easy because it wasn't defended, and you gutted Exeter at point-blank range, as I happen to know since I came home on leave that night in time to tackle the mess. We *were* pulling our dead out of flaming furnaces before you, you know.'

'Köln—' began the German.

'Cologne', said Courtney more good-humouredly, 'is a communications and industrial centre that has been fought over for a thousand years. But no one on my side is proud of what it looks like now. When your chaps bombed Canterbury they actually claimed direct hits on the cathedral in their communiqué and ranked it as a military target.

'Listen. Everybody is the victim of his own propaganda, but we

[1] *Terrorangriffe.*

could try being a little less arrogant about keeping our minds closed. I was one of the first free men in a place called Belsen, which you've never heard of and don't want to hear of, because it's unpleasant. There were hundreds of thin child prisoners moping around there. On what in a school you might call their playground there was a pile of dead bodies of naked women. It was sixty-five metres long and thirty-five metres wide. Now you might have thought somebody would have noticed this. Belsen was at the back of a row of semi-detached houses. It was virtually right inside a village. But to this day nobody in the village admits that they even noticed. There's a name for this psychotic dam you build to stop your glory being flushed out with your guilt—but why start calling names?

'However, I'll make you a simple offer. You say your business sometimes takes you to Munich. Tomorrow I am going to Munich—in my dented car with the Royal Air Force roundel on the top. Meet me there and try a simple test. Ask a few questions to check on what I say. Nine miles from the city limits of Munich is a place called Dachau—which all the records say has been a concentration camp since 1933. But the news hasn't got through to Munich yet. They say there was so much traffic going in and out that they thought it was an industrial centre. When the Americans liberated Dachau they found, beyond the industrial torture-chambers and the industrial crematoria, long lines of trucks. They were filled with dead bodies. There was plenty of traffic, all right. You can even read about it in your own newspapers this very week, because they are trying the commandant and forty guards for atrocities. What do *you* think about it?'

'It's terrible', said the German. 'But you know the newspapers. I'm sure it's all very exaggerated.'

Courtney had been busy in Munich since November 1945, not only on his massive screening of the densely populated cages and camps around it, but in a direct investigation of the Sagan crime that was known to have occurred at or near Munich, the shooting of Lieutenants Johannes Gouws and Rupert Stevens of the South African Air Force.

At a very early stage he had gained access to the Munich City Police records—for the meticulous accuracy of which he never ceased to bless another aspect of the German mind. This led him to two former members of the Munich Gestapo. They gave him information about ten people on his wanted list, some of them known to be in custody in camps in the American zone as far apart as Dachau and Garmisch-Partenkirchen. Courtney split up his team to cover these camps methodically. The Munich murders were their immediate and local interest, but they naturally gathered information on people listed as Wanted, ranging from Scharpwinkel to Ziegler—whom Bowes had heavily emphasized to his SIB after the frustration of the raid on Zell am See.

In a prolonged investigation of the Munich police files Flight

Sergeant R. M. Daniel came across an internal report within the Munich Kripo which exposed three very valuable names. The report, a statement by one Kriminaldirektor (Chief Inspector) Haselsberger, said:

> In the summer of 1944 I was called to Greiner, chief of the Kripo, who handed me a letter from the Gestapo marked 'Reich Top Secret'. This said that by order of RSHA Berlin, the Kripo had to take into safe custody two urns then lying in the Munich crematorium, and keep them until further notice. The two urns must have the names of the cremated and of the crematorium stamped on them. I swore at this, because the Gestapo were always giving the Kripo orders about matters over which they had no control, and I needed better authorization. I did not collect the urns from the crematorium. After some weeks the Gestapo queried this. I telephoned Kriminalrat Schermer of the Munich Gestapo, who said a letter about the urns was on its way and told me that the urns contained the ashes of two British pilots who had been shot whilst trying to escape. Later I told a man from the Kripo to collect the urns from the crematorium and take them to Breslau, as RSHA had ordered.

Courtney now had the names Haselsberger, Greiner and Schermer to concentrate on. But he also started investigations at the crematorium. There were two glaring erasures in the crematorium register—glaring by comparison with the perfection of the rest of the records. The administrator of the crematorium and a magistrate who had signed necessary papers were interrogated. The magistrate recalled that a Gestapo man named Weil had come to see him and declared that two bodies which he was ordered to dispose of were of prisoners named Gouws and Stevens who had been shot whilst trying to escape. The bill for the cremation was to be sent to the Gestapo. Much later, in March 1945, when the Americans were approaching Munich, the destruction of all Gestapo records was ordered. Weil came to the crematorium and said that the names of Gouws and Stevens were to be erased. The magistrate refused to sanction this, and after a few days Weil came to the crematorium administrator, sent for the books, and erased the names himself, saying that it was by order of the Gestapo. Substitute entries were made, saying that the bodies were of unknown male persons killed in an air raid.

Courtney now had the man Weil to seek. He first picked up Greiner, who said he had been away on a cure at the time of the Sagan murders, but could not deny his knowledge of the later disposal of the bodies. Courtney sent him to the London Cage, where they had more time for interrogation. In the meantime Flight Sergeant Williams traced the subordinate of Greiner in the directorate of the Munich Gestapo, Kriminalrat Anton Gassner, whom he found in Garmisch-Partenkirchen. He applied to the

American authorities for Gassner's extradition, but interrogated him on the spot. Gassner described the *Grossfahndung*, for which he had local responsibility, and he knew the details of the recapture of the three officers who had been caught near Munich. Lieutenant Neely, of the Fleet Air Arm, had been taken on an express train, and Gassner interrogated him himself. Gouws and Stevens had not been travelling together, although their intention was to join each other near Lake Constance. One was caught in an express train, and one was on a slow train. Gassner had to go almost immediately to a conference in Dresden, and when he returned he heard that the naval officer had been returned to Sagan, and that the ashes of the two South Africans were in two parcels—that is, wrapped boxes—which were finally sent to Breslau. He could get no details of the deaths of the two officers, because the affair was Top Secret.

Courtney's team was busy all over the American zone. Sergeant S. B. Greet found in the camp at Ludwigsburg a man called Achter who had been in the Munich Gestapo. He remembered the night of the murder of the two South Africans. The Munich Gestapo Chief, Oberregierungsrat and Obersturmbannführer Dr Oswald Schäfer, had called into his office four men—Weil, Geith, Schermer and a driver called Schneider—and had given them instructions which Weil, coming back into the stand-by room, said were Reich Top Secret. Achter took the hint and asked no questions, understanding that an execution was being ordered. 'I assumed', he said, 'that it was an espionage matter with a communistic taint. Weil usually worked on espionage cases, Geith on underground movements and left-wing jobs. This assumption of an execution was made stronger by the fact that Schneider, although a driver, was equipped with an automatic pistol.'

Courtney now had four names as the putative murderers—Weil, Geith, Schermer and Schneider—with Schäfer as the organizing chief. He passed them to his team. Greet interviewed in Ludwigsburg Freiherr von Eberstein, formerly General of Police in Bavaria, who said he believed Schäfer had been killed in April 1945, possibly executed for going slow over an instruction to have the Gestapo shoot all the internees at Dachau, after which the concentration camp was to be bombed by the Luftwaffe—a fantastically impracticable action for its date, 20th April 1945, which illustrates the panic measures contemplated by Himmler to destroy the evidence of twelve years of tyranny.

Courtney did not cross Schäfer off his list, and stormed into renewed activity. He thought he had got both Schäfer and Geith after a comb-out of the records of one of the camps, but found on interrogation that he had got men with the right names but the wrong identity: Schäfer in particular was a very common German name. But the Americans, who were co-operating with great interest, assured him that they were convinced that they had the right Eduard Geith in one of their camps, having a record of an arrest on

5th May 1945, and they would eventually turn him up. The correct Schermer was pretty certainly dead. Kriminalkommissar Martin Schermer had hanged himself in a wood near Munich just before the entry of the American armed forces. Flight Sergeant Daniel collected his death certificate, and was satisfied with its authenticity.

They then went for Schneider. They found the address of his wife and called to see her. She said she had last heard from him in an internment camp at Hammelburg. They tried to reach this camp, but icy weather cut off both the easterly and northerly mountain approaches to it, so they retired to wait for better times while they continued their searches in the south.

They found Emil Weil in Dachau. And Weil talked: not all the truth at first, only enough to lay the major blame on others, without fully realizing he was incriminating himself.

He spoke of the night conference in Schäfer's office in the Gestapo headquarters at the Wittelsbad Palais in Munich, but he said he took no part in it. Later, he said, he was detailed by Schermer to be the fourth man in the enterprise, because there was no one else. He protested, and said that one of the fire picquet should be awoken and sent out. Schermer said, 'Orders are orders. The Chief has laid it on.'

At 4.30 a.m., with Schermer, Schneider and Geith, he got into a six-seater car with two civilians who had been brought from the cells. Questioned as to whether they were handcuffed, he said he did not see. They drove off towards the Ingolstadt autobahn.

After about fifty kilometres, Schermer had the car stopped, and said everyone could relieve themselves. While he was urinating, said Weil, 'Two shots from an automatic weapon were fired in quick succession. I saw the prisoners fall forward. I saw Schneider at the back of the car. He had a sub-machine-gun in his hand. Schermer went to the two who were lying there and told Schneider to fire some more shots at each, which Schneider did. Schermer ordered that a covering should be fetched from the car and put over the bodies. Schermer then said that he had to drive with Schneider to the municipal legal official and the medical officer, and he told me and Geith to remain with the bodies in the meantime.

'After twenty minutes two policemen came along on their beat. Geith showed them his papers and said their officer in charge had gone to the authorities. One policeman went away and the other stayed with us. About an hour or more later Schermer returned accompanied by another car from which a police official and a civilian got out. The civilian went to the bodies, lifted the covering, and said "They're dead". The civilian and the police officer drove away. Schermer told Schneider, Geith and me to put the bodies in a small hollow to prevent their being seen so easily from the autobahn. We also had to cover them with pine branches so that we could take the tarpaulin with us. The policeman remained with the bodies. Schermer, Geith, Schneider and I then returned to Munich. On the way, at Allershausen (or a place with some such name), we stopped at the police station, where Schermer, I presume, telephoned the funeral officer in Munich to collect the bodies. We then went on to Munich.

'On our return to the office we had to swear an oath of secrecy before Schäfer.

'Ten or fifteen days before the entry of the American troops into Munich, Schäfer gave me a note of the persons shot, their Christian names, surnames, date and place of birth, and told me to get the Director of the Funeral Office in Munich to remove their names and particulars from the register. The director's deputy showed me the register, and I erased the two names with a pocket knife and a typewriter rubber. Two days later Schäfer sent me to see that the names were deleted from the prison registers in the Police Presidency and the Kripo office. The Polizeipräsident told me to leave it to him. Kriminalrat Haselsberger in the Kripo sent for a black notebook and crossed out the two names in indian ink. But he said that in any case his instructions were that the notebook had to be destroyed on the approach of the enemy.'

Courtney put out a renewed circulation for Schäfer, whom he now positively believed to be alive. Flight Sergeant Williams had interviewed a man in Moosberg Camp who said Schäfer left the Gestapo offices at Munich on 27th April 1945, thirty-six hours before the Americans arrived and a week after the General of Police had supposed he was executed. The informant said that the man shot after an SS trial for disobedience over Dachau was a Gestapo officer named Bauer. He gave a good description of Schäfer, including a duelling scar on one of his cheeks. Williams then traced and found at Pfaffenhoffen the police doctor, a Dr Max Reber, who had examined the bodies of Lieutenants Gouws and Stevens and pronounced them dead. Williams impounded the doctor's register, which the Gestapo had omitted to order to be destroyed.

At this point Courtney received information from the London Cage that a very junior member of the RSHA staff in Berlin had been picked up, who by a series of coincidences had had full access to the secret Sagan files, which had later been destroyed. This man, Kriminalkommissar Peter Mohr, had an amazing memory of the full sequence of events, and was singing like a bird. With direct reference to the Munich murders, Mohr revealed that, of all the Gestapo offices involved, the Munich office had deducted the cost of the coffins and cremation from the money found in the dead officers' pockets, and meticulously returned the change, and a crematorium receipt, to Breslau with the rest of the officers' effects.

Mohr's emphasis was less on the macabre meanness of the act than on his deduction that the cremation must have taken place at a public crematorium where accounts had to be rendered: it could not, for instance, have taken place at Dachau, where the victims had no money, and the cost of cremations was charitably borne on the State charge. He therefore suggested a search at the only public crematorium available, and gave further hints of novel methods of investigation at the Head Police Office in Munich, where the names of the Gestapo officials handling the prisoners could be ascertained.

Much of Mohr's information duplicated what was already known. But Warrant Officer Williams, as he then was, made an even more thorough search of the Polizeipräsidium in Munich, and found in a cellar another overlooked record which listed Rupert Stevens and John Gouws as having been confined in Cell 32. Courtney went to inspect the cell. 'It was two feet wide and about five feet long', he said, 'and you could see the marks on the walls where the poor devils who were kept there for any length of time had gone demented, and beaten and scratched the wall.'

Williams went back to the East Cemetery and requisitioned as evidence the principal cremation register in which the names against the entries 876 and 877 had been scratched out. But he also found the *Urnenbuch*, the cross-register of urns issued, which the Gestapo had forgotten to deal with. Against the urn numbers 876 and 877 he found the names of Rupert Stevens and Johannes Gouws. In addition, he found the account slips for these cremations, made out to the Munich Gestapo in respect of the disposal of the bodies. The Gestapo had robbed the dead officers to pay these bills, but had kept the cost as low as possible, ordering only fifth-class cremations. Williams also chatted to the crematorium organist, who had been idle at the time of these cremations because the Gestapo had not engaged him, and had taken private notes of the wounds on the bodies, which he gave to the warrant officer.

The Americans had confirmed that Schneider was interned at Hammelburg. As soon as the weather eased he was given a preliminary interrogation and 'frozen' in the camp while the organization of his extradition went through.

Schneider said that Schermer had ordered him to prepare the six-seater car for a night trip, and to bring a machine-pistol with him. He saw Schermer and Geith bring two prisoners from the police headquarters to the Gestapo office. They were chained to each other by one wrist. At 4.30 a.m. the prisoners were brought out to the car. Schermer told Schneider, 'On the orders of Oberregierungsrat Schäfer you are to drive towards Ingolstadt. This job is about two prisoners who have often escaped. They are air-raid shelter burglars and looters. Should these two escape, then you will shoot on my orders.'

Schneider persisted in this not entirely convincing version even when the unfolding and accumulating evidence of the others concerned in the crime declared that he had been a full member of the conspiracy to murder the officers from the beginning of the operation.

He said that on the autobahn Schermer stopped the car and said the men could relieve themselves. When the prisoners had got down from the car Schermer said to Schneider in a low voice 'Out!' and pointed to the machine-pistol under the seat.

'I got out, took the machine-pistol, inserted the magazine, slung the gun, and went to the back of the car. I was leaning against the luggage box about five metres directly behind the prisoners. I stood there without suspicion, as I could not see any danger of escape and because I did not know what was to happen in the next moment. Then I noticed that Schermer was signalling to me with his hands in the direction of the prisoners, and he said to me in an urgent, hushed voice, 'Shoot, shoot!' I looked at him, and it went through my head—he wants me to shoot the prisoners here on the spot.'

Schneider said he fired two short bursts and put the machine-pistol back under the car seat. Schermer said to the others, 'Take the chains off at once'. They covered the bodies with a tarpaulin from the back of the car. Schermer told Schneider to drive the car forward about five metres. He picked up the empty cartridge cases and threw them near the new position of the car, and said to Schneider, 'If there is a commission of inquiry, you shot from here'.

Courtney continued the hunt for Schäfer and Geith. The Americans assured him that Geith was one of the quarter-million persons in their hands, but there had been inter-camp transfers and paper confusion, alongside searches of greater priority, and they requested time to deliver him. Courtney rested his confidence in them, and concentrated on Schäfer. At the same time, because the same locality was involved, he conducted parallel hunts for Ziegler of Zlín, whom Bowes was screaming for, and Müller of Berlin, who was not now so firmly believed as previously to have gone down fighting the Russian tanks in the Alexanderplatz in his best white uniform, with a pistol in one hand and a glass of schnapps in the other. Alongside the search for Müller there was a hunt for his adjutant and brother-in-law, Panzinger.

Schäfer's wife was traced to Wesermünde. She was known to be estranged from him, but it was also ascertained that she had borne him a child in June 1945, and a hope was hazarded that even curiosity about his new offspring might tempt Schäfer to visit his wife. An unobtrusive watch was therefore maintained. In the meantime there was some concentration on his former secretary, whose name had been linked with his by gossip. She was strongly rumoured to have had a child by him. The SIB first found her father, who was so indignant when the scandal was carefully repeated to him that he gave his daughter's address in order that she could refute it herself. She was working as an interpreter at a United States Army Air Forces depot, where she was said to be very popular, and she was living in the house of an American colonel. When interviewed she admitted that, after Schäfer's wife left Munich, he had very occasionally taken her to the opera, but declared that their relationship had been purely platonic. She said she had no knowledge of his whereabouts or of his present false identity. The last time she had seen him was when he had visited her in hospital in February 1945.

She said she had no photograph of him, and he had never written her a letter; and a search of her accommodation, to which she had to submit, showed that at least she had kept none.

Flight Lieutenant Courtney had delayed his release into civilian life in the hope that he could round off the Munich inquiry. Of the two principals still alive and uncaught, Schäfer was to stay on the run for another five years. But Courtney went back to the United Kingdom at least with the satisfaction of knowing that Geith had finally been taken. Geith was a career policeman aged forty-seven with twenty-six years' service. His wife had died in 1944, and his only daughter, Elisabeth, was living with his parents. Eduard Geith told the fullest story of all.

He was not present when Schäfer gave the original order for the killings, but (he supposed immediately afterwards) Schermer briefed him and Weil and Schneider together. He first insisted, on Schäfer's order, that they should exchange the SS hand-clasp which bound them to utter secrecy. Schneider and Weil were certainly in the ring bound by this Service oath. Schermer said that two prisoners had to be shot on the highway on orders from Berlin, and the operation had to be completed during the hours of dawn, before full daylight. Geith said that he and Weil raised an objection that their police pistols were not accurate enough, and Schneider therefore volunteered to use his machine-pistol: 'he would be certain of himself, and could also guarantee that there would be no mistake'. Schermer arranged that he would stop the car and call, in the German term, a piddling pause, and Schneider would fire from the cover of the car. The plan took an hour's discussion to finalize. 'After the conference we passed the time with unimportant conversation, and dozed a little.'

At about four in the morning Schermer and Geith fetched the prisoners from the police headquarters. Geith chained them together by the wrist. In the Gestapo office they were unchained and underwent a cursory interrogation, which Schermer continually interrupted, nervously telling them to keep it short. This interrogation established, however, beyond doubt that the prisoners were 'Royal Air Force' officers, and everyone knew it. The officers were then stripped and searched, and they dressed and were chained together again.

They went to the car. After some distance on the autobahn Schneider slowed. Schermer was looking for open country where a wood was near to the road, so that it could be said that the escaping prisoners were running towards the trees. He saw a suitable place, told Schneider to stop the car, and shouted, 'Get out: piddling pause'. Within seconds the prisoners were shot. One of them was given a coup de grâce. Geith took off the fetters immediately, in case the wrists were marked by pressure through the unnatural position in which the officers had fallen. A ring and a wristwatch were taken from the officers and pocketed by Schermer for safe keeping. The bodies were covered.

Geith and Weil then fired a few shots from their pistols at a telegraph pole in the field, 'so as to leave on it marks of so-called pursuit shots', and Schneider's spent cartridges were scattered around. Schermer had repeatedly called for extreme care in case there was future investigation by an international commission.

Schermer and Schneider went off to find the coroner's officer. Two gendarmes rode up on bicycles. One started to take some notes, but Weil told him to forget it. The coroner's officer arrived and left. The gendarme was left guarding the bodies. The four murderers drove back to Munich.

In the Gestapo office Schermer gave Geith the effects of the dead officers—two little cardboard boxes which they had been carrying, and the ring and the watch—to take in to Schäfer. Schäfer picked out an open packet of cigarettes and said they need not be handed in, and the men could smoke them—Geith was insistent that he had shared out the cigarettes absolutely equally. Schäfer insisted on Geith taking another hand-clasp pledge of secrecy, saying that the consequences of any disclosure would be severe.

Schermer compiled a report for Berlin, but late complained that he had had to write an improved version. Schermer, Schneider and Weil, but not Geith, drove to the scene of the crime to agree a reconstruction of the escape. Schermer mentioned that other Gestapo offices had had to carry out similar killings after the Sagan escape, and the Munich group were lucky, because some of the others had had far more than two prisoners to deal with.

Geith remembered that in the summer the German press had printed official comment on a speech on the radio given by the British Foreign Minister.

'I had to agree beyond question that the statements of Mr Eden were true, while the explanations of the Offices of the Reich stank and lied on all points. I mentioned this to Schermer and said it was a hell of a business, but Schermer did not reply.

'I did not take part in these events', Geith concluded, 'of my own free will or out of personal interest. It was an order for me. I could have refused this order, but I am quite convinced that a refusal would have had the severest consequences. I think no other official would have dared to refuse the order, as Schneider and Weil did not refuse. In my mind I have been a most unhappy man since this occurrence. If I have kept quiet so far, which again was a big mistake on my part, I did this for personal reasons, for the sake of my little daughter, the only member of my family left to me from this tragic war.'

Faced with this full confession, Emil Weil amplified his previous statement. He agreed that he had been briefed by Schermer that two British officers were to be shot that night. Schermer said that he, Weil, was to shoot one of them. He tried to persuade Schermer to delay the action for twenty-four hours, intending to go to his dentist next day, have a tooth pulled, and report sick. Schermer said Berlin had ordered that the killings had to be done that night. The four of them were hesitant how to shoot the officers. Schermer asked Geith and Schneider, who had both served on police duties in Russia, how these matters were tackled there. The answer was that the prisoners were handcuffed and then shot with a tommy-gun. Schermer was impressed, and said Schneider had a tommy-gun and he would do it, during a stop while the prisoners were relieving themselves.

The shooting was done. Geith took off the manacles, and the marks they had made on the wrists were already visible. Geith and Weil made conversation while they waited for Schermer's return, and Geith revealed that both the officers had come from South Africa. On the return of the party to the Gestapo office, Schäfer personally took a pledge of secrecy from them. Later, when a foreign commission was expected, the group revisited the scene and invented a scenario involving a break-down in the car due to a leaking radiator: the prisoners helped to mend the car and then ran off.

'I have now eased my conscience', declared Weil. 'I remained silent until now because of misconceived loyalty. I ask that my silence may be pardoned.'

Schäfer remained untraced. For the British investigators the easing of the pressure of one case meant merely the clearing of decks for another. When Flight Lieutenant Courtney left Germany Flight Sergeant Daniel bore down very vigorously on associates of the senior man on the Wanted List, Gruppenführer Heinrich Müller of the RSHA Berlin. He traced the brother of Müller's former secretary, Barbara Helmut, at his home in the town of Dachau. This man said his sister Babette had been staying at this address, but had reported voluntarily to the United States forces and was now held in Ludwigsburg: Daniel promptly applied for her transfer to a British camp. In any case, said the brother, Babette did not know where her former chief was. Another sister had recently seen Frau Müller in the street at Pasing, a district of Munich. Frau Müller was dressed in black and said her husband had committed suicide just before the capitulation. The brother gave an address for Frau Müller.

Daniel went to Pasing, and found that the street he had been given did not exist. Finally he traced the address of Sophia Müller. He raided the house and searched it completely. He interrogated Frau Müller, who was living with her mother. She said she had left Berlin in February 1945. She had last seen her husband on 31st March 1945 when he came to Pasing for a few hours.

'He did not talk about his intentions, and I did not ask him, because my marriage was not a happy one. About four weeks ago [that is, in May 1946] my father-in-law received a letter from a woman who I think was my husband's mistress. She said that my husband had committed suicide. I can tell you the name of this woman. She is Fräulein Anny Schmid, of Apartment 3, Schützenstrasse 4, Berlin/Streglitz. Go and ask her, because she is the only person who knows about my husband.'

'Do you have a photograph of your husband which I could borrow?' asked Daniel.

'I have never kept a single photograph of my husband', said Frau Müller, 'except my wedding picture, and that was taken in 1924.'

Frau Müller gave the address of her father-in-law, who also lived in Pasing. Daniel went there with his interpreter, Sergeant P. H. N. Linssen. Again they began with a thorough search of the house, but found no trace of Müller. Herr Müller senior said yes, he had had a letter a month ago from Fräulein Anny Schmid saying that Heinrich had committed suicide. But he could not produce it because, unaccountably, he had lost it. However, he could show the flight sergeant two other letters from Fräulein Schmid which had come more recently. He handed these over, and sat in some embarrassment while the interpreter translated them to Daniel.

Clearly Müller, senior, had been prowling round Berlin trying to recover some of his son's possessions, and had been asking Anny Schmid's relations how much money Müller had allowed her, and whether he had cleared his bank account into hers. It was equally plain that Anny Schmid was a woman of fighting spirit, and had responded with belligerence. But one letter did, by implication, refer to Müller's death, and Daniel took a copy for the file:

> My relations have told me of your visits and your nosey questions. During all my thirty-two years I have never known such cheek. It is a shame now that H. [Heinrich] is dead to have to undergo such experiences. H. would be very angry if he knew of your present conduct.
>
> However, I have no wish to quarrel with you, only to give you a clear statement of fact. You will forgive me if I do not go into the details of H.'s awful last days, as I have already dealt with that in two of my letters, and also because my attitude to you has changed after your recent behaviour. I only hope your wife knows nothing of your shady activities. I want at least to keep my faith in 'H.'s dear loving mother.'
>
> You are very curious about his bank account and my allowance. I could afford to pay for my own holidays and for his leaves as well. As for the fur coats—what are you insinuating about my fur coats? I still have the receipts in my possession. The same goes for all your other insinuations.
>
> The whole of the private property including furniture, bank account, etc., were confiscated by the State. What Heinzel and I intended to keep after the Russian occupation were one carpet and two photographs which I wanted to keep as a souvenir, and later as a keepsake for Reinhardt [Müller's son].
>
> As for your fairy tales about your poor wife having to go out as a washerwoman, find somebody else to tell them to. You must think that my relations and I were born stupid. Even if your wife does have to set her hand to earning a living, she has been doing for only one year what I have been doing all my life. Perhaps you will bear that in mind, Herr Müller.

In the same registered envelope containing this letter Anny Schmid had sent a mollifying note to Frau Müller asking her not to take anything personally, 'as I know you are not connected with your husband's low activities . . . otherwise you would not have been H.'s mother'. Here she made one explicit reference to Müller's death:

> Perhaps we can meet somewhere, because there is a lot on my mind which I would willingly confide to your motherly heart. We were together until the very last moments of his life. Perhaps it may be possible to meet Reinhardt.

An unhappy witness of this recital was Müller's son Reinhardt, who was now living with his grandparents. Then aged nineteen, he had served in the Wehrmacht during the last stages of the war. Afterwards he had been interned by the Americans, but had recently been released as being no security threat. He told Daniel that he had seen his father briefly in Berlin in February 1945. He had received a letter from his father, which he could not produce now, postmarked Berlin and dated 28th April 1945. He also had no photograph of his father which he could show, and he said he believed he was dead.

Flight Sergeant Daniel did not recommend a raid on Anny Schmid's apartment in Berlin. He reasoned that if her report of Müller's death was a ruse she would be unlikely to admit it on a mere confrontation, judging her strength of character from the force of her letters. He suggested that a permanent watch on her house, and regular shadowing of her person, might be more effective than a heavy-footed raid or the arrest of Fräulein Schmid. And this policy was followed.

Daniel then turned to Kriminalrat Hans Ziegler, head of the Zlín *Grenzpolizei*. He obtained information that Ziegler's mother was living in Munich. He found her house, and raided it. Ziegler's mother, Thérèse Ziegler, was living with her daughter Maria Grüber, whose husband was a former Gestapo officer in internment, and with Maria's three-year-old son. A search of the house produced nothing. Daniel confined the two women in separate rooms and subjected them to long interrogation. Maria Grüber was extremely hostile and said nothing. Thérèse Ziegler finally admitted that her son was alive and had visited the house recently.

'What name does he use?' asked Daniel. Frau Ziegler said she did not know that her son had another name.

'How long ago was he here?'

'Three weeks', said Frau Ziegler unconvincingly. Daniel nodded at the interpreter, who went out of the room. He had already made friends with the little boy. He knelt on the floor and played with him, and asked him casually when he had last seen his uncle. 'On Sunday', said the little boy—that is, four days previously. 'Has he got a new name?' 'Don't know.' 'Where is he now?' 'Don't know.'

The interpreter came back and quietly told Daniel his information. Daniel then announced that all three in the family would have to be taken to Dachau—not so grim a fate as it would have been fifteen months earlier—and the interpreter should go to arrange the transport. Daniel had, of course, no authority over entries to an internment camp in the American zone, but the name had its own impact on these professional police families who could never plead ignorance of the existence of the place. Ziegler's mother collapsed in tears. Daniel strongly pressed her about the whereabouts of her son. But she would give no more information. Daniel and Linssen left. The 72-year-old Frau Ziegler had put up a good fight.

Daniel went to the Munich Public Safety Officer, Lieutenant Moran of the United States Army, who promised to have the apartment put under continuous observation by the Kripo. The United States Counter-Intelligence Corps was alerted to Ziegler's probable presence in Munich and was given photographs. Counter-Intelligence gave in return the information that on their instructions an undercover man had struck up an acquaintance with a woman in Mittenwald, Bavaria—the birthplace and former retreat of Zacharias, Ziegler's former subordinate at Zlín—who was known to have been visited by Zacharias before his capture, and was believed to be in touch with other Zlín personnel, possibly Ziegler. The clandestine acquaintance had produced no more information, and Counter-Intelligence suggested that it was time to arrest the woman, interrogate her and search her house. All this was done.

The woman admitted that Hans Ziegler had stayed a night in her house during the previous summer. He had come to ask if any other Zlín officials were around and to take advice about starting a business in the Garmisch area. She said he had obtained a false identity card and had used it to get a job. She said he was thinner than he had been, and had grown a moustache. He had said that he had no intention of seeing his ex-wife, but he did mean to see his mother and then perhaps slip back over the Czechoslovak border, to join the mistress he had kept in Zlín. Daniel traced Ziegler's ex-wife to Babbenhausen, near Augsburg, and raided the house, not in any expectation that Ziegler was pining for his divorced wife, but hoping that he might have been in correspondence with his daughters.

Back in Munich, Lieutenant Moran persuaded the Kripo to arrest Ziegler's sister, Maria Grüber, and hold her for the maximum of three days which were permitted before a charge. An undercover man was then sent to call on Frau Ziegler. He carried a small parcel and asked to see Maria. The mother said she had been arrested.

'That's too bad', said the agent. 'I had some private business with her about Hans.'

'What is it? Perhaps I can help.'

'No. It's very good of you, but it's impossible.'

Frau Ziegler was worried about missing an opportunity to help her son. The agent played a reluctant surrender, saying that the matter was much too confidential and dangerous. Finally he revealed that he was the man who had supplied Hans Ziegler with his false papers, and it was now necessary to alter them.

'Oh!' said Frau Ziegler. 'Isn't he using the name Hans Berger any more?'

'No', said the agent.

'Perhaps that's why Maria could not get hold of him two days ago. She tried to telephone him but could not get in touch with him.'

The agent spent a long time probing for any hint about Ziegler's new identity, occupation and residence. But suddenly Frau Ziegler seemed to know that she had said too much. The man said he would try to get in touch with Maria, and would call again. He went to see Maria Grüber in the police cell and made the same careful approaches, but she refused to speak, and the agent went away.

The police officials told Maria Grüber that she had permission to write a letter to her mother on any domestic subject. She wrote one, which was immediately studied, telling her mother to refuse to speak to anybody or to answer any questions. With this model in front of them the police brought in an expert forger, who wrote a letter to Frau Ziegler, purporting to be from Maria, saying that Frau Ziegler could tell everything to the bearer. This letter was then given to the undercover agent, who went back to the house. Frau Ziegler was deceived by the handwriting, but when she began to 'tell everything' she confided to the agent that she had invented the name 'Hans Berger' on the previous day to test him, because she had an idea he was a Counter-Intelligence Corps man. 'The truth is, I don't know where Hans is staying, what he's working at, or what his new name is. They won't tell me. They say I'm too old and feeble to have the responsibility of such knowledge, and I'll crack under interrogation.'

The agent went away with no more information than that. Flight Sergeant Daniel was left to wonder if Frau Ziegler was at last telling the truth, or whether this formidable old lady was now launching out into treble bluff. He could only fall back on routine counter-measures. He sent a man to the Labour Exchange to list every Ziegler and Berger in the register, with their place of work. He put Ziegler's photograph and description in the Bavarian *Police Gazette* and arranged for the same information to be sent to every public safety officer within fifty miles. He arranged for all mail —outgoing as well as incoming—linked with this address to be censored indefinitely.

Wing Commander Bowes, presiding in Rinteln over a now not unsuccessful progression in the Stalag Luft III inquiries, commended Daniel for clearly doing his damnedest. He himself had just returned with Flight Lieutenant Lyon from Poland, where he had found that the SIB's damnedest was not damned overpowering enough to counter organized political intransigence.

Bowes and Lyon had first gone back to Liberec to add to their file on the murder of Squadron Leader Williams, Flight Lieutenants Bull and Kierath, and Flying Officers Mondschein and Stower. The first four had always been presumed to have died together, and at the crematorium at Most (marked Brüx on the urns, under German administration) Bowes and Lyon found full records of their being burnt there by authority of the Gestapo. There was no record for Stower. But the officers discovered an entry in the files. Bernard Baatz, Gestapo Chief at Reichenberg (later Liberec) had signed a cremation order in respect of all five of the captured airmen *on the day before the known date of the killing of four of them*, which was certainly before the death of Flying Officer Stower. Baatz was therefore a priority as a man wanted not only for complicity in murder but, *ex officio*, as the instigator. Lyon also obtained from the crematorium keeper at Most a description of the Gestapo officers, and especially of the senior official, who had delivered the bodies to him. His careful delineation of the insignia of rank indicated an SS Sturmbannführer. Bowes and Lyon went through a list of the Gestapo staff at Reichenberg. There had been only two men of that rank in the station. They promptly added Sturmbannführer Robert Weissman and Sturmbannführer Robert Weyland to the urgent circulation list.

The Royal Air Force investigators were hampered in Liberec by the almost total ignorance among the inhabitants of what had gone on in 1944. Reichenerg had been part of the Sudetenland, strongly populated by the former Czech nationals of German descent whose grievances had given Hitler the excuse to annex Czechoslovakia. The Gestapo, escaping after the capitulation, had been able to rely on local sympathy and local silence. They evaded the net which caught so many Gestapo in southern Czechoslovakia and set them in gaol. After the war over three million Germans were evicted from the Sudetenland. The Czechs who took their place were almost as new to the areas as the British visiting officers. Baatz, Weissman and Weyland, and all the small-fry informants who had been so useful in Brno and Zlín, would not be found in Czechoslovakia, but had to be hunted amid the general self-defensive chaos in Germany.

While they were in Czechoslovakia the SIB officers heard that they had been granted permission to visit Poland, and they took the opportunity to get from the Polish consul in Prague visas to enter the key towns of Breslau, Görlitz, Hirschberg, Liegnitz and Danzig, where so many of the murders had been committed. These towns, now in Polish territory as Wrocław, Zgorzelec,[1] Jelenia Góra, Legnica and Gdańsk, had been barred to the investigators so far.

On 13th April 1946 the Air Attaché in Warsaw, Group Captain C. B. E. Burt-Andrews, received an Air Ministry signal: 'Bowes Lyon arriving tomorrow'. He spent some frustrating hours discussing

[1]This is part of the former Görlitz; the rest remains in Germany.

with his Ambassador, Mr V. F. W. Cavendish-Bentinck, how to receive this unsuspected member of the family of the then Queen—*née* the Lady Elizabeth Bowes-Lyon. But at the airfield he found Freddie Bowes and Dickie Lyon. During the next days he conducted them to a number of conferences at the Polish Foreign, Defence and Interior Ministries, but it was soon fairly apparent that the Polish authorities had no wish that any inquiries should be made by British personnel in Poland.

The well-worn tactics of delay were introduced. Bowes suffered as patiently as possible. Whenever the officers left their hotel they were aware that they were being tailed by the secret police. There was nothing for them to do while the diplomatic obstacles were being negotiated except to eat and drink, but their meagre allowance largely forbade this. They found a small restaurant on the road to the Poniatowsky Bridge which served magnificent but expensive roast goose, and they occasionally allowed themselves to enjoy the smell. They were sitting in this restaurant one evening when their shadow came in, and sat at a table on the other side. 'Come on, let's send the poor bugger a drink', said Bowes. They gave the order to the waiter. The plainclothesman looked sheepish, but he did raise his glass to them. From that time on he never tailed them without getting his ration of vodka.

After nine days they were told that their inquiries would be permitted, and they set off for Breslau in a staff car with a Polish liaison officer and the inevitable security officer. They were told that there were Gestapo prisoners in Breslau gaol whom they could interview.

When they arrived in Breslau all the information which they had given at the Warsaw conferences was requested again, and the liaison officer, Captain Kurz, said that the matter would take some time. He said he had been unable to contact the general in command of the district. Bowes, judging the occasion to be a time for strong words, protested in the appropriate language that all arrangements had already been made at the highest level with the Minister of the Interior. The atmosphere began to get tense. On the next day the liaison officer said, 'We have good news for you. All the names on your list except two are on our register. The attorney is sending for particulars of the other two.' Bowes could hardly believe his ears. He had put in a list of 126 men wanted for interview who had served in the Gestapo within the Breslau military area—and the Poles had particulars of 124 of them! 'Fine!' said Bowes. 'Then we shall be able to examine this register and get the men's particulars from it.' 'Of course', said the liaison officer. The security officer spoke to the liaison officer, who laughingly said, 'Don't think that this means that we have got all of the men here. But we have got their names.' Bowes said, 'I understand. But I am sure we can get some useful information from the register.'

The register was mentioned frequently on four subsequent days of utter inactivity. Captain Kurz said that, on the summons of the attorney, a constantly referred to *deus ex machina*, one Gestapo man was arriving in Breslau on one day and several others were arriving from various localities on subsequent days, and they could all be interviewed. The days passed and no interviews were arranged. Bowes demanded to see the attorney. When this meeting finally took place the attorney said that there were no members of the Gestapo available for interview, he had never said that there were, and there was certainly not a register with even one Gestapo name in it, not to speak of 124. Finally, the visits to Görlitz, Hirschberg, Liegnitz and Danzig which had been mentioned were impossible.

Bowes demanded to see General Siedwidski, military commander of the area. After three days this was granted. The atmosphere was icy. The general would not listen to Lyon's arguments in the German language, which he said he did not understand. He refused permission to visit any of the towns for which the officers had visas, but said he would allow them to go to Sagan.

Altogether Bowes and Lyon spent ten fruitless days in Breslau. Whenever they left their hotel they were pursued by young German boys, apparently near starvation, grasping their greatcoats and begging for a zloty—something under a penny. The officers stuffed their pockets with small change, but it was never enough; and if a weak boy got a zloty it was generally wrenched from him by a stronger. The town was still full of seedy Germans waiting to be evacuated in the violent transfer of population that was taking place. Many of them thought that the Royal Air Force officers were members of an international commission arranging the evacuation, and they sought them out in the hotel with pleading narratives of special circumstances which they thought might influence the British.

Breslau, after its long siege, was in graceless ruin. It seemed exhausted still by the massacre and looting that had followed its capture. In a basement shop where a few pieces of porcelain were sold, Bowes and Lyon were told of the fate of the former proprietors, an elderly husband and wife. The woman, aged seventy-five, had been raped in the shop successively by sixteen Russian soldiers in the presence of her husband. They took poison immediately afterwards.

Bowes and Lyon accepted the solitary concession of a visit to the site of Stalag Luft III at Sagan. The camp was a vast sandy expanse, still bounded by its perimeter wire. Some of the prisoners' huts were occupied by displaced slave labourers returned to Polish territory. There was an air of desolation and decay over all. The officers walked to the cemetery outside the wire, where the comrades of the fifty had built a monument in a grove of trees. Bowes and Lyon stood at the salute, and came away.

Wing Commander Bowes entered his account for the killers of Lieutenants Johannes Gouws and Rupert Stevens:

Martin Schermer suicide 25.4.1945.
Johann Schneider in British custody 18.3.1946.
Emil Weil in British custody 16.5.1946.
Eduard Geith in British custody 20.8.1946.
Oskar Schäfer: WANTED.

In the space kept for Squadron Leader Kirby-Green and Flying Officer Kidder he amended the entry on Hans Ziegler—Known to be alive: WANTED

Against the names of Squadron Leader Williams, Flight Lieutenants Bull and Kierath, and Flying Officers Mondschein and Stower he wrote:

Bernard Baatz, Robert Weissman, Robert Weyland: WANTED.

In the box reserved for Berlin he entered:

Heinrich Müller ?suicide? Spring 1946?

Against the names of the twenty-nine of Breslau he could, after all his impetuous effort, write nothing at all.

6 'HE is for it: but this man is so young'

At the end of May 1946 Wing Commander Bowes reported to London that the speed of demobilization had reduced his Stalag Luft III team to three officers and four NCOs. The fact was to be that, apart from temporary attachments for interpretation, the team was never to be any bigger, and the forty-eight people to be erased from the Wanted List were all its own responsibility.

At the time of writing of Bowes's report, his actual muster was even fewer. McKenna was in hospital at Rinteln for exploration of a physical breakdown which was to take him out of action for two months in the autumn. Lyon visited him in hospital, and passed on a message he had taken on the telephone from Major Barkworth.

Major Barkworth was a member of the War Crimes Investigation Unit specializing in tracing the guilty men responsible for the many atrocities committed against the Special Air Service. McKenna had closely co-operated with him and with Miss Vera Atkins, a member of the Special Operations Executive, the secret organization created by Winston Churchill after the fall of France to 'set Europe ablaze from the inside and develop a reign of terror so that the lives of German troops be made an intense torment'. Vera Atkins was particularly occupied with the torture and murder of women agents of the Special Operations Executive. Much of the territory covered by SAS and SOE operations had been around the French border country with Germany, whose Gestapo headquarters had been located at Karlsruhe. Karlsruhe was known to have sent many of its victims to the concentration camp at Natzweiler, or forward on the fatal journey to Dachau. McKenna had carried in his head an obtrusive mental headline about Natzweiler, because that was the location of cremation stamped on the urn in which the ashes of Flying Officer Dennis Cochran had been returned to Sagan. He had more than once mentioned to Major Barkworth and Miss Atkins that he was particularly anxious for details of a young lad called Cochran who had been murdered by the Karlsruhe Gestapo and cremated at Natzweiler.

Lyon told McKenna in hospital that Barkworth had telephoned to say that he had picked up two men in connection with his own inquiries and had had them lodged in the civil gaol at Wuppertal. One was Ganninger, who had been adjutant at the Natzweiler concentration camp. Immediately after his first interrogation Ganninger had commited suicide in his cell by cutting his throat with a razor blade sewn into his jacket. The second man was Herberg, and after prolonged interrogation Barkworth had decided that he had no further interest in him. But Herberg had admitted that he had been a member of the Karlsruhe Gestapo, and when pressed had let slip some slight admission of knowledge of a British officer having been burnt at Natzweiler in 1944. Barkworth said that Herberg was still held in gaol at Wuppertal, and McKenna might like to know of it.

'What would you like me to do?' asked Lyon.

'I'll tell you what I'd like you to do', said McKenna. 'You get a car and come back here immediately, and by the time you're back I'll be out of this flaming bed and waiting for you.'

'It's a long way', said Lyon. 'It's in the Ruhr.'

'It's only a hundred and fifty miles. Let's go down and try to get back by sunset.'

'It's three hundred there and back', said Lyon, and went off for a car.

McKenna waited until the nurses were out of the ward, then took his clothes, dressed in a bathroom, and stayed there with his head out of the window. He heard the crunch of the tyres on the gravel path, and made a swift exit from the hospital. 'I hope to hell Herberg's still there', he told Lyon as he got into the car. 'I can't trust the civil police to hold him.'

Lyon drove fast, and they reached Wuppertal. Herberg was still in the gaol. He was an intelligent man of forty who had studied law, given it up in the confusion of Germany in the mid-twenties, become a sports instructor and then a sports editor, and joined the Gestapo in 1934, finally specializing in anti-communism, anti-sabotage and counter-espionage against parachute agents.

McKenna had no time for cat-and-mouse tactics, but applied a little finesse. He asked a personal question or two: name, Walter Herberg, married with one child. He ascertained that Herberg had been on the staff of Oberregierungsrat Josef Gmeiner, the Chief of the Gestapo at Karlsruhe. 'Were you there in March and April 1944?' McKenna asked.

'Yes.'

'Have you anything on your conscience from that time?'

Herberg began to speak, but failed. He broke down completely into tears. McKenna left him alone for some time. The man recovered sufficiently to tell his story. He was a tall, slim, dark-haired and quietly spoken man who had clearly been under stress, and possibly remorse. But, as was the case with many first statements, his confession was occasionally lenient at points of potential self-incrimination.

He said that in March 1944 he had spent a few days leave with his parents in Mainz, and there he became aware of the *Grossfahndung*. He came home to Karlsruhe before his leave was ended, but almost as soon as he got in he was telephoned with instructions to report to the office. He went in, and his departmental chief, a Kriminaldirektor Dr Faber, said there was a special job for him. They went into the Head of Gestapo, Gmeiner, who read out a secret teleprint he held in his hand, and passed it across for Herberg to study.

Herberg, and later Gmeiner, agreed to McKenna's request that they should try to reconstruct the contents of this key message from memory. All copies had been swiftly destroyed, and their reconstructions were convincingly similar. The following is a composite version of their impression:

> REICH TOP SECRET. RSHA to Chief of the Gestapo office, Karlsruhe, or his deputy. By order of the Führer the Reichsführer SS [Himmler] has ordered that the British airman Cochran who escaped from Sagan and is now held by the Kripo at Ettlingen, Karlsruhe, will be taken over by officials of your office and during transport in the direction Breslau will be shot whilst trying to escape. The shooting will be done in such a way that the prisoner concerned will be unaware of what is going to happen. The corpse is to remain on the spot until inspected by the local gendarmerie and a death certificate has been issued. The body is to be cremated in the nearest crematorium. The urn is to be kept by the Gestapo office. Further instructions about the urn will be issued at a given time.
>
> The death certificate is to be returned to me with a description of the spot where the shooting took place. Only persons strictly concerned with this matter will be allowed to know of this teleprint. These persons must be pledged to special secrecy. The teleprint must be destroyed after the order is carried out. Destruction of the teleprint must be notified to me by teleprint. The Kripo, Karslruhe, have been given relevant instruction.
>
> (signed) Müller, SS Gruppenführer and
> Lieutenant-General of Police

Herberg read the teleprint and handed it back to Gmeiner. 'We shall now take the pledge of secrecy', said Gmeiner.

Gmeiner, Faber and Herberg ceremonially shook hands with a slap of the palms and a hand-clasp. Gmeiner looked at Herberg.

'You are the one who will carry out the order', he said.

Herberg said he was dumbfounded at this and protested immediately, begging Gmeiner to give the task to someone else.

'I am not giving it to anybody else now', said Gmeiner. 'You have already taken the pledge of secrecy, which is restricted to those concerned in the actual act. Come on, it's not so dreadful. You don't have to *do* anything. I have selected Kriminalsekretär Boschert as the driver, and Kriminalsekretär Preiss will do the actual shooting. You are going along only because you can talk. Somebody will have to smooth over the State Attorney and the crematorium authorities, and neither Boschert nor Preiss have got the education for this.'

Herberg played his last card. 'But I'm still on leave', he said.

Gmeiner promised, 'I'll give you an extra day off afterwards'.

'Thank you very much, Herr Oberregierungsrat,' said Herberg.

The three men began to discuss the details of the operation. Gmeiner and Faber, having passed the buck, indulged in a little cautious insubordination and agreed that the order had been issued by one of 'Them', the faceless men behind a green table, who knew nothing of conditions in the field. Faber and Herberg pointed out that no State Attorney would formally condone such an act by issuing a death certificate. Also, there was no handy crematorium on the route from Karlsruhe to Breslau. Gmeiner, a trained lawyer, said the solution was to drive away from Breslau, to the west towards Natzweiler, where there was a crematorium in the concentration camp and there would be far less fuss about issuing a death certificate. He then suggested, with some air of self-congratulation at his own brilliance, that a suitable occasion for the shooting would be for Herberg to stop the car and propose that the prisoner should relieve himself. They aranged the details of the killing. Herberg left the office. Boschert and Preiss were called in, pledged to secrecy by Gmeiner, and given their briefing.

Early next morning they drove to the Kripo prison at Ettlingen to pick up the prisoner. Flying Officer Cochran had been caught right on the Swiss frontier, south of Lörrach, opposite Basel, and had been brought a long distance to a place of custody convenient to the Karlsruhe Gestapo. He was taken from his cell, handcuffed, and put in the back of a green Mercedes car. Herberg described him as very young, about twenty-one [he was one year older] about one metre 84 [six feet tall] with a long, slim face, reddish-blond hair and a freckled complexion. He spoke very good German, and at first conversed easily and unsuspectingly. Herberg asked him his rank, and then inquired what the equivalent of Flying Officer was in the American Air Force. 'Never mind the title,' joked Dennis Cochran, 'the important thing is that in the American Air Force he gets paid four times as much as I do.' Herberg asked him how he had managed to get so far from Sagan, and he politely answered that he was not going to give any details about his escape. He was wearing a converted uniform which had been dyed a violet colour, and had no gilt buttons or military insignia: it was, indeed, the characteristic dress of the displaced persons with whom he had been coolly sweeping the street when Van Wymeersch had seen him in Frankfurt.

The car was driven through Strasbourg and towards Natzweiler. Herberg explained to Cochran that they were taking him to a transit camp before going to Sagan. After that there was no conversation in the car at all. A mood of uneasiness and introspection seemed to affect everybody. Boschert, the driver, was so preoccupied that the Germans suddenly found that they had driven right up to the entrance of Natzweiler concentration camp. They had arrived at their destination with the prisoner alive instead of dead. Herberg muttered to the sentry that they had lost their way. Boschert reversed the car, and they drove back on the road by which they had come. After two kilometres a track branched off the main road, leading up a slight incline into some woods, and Boschert took it and stopped forty metres past the junction. Herberg got out and said he wanted to relieve himself. Cochran was invited to get out, and did.

Herberg said to McKenna, 'I walked another twenty metres along the road. I saw that Preiss and Boschert and the officer had also got out of the car. I could not possibly watch what was coming, and I turned my back. Shortly afterwards I heard a shot, and then another one. I walked back and saw the officer lying on the ground face downwards about three metres from the car.

'Preiss stood beside him with a pistol in his hand, and Boschert was standing near the car. I could see that the officer was dead. He had been shot through the back near the heart and through the back of the head. The bullet through his head had come out through the right eye. None of us spoke a word. Boschert took off the handcuffs.

'We wrapped the body in a blanket and put it on the back seats of the car. We had difficulty in getting it into the car, and Boschert slid back the roof and we lifted it over the windows. We drove up to Natzweiler Camp and I asked to see the Commandant. He was absent and I was referred to his adjutant, whose name was Ganninger. I told him we had been unlucky, and had had our prisoner escape, and he had been shot in flight. Ganninger smiled knowingly and said he was already in the picture. I do not know where he got his information from, and I did not ask. Ganninger asked if I wanted a death certificate, and when I said I did he took me to another building. But the Camp Registrar, a Kripo official called Wochner, refused to issue a certificate on the ground that the death had taken place outside the camp. The Camp Doctor was called and made the same decision. Even when I demanded the certificate on the authority of the Reichsführer I was still refused. I went back to Karlsruhe and was reprimanded because I had not got the death certificate. The body had been taken to the crematorium, but I do not know by whom.

'A fortnight later I was sent for by Gmeiner and told that he had had a teleprint from RSHA Berlin saying that the Karlsruhe report of the shooting was inadequate. I was to take blank office notepaper signed by Gmeiner to Berlin. Because of an air raid I was a day late getting to Berlin, and in Müller's anteroom I saw other Gestapo officials from, I think, Munich, Strasbourg and Vienna, who were on the same errand.

'When I saw Müller he said that nobody in the Gestapo had any imagination. Every unit had reported that their prisoner had run away during a stop for urination. He wanted the reports to vary. He dictated to me a report that said we had to do some repairs on the car, and that was the occasion when the prisoner escaped. But he said, since he did not know the locality well, I was to go back to Karlsruhe, visit the scene again to put in local details, and send the revised report by special courier.

'I hope I have remembered every relevant detail. This matter has been so dreadful to me that I have tried to block it out of my mind. It is horrible how a man can be thrown into agony by orders that destroy his piece of mind and leave his conscience tortured. It was impossible for me to let the officer escape, because I could not give orders to that effect to my subordinates. If we had let him escape the concentration camp would have been awaiting us, and I could not be expected to let myself down in front of my subordinates.'

McKenna listened to Lyon's intermittent translation of this confession in silence. He had prompted the last remark with an inquiry, asking how Herberg had been able to go through with his task, but he made no further comment. They took Herberg from the police prison in Wuppertal and drove him back to the holding prison in Minden. Lyon dropped McKenna at the hospital, and he crept into bed.

The ward sister came round with a nurse and demanded, 'What have you been up to?' 'Well,' said McKenna, 'I had an urgent bit of business to deal with.' 'What kind of business?' 'Something terribly urgent, I just had to go. There wasn't anyone to ask.' 'Don't give me that. Did it ever occur to you to ring the bell?' Group Captain Williams, in charge of the hospital, came round the next morning.

'What's this you've been up to?'

'I had to go out and do a job in Wuppertal.'

'What was it?'

'I had to arrest a man for the murder of one of the Stalag Luft III officers.'

'You mean to tell me you crept out of a hospital bed, whisked off to Wuppertal, got this man, and put him inside?'

'Yes, sir.'

'And you've come back here?'

'Yes, sir.'

'Nothing like this ever happened in my confounded life. And it's not to happen again, you understand?'

'Yes, sir.'

'Did you get the right man?'

McKenna got out of hospital as fast as possible under the warning that he had better take things easily because he was due for an operation later. He took a full statement from Herberg and sent him back to London. He drove to Wuppertal with Sergeant J. Van

Giessen and saw Major Barkworth, who said that Magnus Wochner, the Camp Registrar and also Police Chief at Natzweiler, had gone down for ten years for war crimes—a comparatively light sentence at that time for complicity in the injection and cremation at Natzweiler of four women agents. But, Barkworth said, he had already secured a statement from Wochner on Cochran's death, and he passed it over. McKenna went on into the American sector and browsed through their registers. He was searching for Preiss, one of the most common names in Germany. Taking on one camp a day, he combed Dachau, Ludwigsburg, Mannheim and finally arrived at Darmstadt. There were a number of Otto Preisses in internment here, and McKenna asked for them all in succession. When he had established that their Gestapo records did not qualify them for interrogation he dismissed them.

A man was shown in, some forty years of age, a big-boned, heavily built blonde southern German type. 'You are Otto Preiss, former Kriminalsekretär, Gestapo Karlsruhe?' said McKenna. 'No', said the man, 'no, Herr Major.' 'Oh?' asked McKenna. 'Where do you come from?' 'Heidelberg', said the man. 'Served in Heidelberg?' 'Yes, Herr Major.' 'In what department of the Gestapo?' 'Department 4 (1) C, Herr Major. Foreign labour and economic sabotage.'

'Who was the head of Department 4 (1) C?'

The man hesitated.

'You weren't going to say Kriminalkommissar Reise?'

'No', said the man. But his eyes were very troubled.

'Or Kriminaldirektor Faber as the boss of the entire Department 4?'

'No, Herr Major.'

McKenna shook his head sympathetically.

'It's this wretched camp', he said. 'It's affecting your memory. Now I have a piece of paper here, and it has a very good description of you. It says you were *born* in Heidelberg, not that you served in it. It says that you were a Kriminalsekretär under Reise and Faber. Now the reason I'm interested in you is because I am an officer of the Special Investigation Branch of the Royal Air Force and I'm making inquiries into the murder of Flying Officer Cochran of the Royal Air Force, who was shot in the neighbourhood of Natzweiler concentration camp at about eleven o'clock in the morning of 1st April 1944. Now, I know you know something about it, but I want to tell you something of what I know. I know that you and Herberg and Boschert were in it together, and I know who did the shooting. I know that it was not your idea. I know that Gmeiner ordered the shooting because Himmler ordered him, and Hitler ordered Himmler. Now you tell me what you know about it.'

Preiss obliged with a fairly full confession. The significant difference from Herberg's statement was that Dennis Cochran had walked along the path from the car with all three of his escorts. Preiss was on the right of him, Herberg on the left, and Boschert in the rear.

Herberg told Cochran to turn right and face the woods, and nodded his head to Preiss. Preiss walked forward and shot Cochran in the back of the head. Death was instantaneous, but Dennis Cochran's body was twitching, and Herberg told Preiss to fire a *Gnadenschuss* (coup de grâce) below his shoulder towards the heart. Preiss also said that eight weeks later they had combined a car trip to Natzweiler to pick up the urn with a faked reconstruction of the incident, fabricating details of an escape after a wheel-puncture. And a week after that, Preiss took the urn to Breslau.

Preiss, who warmed to McKenna's interviewing sufficiently to boast that he had carried out a number of other 'executions'—but firmly denied this in every written statement—said he had shot Flying Officer Cochran because of superior orders, not out of personal malice, and gave as an illustration of his attitude to the prisoner the fact that he had put peppermints in his mouth and given a light for his cigarette as he had sat beside the manacled man before getting out to shoot him.

McKenna obtained the necessary clearances and brought Preiss back to Minden. Herberg had said that he thought Boschert had been taken prisoner by the French, and McKenna telephoned Baden-Baden. The French said that Boschert had been the subject of inquiries by their war crimes investigators, but he had been later cleared to the Americans, who also wanted him for interrogation. McKenna then asked about Gmeiner. The French had a note of him too. He had been arrested about April 1945 at Freiburg, but they were unsure of his present location. However, they would circularize their camps.

McKenna checked with the Americans at Frankfurt for news of Boschert. They located him at No. 2 Internee Hospital in Karlsruhe itself. McKenna went to see him. He found him in bed with a broken back. 'What happened?' asked McKenna. Boschert said that while he had been in a French prison for interrogation he had fallen downstairs and broken his spine. 'Fallen, pushed or thrown?' asked McKenna. Boschert said nothing, and McKenna did not pursue the matter. 'You know what I've come about', he said. 'Do you want to speak?' Boschert spoke. His story corroborated all the others, except that he said he had stayed by the car when the other two walked along the path with Cochran, and he heard the shots only from a distance. McKenna got assurances that the Americans no longer required Boschert, and arranged to have him moved north by ambulance.

The French now informed McKenna that Gmeiner had been in Freiburg gaol all the time, but they would not release him because they intended to pursue capital charges against him themselves. McKenna asked, and was given, permission to interrogate Gmeiner at a later date, and turned to Faber. He learned that he had probably been captured by a British commando near Osnabrück, and might be in a British internment camp under a false name.

McKenna consigned the search for him to a slower hunt through the records. The Karlsruhe case had virtually been cleared up within a fortnight of the original interview with Herberg. Eventually the French did hand over Gmeiner under strict assurances that they could have him back if the British charges did not stick. Gmeiner claimed under interrogation that he had merely passed on orders from above, and refused to say more. McKenna left him to work out any fresh attitude under interrogation in the London Cage.

When Flight Lieutenant Lyon returned from Poland with Wing Commander Bowes he went immediately to a new assignment at Esterwegen. Into this camp near the Dutch frontier, historically the first concentration camp ever set up by the Nazis, Bowes had siphoned 134 prisoners who had been extradited from the American zone as deserving lengthier interrogation than could be given by the vagrant officers, pending a decision whether or not to send them on to London. Lyon set about the wearying task of reinterrogation. It was tiresome because the internees tended to be garrulous about every subject except their own personal careers: interrogation advanced very little an officer's knowledge of the man opposite him, and yet it was valuable because it added to his general knowledge of the Gestapo scene.

Lyon was joined at Esterwegen by Flight Lieutenant H. E. Harrison, who had been recruited into the team by Group Captain L. G. Brown, the BAFO Provost Marshal, and Wing Commander Bowes, head of SIB in Germany. Harrison had been a navigator in 115 Squadron, Bomber Command. At the end of the war he had spent two months on food drops to the Dutch, and flying prisoners of war from the Continent to England on repatriation. He badly broke an arm, was grounded, and served in Germany on runway control and then German administration duties, being a useful speaker of the German language. He was then taken into SIB to join McKenna and Lyon as the only surviving officers under Bowes.

Working continuously at Esterwegen, Lyon and Harrison narrowed the 134 internees down to seven of primary importance who were transferred to the London Cage, and twenty-two whom it was still valuable to be able to consult for further background information. Among the latter were two of more than passing interest. Paul Kempka, Hitler's chauffeur, was considered to be potentially more informative than he himself had conceded about the fate of Müller, who had been on the fringes of the Hitler circle in Berlin until the end. Kempka had been in the Berlin bunker when Hitler shot himself and Eva Braun took poison. He told Lyon that he himself had brought a dozen cans of petrol to pour over the bodies, which were placed in a shallow depression near the exit to the dugout; but the cremation had not been immediately successful.

Far more useful for information on the Stalag Luft III case was Dr Hans Merten, a 42-year-old graduate who had been an intermediate officer in Amt V, the Kripo department of RSHA Berlin. Panic stations were sounded in the department one morning at the end of March 1944 when, owing to air raids and sickness, General Nebe's personal aides had not come to the office. Merten was sent to the general as an emergency stop-gap. Merten told Lyon:

'Nebe was blowing his top, screaming to know if he was expected to run the Sagan case entirely by himself. When I came in, he said:

' "Take the teleprints which report the individual recaptures. Write down the names of the recaptured men and the places where they are now. Then bring me the personal file cards of the recaptured men.

' "You have heard about the Führer Order? Then you know what to do. Müller, Kaltenbrunner and I are lunching together. I will take him another list of men to be shot when I see him at lunch-time." '

Merten then went on, 'I gave Nebe the personal file cards of those reported captured since the last list was made up. Each card contained a photograph and personal details of the officer concerned. Nebe was very excited. In my view his agitated, uncontrolled behaviour was due to the fact that he was very keenly aware of the monstrous thing he was about to do.

'I gave Nebe the cards. He threw several in front of me, saying, "Have a look whether they have wives or children". He put the other cards in two piles. Then he took my cards. I gave him briefly the personal details of the officers he had put aside. I remember Nebe said of one of them: "HE is for it" ["*Der muss dran glauben*"] and he put that card on the pile in front of him. He looked at the photograph of another officer and said, "He is so young. No!" He took another card and looked at it and said, "Children? No." And he put it on the stack in front of him.

'He looked at the two piles in front of him, suddenly changed a card from one stack to another, and handed me a pile with the order "Make a list of those. Quickly." '

Merten dictated the list to Nebe's secretary. He said he deliberately dictated the wrong places of recapture, so that orders to shoot officers would be sent to locations where nobody had been caught. But the errors were noticed before teleprint transmission. Merten was immediately removed from the job as a man affected by recent nervous illness, and was posted to a school in Fürstenberg as a teacher in criminology. It was an odd appointment, but at least he was an example that a man could try to sabotage the Führer Order and could still live.

Meantime, the count in the office in Amt V went on. When Nebe had completed a pack of fifty cards the operation was over. . . . Or had it only started?

Dennis Cochran, the independent loner who had died on his second great escape, had an individual entry in the last column of the list kept by Wing Commander Bowes:

Walter Herberg in British custody 28.5.1946.
Heinrich Boschert: confession obtained 8.6.1946, body receipt 2.7.1946.
Otto Preiss in British custody 14.6.1946.
Josef Gmeiner in British custody 3.8.1946.
Dr Faber believed taken by British Commando during hostilities.
Ganninger (Natzweiler) suicide 26.4.1946.
Magnus Wochner (Natzweiler) 10 years imprisonment for other crimes.

Flying Officer Harold E. Harrison (almost immediately advanced to Flight Lieutenant), who came into the SIB team relatively direct from a navigator's cubby-hole, was able to provide an appreciation of the tasks and trials of an investigator which is valuable for the freshness of its approach:

'I entered the investigation as a complete and utter babe. Having been accepted as a member of the team, I was placed under the guidance of Dick Lyon, and always acted in his shadow until I was capable of flying solo.

'I was never trained as a police officer. I didn't have the inquiring, disbelieving mind. To speak the German reasonably well was not the prime quality. It was to understand the situation and to be able to interpret the type of information that was fed back in response to questions. The basic art of interrogation is to understand what is required and why it's required, so that you can interpret the answers coming back. It doesn't really fall into yes-or-no, false-or-true situation. Having asked the basic questions, you can't say "Oh-er", but you must carry on and not lose the initiative. The man is being interrogated because he is withholding something, and as long as one treated the situation as such one had the upper hand. But if I lost that domination I should lose all direction in the interrogation and—more important—spoil the situation for anyone else.

'Working with Dick Lyon in the Esterwegen programme, I was being moulded. The Gestapo types there were arrogant in that, although they were cowed, they were fighting for their very existence. They were often congenital liars, and good at it with their police background. One had to learn to analyse the nuances in the answers and then come back, trying to crack the alibis they might have produced or fill in the holes in their stories.

'Moving about Germany, I was shot up, as I suppose many people were. They hit the truck but missed me. All our jeeps had wire-cutters built on to the bonnet, angle-iron supporting a sharpened jaw which saved one from decapitation. One was shot at, bricks were thrown and bottles broken on the road. A lot of driving was done at night, which was an additional strain since headlamps were still masked and dipped. Because of the shortage of transport the Germans used to use lorry-tugs towing up to four trailers. To overtake five linked vehicles in the dark on a road with reverse camber and limited vision was not relaxing.

'It was a completely depressing experience. I had been fully involved in aircrew and I tended to look on life as something to be enjoyed. I liked flying,

even if I did not particularly enjoy dropping bombs, but it was something that had to be done, and one did it to the best of one's ability with justification in the cause. This of course was the very point which cropped up during interrogations, when the subject under discussion was how the situation arose that they would point a gun and kill someone without passion, looking them in the eye. People would recognize my aircrew brevet and say: "You must have been on that fire-bomb raid on X or Y. My wife, or my kid, was killed there." I learned in the end not to start the arid argument that I had killed on the field of combat and they performed cold-blooded murders. The answer always was: "We were both acting under orders." I could only wrap the answer up in the beautiful German word vielleicht—"*Perhaps. . . . Take out of it what you will.*"

'*I remember in particular a challenge from a man named Julius Gehrum who was held by the French in Baden-Baden. He was in terrible shape, because in the usual crude way he had 'fallen down the stairs' and broken his leg and arm. He was a brute of a man, some six feet three high, built originally like the side of a house, but then rather emaciated and obviously in great pain. He was under sentence of death for having committed a score of murders. He told me: "Why should I admit to one more? I didn't do it. If I had done it I should have told you, because I'm a dead man in any case." He pointed to my wing and said: "You're a terror-flier. Did you bomb anyone? Did you go to Dresden?" I said "Yes". "What was in Dresden?" Nothing. It was the pottery sector, but we were told to go there. If I hadn't gone I should have been court-martialled. You could see the line of the argument although you didn't particularly want to believe it. The difference, of course, was between an operational sortie and a cold-blooded murder. But, yes, it did come home. . . .*'

7 Find the woman, and you will find the man

The site of the Esterwegen camp had been earmarked for other purposes than the Stalag Luft III inquiry. As soon as the in-depth interrogations were over it was intended to remove some of the prisoners to other camps and release others. And it was with the object of getting some way towards release that a man named Kurt Achterberg approached Flight Lieutenant Lyon in the camp a few days before its closure.

Achterberg was from the Danzig Gestapo. A number of others in the camp were also from there. The murders of the four officers at Danzig (Flight Lieutenants Edward Brettell, Romas Marcinkus and Gilbert Walenn, and Flying Officer Henri Picard) were still an area of the Stalag Luft III case which was almost completely unprobed. It was impossible to do field research in Danzig, because the place was barred to the British. Very little casual information had emerged during the massive general interrogations that had now been completed in almost every camp in the British and American zones. The few ex-Danzig men who were unearthed seemed to have little knowledge even of the occurrence of the crime, and were kept as potential witnesses when something more solid was mined on which to interrogate them.

The only suspects as yet listed in the Danzig case had been culled from the interrogation of Kriminaldirektor Erich Graes, who had been deputy director of the Kripo in Danzig.

Graes had applied the *Grossfahndung* after the Stalag Luft III escape. Four Royal Air Force officers had been taken off a train at Schneidemühl and put in a prisoner-of-war camp at Marienburg. Graes had had them brought in by truck to Danzig and lodged in the police prison. Graes told the prison commandant that the prisoners were officers, they should have the best room, and they should be given good treatment.

Graes never saw these officers. They arrived at the prison at night, and when he telephoned the commandant next morning he was told that the Gestapo had taken the officers away. He only knew that a Top Secret message was later received ordering that urns containing the ashes of the officers should be taken to Breslau.

The head of the Danzig Gestapo was Dr Günther Venediger. After the deaths of fifty officers had become international knowledge, Graes directly challenged Venediger that he had had the four officers shot in the Gestapo prison at Matzkaw. Venediger merely replied, 'We don't do that sort of thing in Matzkaw'.

Graes told his British interrogator that there were two people who must know all the details of the killings:

SS Standartenführer, Oberregierungsrat and Kommandeur der Sicherheitspolizei Günther Venediger; now thirty-eight years old; 1·82 m. high (almost six feet); dark hair; remarkable steel-blue eyes; a saddle nose; would certainly have false papers; and

SS Brigadeführer, Generalmajor der Polizei Helmut Willich; now aged fifty; height 1·74; greying brown hair; many wrinkles on face; alcoholic complexion; blue watery eyes with bags under them; walked with short steps; would certainly have false papers.

A third man was probably partly in the picture:

SS Sturmbannführer, Regierungsrat Kurt Achterberg, deputy to Venediger; now aged forty; height 1·80; wears glasses; very unruly brown hair brushed back; grey-blue eyes; rather unmilitary gait; big feet; big ears; lower lip underslung; bad teeth, yellow and irregular with some gold fillings.

Achterberg did not have false papers, and had in fact been caught. It was this rather clumsy man—who proved in the event to be most competently controlled—Kurt Achterberg, who now came conspiratorially to Flight Lieutenant Lyon in Esterwegen and asked for a private interview. He had always declared that he had known nothing about the Danzig murders, but now, after discussion with his colleagues, his memory had been prompted.

'I have been in conference', he began a little pompously, 'with some of my colleagues from the Danzig Gestapo who are interned here, and they have decided that I should come to see you and give you a lead on Kriminalsekretär Reinhold Bruchardt, who was the hatchet man for special assignments in Danzig and, we think, may be able to help you in your inquiries. We want to suggest to you how you can find Bruchardt—*wie Sie auf Bruchardt kommen können*. The reason is that none of the Gestapo members interned here, including me, was involved in the murders, and we consider that, as we have been inside for over a year, it is time to inform on Bruchardt so that the whole matter can be cleared up and we can be released. We are able to give you the address of Bruchardt's wife, and it is at this place in the Hamburg area.' He passed over an address. 'We know nothing about the whereabouts of Dr Venediger, but we believe that Frau Bruchardt will be able to give you information that will lead to your coming up with her husband.'

Achterberg paused.

'I must give you a warning', he said. 'Bruchardt was a terror. He has shot people in his office and in the street. He always had a rawhide whip soaking in a bucket of water by his desk, and he used this personally and often. Herr Hauptmann, if you do find Bruchardt, for God's sake be careful. He is a dangerous man, and he is always armed. I advise you to shoot him dead if he flicks an eyelid.'

Lyon swiftly sent men to the Hamburg address, in the hope that they might pick up Bruchardt. There was no trace of him, but Frau Bruchardt was volubly in evidence. Her husband had deserted her, she said. He had run away with his mistress after the war. She knew the town where he was now working, presumably under another name. It was Kempten, in the Allgäu, in the extreme south-west of Germany.

Immediately after his revelation to Lyon, Achterberg had been moved in the evacuation of Esterwegen, and had been transferred to Neuengamme, an internment camp near Hamburg. McKenna, who had been busy taking and interrogating the Karlsruhe murderers, was out of touch with Lyon, and independently called at Neuengamme as soon as he had finished his paper work. He had decided to concentrate next on the Danzig murders, and the only means he saw in his power was to conduct another sweep of the camps.

He called at Neuengamme with his interpreter, Sergeant Van Giessen, and sent for the head clerk of the documentation team. 'You know me', he said. 'I want to do a quick sweep on all internees who were in the Danzig Gestapo and Kripo during March and April 1944. Please let me have the list.' He went to the interview room and waited, and the clerk brought in a list of about twenty names. 'Will you have them sent in at intervals?' McKenna requested.

They were a varied selection up for interrogation. Some, McKenna could judge from his experience, had no relevant information at all, and he dismissed them quickly. There were others of whom he was not too sure, and he put all his skill into a deep interrogation. But he went right through the day without success. He looked at his list and found there was one more man to appear, and he waited for him. Van Giessen said, 'I've worked with you on many of these cases and you never stop, you never give up. I would give you the Victoria Cross.' McKenna said: 'Thanks very much, but I'll settle for a pint of milk. This is what most police work is, for most of the time: very exhausting routine, but you learn to do it. Anyway, we'll see what this fellow has to say.'

The last man came in. McKenna swiftly concluded that he was dim and useless. He dismissed him, and shut his book with a bang. The man was just going through the door with his escort when McKenna stopped him. 'Just a minute. Come back.' The man came back to the table.

McKenna said, 'Listen carefully to all these names.' He read through the list of men he had interrogated that day. 'Now I've seen all these men from Danzig. Do you know if there is anyone else in this place from Danzig Kripo or Gestapo?'

The man really tried. His face moved as he seemed to be going over all the likely people in camp in his mind, shaking his head as he rejected them. Then he said:

'Well, there's Achterberg.'

'Achterberg? Who's Achterberg? He wasn't on this list. Why isn't he on this list?'

The man shrugged, as if it might have been his responsibility.

'Who is he? Who was he?'

'A very big man in Danzig Gestapo.'

'Don't give me that.'

'A very big man. A friend of Dr Venediger's.'

'Right', said McKenna. 'He's here, is he? I must get with him.' He dismissed the man and telephoned the documentations clerk: 'You've missed one. What about Achterberg?' The clerk gave a groan. 'I'm sorry, sir, I missed him. He is only just in and I suppose he wasn't on my register. I'll send him in.'

Achterberg came in under escort. He looked very tall, very massive, and pretty surly. When McKenna told him the subject of his inquiries he protested that he had been answering questions on that subject in interrogations all over Germany. 'Well, never mind.' said McKenna, 'I'm not saying that you had anything to do with it, but I know some names of people who probably did. Now, can you tell me anything about Hug?'

'No.'

'Asal?'

'No.'

'Voelz?'

'No.'

'Bruchardt?'

Achterberg's expression changed. 'Well, yes, I do know a little about Bruchardt. I haven't mentioned it before because it had gone out of my mind. But I've been discussing this case with some other Danzig people, and two things have come back to me.'

'What?'

'I remember that in the late summer of 1944 I was standing in Dr Venediger's anteroom when Bruchardt came in, on his way to see Venediger. He said to me, "It has been damned difficult to get the Red Cross to believe that the British officers had been shot while escaping". I was very surprised by this remark, but I did not say anything. I was later talking about this case with a man called Weidgen, and he said he had seen Bruchardt packing away some personal effects of dead men which had to be sent to Berlin, and he thought it was something to do with the British officers.'

'Well', said McKenna, 'that's very interesting. Now, how do we get hold of Bruchardt?'

'I don't know.'

'Is he in custody?'

'No.'

'How can you be so sure?'

'Oh, he can look after himself all right.'

McKenna thought: 'He's keeping something back. I wish I knew what it was.'

Achterberg seemed to sink into a brooding brown study. McKenna let him sit in silence. Suddenly he interposed and said:

'A penny for your thoughts.'

Achterberg did not answer immediately. Then he said:

'Bruchardt is having an affair with my wife.'

McKenna took it slowly. 'Are you sure?'

'Yes.'

'How do you feel about it?'

'I feel very badly. But what can I do, in here?'

'Well, you can put a stop to that for a start by helping me to find Bruchardt.'

Achterberg thought, and said: 'There's one way you might do it, but I don't know if it will work. Make a note of this lady's name. Frau Blum.'

'Frau Blum.'

'She lives at a town called Kempten in Allgäu. I don't know her address more precisely than that.'

'What has she got to do with Bruchardt?'

'She is a mutual friend of Bruchardt and my wife. She is acting as a poste restante between the two, forwarding their letters. She must know where Bruchardt is. Find her, and you will find him.'

'I'll do my best', said McKenna.

McKenna went straight to the commandant at Neuengamme and said that he was arranging right away for the extradition to England of Kurt Achterberg, and requested that he should be kept very secure and not allowed to communicate. He drove the 150 miles back to base. As he was driving in to see Bowes he met Lyon. 'I've got a lead on Bruchardt in a town called—'

'Kempten', said Lyon.

'Where did you hear that?'

'It's a funny story', said Lyon. 'I'll tell you sometime. Let's go in and see Freddie.'

Bowes said, 'This is in the American zone. We are not going to have the same trouble in holding him as we did with Zacharias, I hope.'

McKenna said he would try to get a provisional clearing in advance, and not go for Bruchardt until they had got it. He and Lyon drove to Wiesbaden and saw the British War Crimes Liaison Officer. After a day spent going round the offices they got from the Provost Marshals of two American Theatres a provisional clearance to take away Reinhold Bruchardt, badly wanted in connection with the murders of four officers from Stalag Luft III. They set off south next day, and it was evening before they arrived at Kempten.

They went to the Field Office of the United States Counter-Intelligence Corps, where they were welcomed by Special Agents John Kiselyk and Roger Cope of the American Army. They explained their mission, and gave the name of Frau Blum. 'No address,' said McKenna, 'this is our only lead'. 'Come on', said Roger Cope, and they started going through the books.

Cope found an address for Frau Blum, a villa in a place outside the town. The time was now midnight. Cope brought in some American soldiers to guard the exits, and they went out to the villa. They hammered on the door for a full quarter of an hour. Lyon shouted that it was useless for the occupant to think they would go away, and eventually the door was opened. McKenna walked in without invitation. 'Frau Blum?' 'Yes.' 'We're looking for Bruchardt.' There was no change in the expression of Frau Blum, a well-groomed woman in a dressing-gown. 'I don't know him', she said.

'Oh, yes, you do,' said Lyon, 'And you know Frau Achterberg. What about the letters?'

'I don't know what you're talking about.'

'Very well, we shall have to search the house.'

A thorough search of the house revealed nothing: no sign of male occupation, not a trace of any letters. Frau Blum was very cool, very much in control, a little unnaturally so.

McKenna was, in his own term, peevish. He had had four successive fifteen-hour days on this mission. It was one in the morning, and he sensed that a breakthrough could be gained. He said something which he always remembered, knowing that it was a last resort, knowing that it was a threat, and knowing that he could never have carried it out. It was completely out of character, and it is a measure of the man that to this day he regrets that the threat was made.

'Please tell Frau Blum', he asked Lyon, 'that she has probably heard a lot about the British officers, and British police officers, and how kind they are to women. Please tell her not to believe it. Because some of us here are going to alter the shape of her face unless she is very careful. And I personally am going to take a leading part in this. She is in very great danger of being severely beaten up.'

There was a long pause while Frau Blum considered this. She had been half sitting, half standing against the edge of a table, with her dressing-gown occasionally falling open to display a short slip. Now she sat down.

'He is not called Bruchardt any more', she said. 'He is called Brandt.'

'Where is he?'

'Rathausstrasse 22 in Kempten.'

McKenna glanced at Cope. 'Can we bring two men in here to see that she doesn't telephone?'

'Help yourself. But we can always pull the phone out of the wall.'

'I'd rather have her under surveillance.'

Cope left two escorts at the villa and led McKenna's car to the Rathausstrasse. 'The bitch!' said McKenna as he saw Number 22. It was the police station. He went in with Lyon and asked if anyone lived at 22 Rathausstrasse. 'Oh, yes,' said the duty man. 'There are flats above.'

They had to awaken the concierge to get into the flats. They were afraid that the noise might rouse Bruchardt. They went up the stairs, the Americans Cope and Kiselyk with sub-machine-guns, Lyon with a small German automatic, McKenna without arms. They had digested Achterberg's information that Bruchardt was quick to shoot, and they allowed the concierge, who had the key, the privilege of leading the way. The pattern changed outside the door with the card: R. Brandt. The door was very quietly unlocked. They could hear heavy breathing, and there was the sour smell of a closed house. On the right of the corridor they could see that a room door was slightly open. McKenna pushed it a little more open and started feeling for the switch, which the concierge had said was on the left-hand side. Suddenly there was a movement. The occupant was sitting bolt upright in bed. McKenna realized that the switch was on the right of the door, and plunged it on. Bruchardt literally leapt—the highest that professionals like Lyon and McKenna had ever recorded—upwards in the bed, and tried to get over to a cupboard in the corner where they later found his revolver. The four hurled themselves on him and subdued him. He was a huge fellow, of much the same build as Achterberg, and his wrists were far too large to get any handcuffs round them. Under cover of the armament, he dressed and was driven to the local prison, where two American Negro military policemen were put in his cell to guard him intimately: a fact which he long resented.

In the morning Lyon and McKenna thanked the Americans profusely, left them to sort out Frau Blum, collected Bruchardt into their car and took him, under Lyon's careful eye and poised trigger-finger, to Minden in a two-day journey. McKenna had deliberately laid off any forceful interrogation of Bruchardt, knowing that even the familiarity hatched by a long car-trip had its value. He put Bruchardt into the holding prison at Minden and went to his quarters to sleep. Next day he came into Bruchardt's cell, ready to hear what the man had to say after two days' reflection. He was shocked to see that Bruchardt's eyes were almost completely closed and there was a gash and heavy bruising on his face. He asked what had happened. Bruchardt said, 'You should know. You're in charge.' McKenna went outside and began questioning. He learned that the second-in-command of the military gaol, a warrant officer with a leaning towards alcohol, had come in late at night, scanned the register for new entries, found that someone was entered in connection with the Stalag Luft III murders, and gone into Bruchardt's cell and beaten him up single-handed.

McKenna went to the commanding officer of the War Crimes

Investigation Unit and had the warrant officer posted to other duties the same day. But the damage was done. All the psychological softening that McKenna had been exercising had gone for nothing. Bruchardt refused to make any confession, and when he was invited to make a statement said that the murder of the four Royal Air Force officers had been carried out by a special group of Ukrainians who were employed in Danzig for terroristic action against the Polish Resistance. No valid refutation of this could be obtained for over a year. Eventually witnesses were traced and gave evidence which led to Bruchardt's conviction. But his trial was delayed for fifteen months, and had an ironic result. Bruchardt was eventually condemned to death, but in 1948 the British Government introduced an experimental period when capital punishment was suspended. Sentences for war crimes were also commuted, and Bruchardt, alternatively given life imprisonment, was released under a general amnesty after serving less than eight years. Other people condemned for the Sagan crime died on the hangman's rope. The warrant officer who had reserved to himself the dispensation of vengeance must have been sorely chagrined.

McKenna could not know of this at the time. He came back to his office, relaxing after the exhaustion of a punishingly concentrated operation. Bowes met him, full of a suppressed excitement which McKenna could not fathom.

'It's a pity you never heard about Scharpwinkel', he said.

'That Russian general in Berlin hasn't answered a letter in seven months', said McKenna. 'I'm sure we'd do better if we went to the highest levels. You know, Monty and Zhukov must be very close. I believe they're real kindred spirits, those two. They are military men, hard and fast. Right from birth they were destined to be leaders of men. These two together have spent all their effort on the defeat of Germany. They have been pressing the Germans from both ends, and they've met in the middle. Now what better could we do than to get old Monty to drop Zhukov a line and say, "Look, George, get on to the Lubianka and see if you've got Scharpwinkel in gaol in Moscow". Surely this can be done.'

'Not necessary', said Bowes.

'It would be better than defeatism, just tamely accepting the silence.'

'Not necessary.'

'Why isn't it necessary?'

'I have a fourth-hand signal here', said Bowes, producing it. 'Moscow to Foreign Office to Provost Marshal to Command Provost Marshal to me. Message from George Zhukov to Frank McKenna, care of Monty. Dear Frank: Thanks for all your post-cards, having a wonderful time, too, wish you were here. Yes, we have got Scharpwinkel in Moscow, but you can't have him. He is a sick man and would not be fit to stand trial, so we are not handing him over. However, you are welcome to come and interview him in Moscow." '

'Is that what it says?' asked McKenna.

'Well, words to the effect of.'

'I can't believe it. May I see it?'

'You really are a lucky bastard', said Bowes in the greatest good humour.

'There's no luck about it at all', said McKenna. 'This is the kind of thing you do in the real police, tracing people when everyone else has forgotten them. You wanted to write him off, didn't you? By the way, I don't see that it says anything here about my going to Moscow.'

'You aren't', said Bowes. 'I'm going. I'm taking Dickie Lyon.'

McKenna put a military scrip banknote on his desk. 'What's that for?' asked Bowes.

'That says you will never get there.'

Wing Commander Bowes amplified his entries against the names of Flight Lieutenants Gordon Brettell, Romas Marcinkus and Gilbert Walenn, and Flying Officer Henri Picard:

Reinhold Bruchardt in British custody 18.7.1946.
Günther Venediger: URGENTLY WANTED.
Helmut Willich, Julius Hug, Walter Voelz, Asal: WANTED.

Later, Squadron Leader McKenna established the name of Willy Reimer as Venediger's personal driver, and instituted an all-out search for him. But it was two years before he was caught. McKenna himself was most eagerly awaiting the result of the delayed interrogation of Scharpwinkel in Moscow. This would provide the most direct lead to clearing up the twenty-nine Breslau murders. But when Scharpwinkel's statement was finally obtained it threw, in addition, the first clear light on what had been the most obscure of all the sequences of killings.

8 Day in the life of an investigator

While Squadron Leader McKenna and Flight Lieutenant Lyon were driving to Wiesbaden and Kempten to take Reinhold Bruchardt, Flight Sergeant Stuart B. Greet and his interpreter, Sergeant J. W. Venselaar, were on almost the same course, with only a few hours separating them, to Frankfurt. There they were to interrogate and arrest Walter Breithaupt, the first man to be caught up with in regard to the Saarbrücken murders.

There had been a long lapse in progress towards solving the murders of Squadron Leader Bushell and Lieutenant Scheidhauer. It had been partly due to lack of liaison. As early as September 1945 an American war crimes investigator, Lieutenant Ernest Neidorff, had made a full series of interrogations with regard to these deaths, which he knew were related to the Stalag Luft III escape. He took statements testifying to details of the capture, imprisonment, interrogation and cremation of these officers: the most cynically macabre was the testimony of a Kripo typist who had seen both Bushell and Scheidhauer and almost immediately was asked to type out an instant funeral certificate: 'I was frightened, and asked the Gestapo Kommissar if the two officers were already dead, and he replied, "Yes, one of them died of appendicitis".'

Lieutenant Neidorff had been recalled to the United States, and at some unspecified time later the statements had been collated by another American investigator, Captain Werner Dietrich, who had activated the case and was urgently seeking Dr Leopold Spann, Gestapo Chief in Saarbrücken, who had signed a falsified report about the officers having been shot whilst trying to escape. Others among the statements had tended to show that Spann himself had shot the officers, possibly even single-handedly. He was the only Gestapo area chief apart from Scharpwinkel who obeyed the Berlin instructions to the point of shedding the prisoner's blood himself rather than passing on orders which kept his hands physically clean.

A further strong statement on the murders had been taken by

investigators of the French Army from Fritz Schmoll, a police inspector at the concentration camp of Neue Bremm, near Saarbrücken, who was charged with atrocities committed there. He said that Dr Spann had come into the camp one morning and told him that he had in a truck the bodies of two prisoners shot whilst escaping. He said he needed to have them burned, and Schmoll arranged to have this done in Saarbrücken. Schmoll later learned that these were the bodies of Bushell and Scheidhauer, who had originally escaped from Sagan. He said that with Dr Spann in the truck were a Gestapo official named Emil Schulz and a driver named Breithaupt.

The French had a legitimate interest in reserving to themselves, if they wished, investigations into the death of a French national. But Bernard Scheidhauer, who after the fall of France had served as a Free Frenchman in the Royal Air Force, had been in a British arm of the Services and had been murdered side by side with a British squadron leader. A specialized investigation team was working on the entire crime for the Royal Air Force, and they could have expected to have received the valuable information contained in the statement of Fritz Schmoll earlier than they did. It was an appreciation of a need to cut intra-national red tape and bring a criminal speedily to justice that governed certain of McKenna's actions later in this investigation.

The statement by Schmoll, which was taken on 13th February 1946, was only tardily forwarded to the British Army of the Rhine, and was sent to the War Crimes Investigation Unit on 10th May. It was the first reference known to the names of Schulz and Breithaupt as having been concerned in the murders. Spann had long been suspected, and had been named by the head of the Saarbrücken Kripo, Gustav Dingermann, who had been interrogated by Flight Sergeant Williams in January 1946. But Dingermann later heard—and passed the information across when he came into British hands in London—that Spann had been killed during an air raid on Linz, in Austria.

The SIB at Rinteln asked for American aid in tracing Schulz and Breithaupt, and it was given as generously and efficiently as in the past. By early July the Americans had located Walter Breithaupt as probably living at his parents' home in a suburb of Frankfurt am Main. They prepared a clearance for him, and Greet was dispatched to pick him up when found.

It was a model arrest. Greet put a man at the back door and knocked at the front with his interpreter. He asked for Breithaupt. His parents said he was still in bed. Greet went upstairs and established his identity. Breithaupt was arrested, and made a full statement.

He was a 38-year-old bachelor who had been Dr Spann's driver-mechanic. Spann had warned him of a dawn run to take two recaptured pilots to, he said, Mannheim. With Kriminalsekretär

Emil Schulz, Breithaupt fetched the handcuffed prisoners from the Kripo prison, and they were put in the car. Spann and Schulz both wore Gestapo uniform, and got into the car. After forty kilometres, soon after they reached the autobahn, Spann ordered the car to stop.

'Dr Spann and Schulz stepped out of the car and went a little to one side and talked, having lit cigarettes. I stayed with the prisoners in the car and could not hear what they were talking about. Day was breaking, but it was not yet full daylight. After they had finished their cigarettes Dr Spann called me out of the car. Dr Spann took me to one side, so that the prisoners could not hear, and said he had received a teleprint order from Berlin to shoot the prisoners. He said I was to say nothing about it, tell nobody of the incident, otherwise I would be sentenced to death. He said, "You don't have to be frightened. Just think of what happens to our wives and children during an air raid."

'The prisoners were told that they could come out of the car to relieve themselves. One of the prisoners pointed to his handcuffs, but I do not remember if they were taken off. The two prisoners went to the bushes a few metres to the right and rear of the car, and Spann and Schulz followed, each with their pistol in their hand. As the prisoners were walking they were told that they would be shot immediately if they tried to escape.

'I stood next to the car, and could see everything. Both prisoners were just unbuttoning their trousers with Spann and Schulz standing a metre behind them with their pistols in their hands. Spann gave a sign, and Spann and Schulz each fired one shot at the same time in the neck of the prisoners. Both prisoners dropped on the earth at the same moment. I swear that I did not shoot.'

Breithaupt said that Spann left Schulz guarding the bodies, and drove with Breithaupt to Saarbrücken, where he ordered Breithaupt and another driver to fetch a large double coffin and bring in the bodies, which they took to a Gestapo prisoner-of-war camp near the main cemetery in Saarbrücken.

McKenna now had a double lead implicating Schulz. He decided to start the hunt from Saarbrücken itself, and drove down there with Sergeant Jean Van Giessen, and met Warrant Officer H. J. Williams in the town. In the course of one remarkable day (10th August 1946) he located, arrested and removed from the French zone a man of whose precise whereabouts he had had no knowledge at all.

He went first to the French military security unit, a branch office of the organization run by the French Army from Baden-Baden. He explained his quest, and asked for information leading to any people in Saarbrücken who might have known Emil Schulz at the time he was serving there. They had no information on Schulz themselves, but put McKenna in touch with several former officials in the town who at least confirmed that Schulz had been on duties there at the relevant time. But nobody knew where he was then. McKenna went back to the security unit, not much farther forward, working out his next move.

He rememberd Gustav Dingermann, former chief of the Gestapo Kripo, who was now in the London Cage. McKenna had found him a pleasant enough person when he had interviewed him. Dingermann had been ordered to hand over Bushell and Scheidhauer, whom he held, to the Gestapo. He had been severely shocked by the crime, and had given all the information he could, but had not mentioned either Breithaupt or Schulz. McKenna asked the French if it was possible to telephone to London. They agreed, and explained the routine. McKenna was put through via Baden-Baden to 21 Army Group in Bad Oeynhausen, and asked them to put in a London call to Bayswater 6666, the number of the London Cage. He was put through, asked for an old friend, Major Terry, and requested to speak to Dingermann. Dingermann was put on the line, and began a cordial conversation which McKenna cut short:

'Thank you for what you have done in the past, but there have been some developments, and I wonder if you can help. Do you remember a man called Breithaupt of the Gestapo and another called Schulz?' Dingermann did remember them. Breithaupt was the driver who did special jobs for Spann, and Schulz was close enough to Spann to be the man who would be asked to do anything questionable. 'I'm trying to find Schulz', said McKenna. 'Have you any idea where I could get him?'

Dingermann said he knew where Schulz used to live, but he could not remember the address. He described a rectangular block of flats near the centre of the town, which McKenna instantly recognized. McKenna rechecked the location of the place, rang off, and went back to the French military officers. The French recognized the flats, and said the block was of no military significance. 'We'll race down there', McKenna told Bill Williams, and they drove away. McKenna let himself in by the front door, which was insecure, and rang the bell for the janitor. 'I'm looking for Herr Emil Schulz.' 'There's nobody of that name in this place.' 'Do you remember a man of this name?' 'Well, there was a family of that name on the next floor above.' 'Show me the apartment.' They went up the stairs to a door bearing a very faded card which read 'E. Schulz'. McKenna knocked, and there was no response. He looked through the letter box into an empty hall, and he could see that a far window over the street was dirty enough not to have been cleaned for years. The porter had no more information on the Schulz family, but neighbours said that Frau Schulz and her little daughter had gone to live in a small village outside Saarbrücken which they thought was Frankenholz.

McKenna drove seven miles to Frankenholz, asked at the general store, and was immediately directed to Frau Schulz at No. 8 along the street. A woman in a white dress answered the door.

McKenna reflected that she was beautifully turned out, and her face shone as if she had just scrubbed herself with soap and water. A little girl of six or seven was by her side. 'Frau Schulz?' asked McKenna. 'We are just making inquiries about your husband. May we come in?' McKenna, Williams and Van Giessen were invited in.

Frau Schulz said she had no idea where her husband was. McKenna asked her if he had been in the Gestapo during the war. Yes. Was he in Saarbrücken in March and April 1944? She could not be sure, she had no memory for dates. Where was he now? She did not know, she did not even know if he was still alive, whether he had been captured or whether he was killed.

'May I look through the house?' asked McKenna. They went from room to room, with Frau Schulz and her little daughter anxiously following them. There was no sign that a man had been there, no cigarettes or pipes or male clothing that seemed recently worn. 'I'm afraid', said McKenna, 'that we must search the house very thoroughly'. They began to open drawers, looking particularly for correspondence.

There was a letter in a drawer, on ruled notepaper with a serial number at the bottom. McKenna could not read German, and passed it to Van Giessen. He saw his face brighten. 'What is it?' he asked. 'Get her out of the way', said Van Giessen. When the door was shut he said, 'If this letter is from who I think it is, we shouldn't have much difficulty. It must be from her husband.' 'Read it.' It was a letter written in very intimate terms, and could only have come from a lover or a husband. It was not signed with any name that could be taken for Emil Schulz. 'Is there any indication where it's from?' 'No, there is no address at all.'

McKenna asked Frau Schulz to come in. 'Who is this letter from?' he said. She was very near to breaking down. 'This is from your husband, isn't it?' asked McKenna. 'No, it is from a friend.' 'Where is he? Where is he writing from?' 'I don't know.' 'When did you receive it?'—for there was no date on the letter. She could not remember.

'We shall have to take this letter away,' said McKenna, 'and we shall make further inquiries.' They left Frau Schulz in a state of paralysed anxiety. They drove back to the French security office. 'What kind of paper is this?' asked McKenna. 'This is prison paper', he was told. 'It is what they issue to French prison governors for general administrative purposes, and it is quite possible that a prisoner could be given this for letter-writing.'

'How many prisons are there round here?' McKenna asked, and he was told of a number in Alsace-Lorraine. 'What about concentration camps?' 'There is one outside Saarbrücken.' 'We'll try that one first, Bill,' said McKenna to Williams, and the interpreter checked the location.

It was now about four o'clock on an overcast, humid August afternoon. The camp lay about eight miles from Saarbrücken.

McKenna went in, asked for the camp commander, and introduced himself: 'Squadron Leader McKenna.' What rank is that?' asked the officer, a very dark, heavily built, bucolic man. 'It's the same rank as yourself,' said McKenna, 'it would be Commandant in the French Army.' The commandant became genial. McKenna said, 'I'm looking for a man called Emil Schulz who was formerly in the Gestapo at Saarbrücken. He is wanted for the murder of an English officer, Squadron Leader Bushell.' He did not mention Bernard Scheidhauer, and he was grateful for it, for the commandant interposed, 'This man Bushell, what was his nationality?' 'He was South African born but of British nationality, a British national serving with the Royal Air Force.' The commandant considered.

'It *is* murder?'

'Oh, yes. He was shot by this man Schulz. I'm quite certain of that.'

'Very well. I'll help you. What can I do?'

'I've got a letter here to the wife of this man, who is living not far away. Although it's not in this man's name, I think he is the writer, and, if you like, my interpreter will read it to you.' Van Giessen did so. The commandant seemed quite interested. He asked to see the letter. 'A prisoner has got to put his name somewhere on a letter', he said. 'What is this? It could be Ernst Schmidt. I can tell you that the paper could be from here.' He looked through a register. 'I've got a man here of the name of Ernst Schmidt.'

'Can you produce him?'

'Yes', said the commandant, and sent for one of his aides. McKenna carefully pocketed the letter. After ten minutes a man was escorted into the office. He was aged about thirty-eight, slimly built but with broad shoulders. He had a sharp, narrow face and a high forehead, and no obviously commanding personality: a very ordinary man. As he came in at the door he looked with sudden concentration on the Air Force uniforms of McKenna, Williams and Van Giessen, and he drew a breath and seemed to go on guard. McKenna went straight to the point:

'We are making inquiries about the murders of Royal Air Force officers who had escaped from Stalag Luft III. Can you help us?'

'No. I can't help you about that.'

'How long have you been known as Schmidt?'

The man shook his head.

'I believe you are Emil Schulz, who served in the Gestapo at Saarbrücken under the command of Leopold Spann.'

The man denied that he had ever been in the Gestapo, ever served in Saarbrücken, ever known Dr Spann.

McKenna produced the letter from his pocket. 'I have a letter here, written from this prison to Frau Angela Schulz, the wife of Emil Schulz. Did you write this letter or not?

He showed the letter. The man gave a hopeless glance at the camp commandant.

'I am quite convinced that you are Emil Schulz, and, if we have to, we can easily confront you with your wife.'

The man was silent for some time, and then he said:

'*Ich bin Emil Schulz. Angela Schulz ist meine Gattin.*'

McKenna paused, and glanced quickly towards the interpreter before putting the next questions through him. 'Well,' he said, 'I know the man with the real responsibility for this is Spann, and he's already rotting in his grave. He's the man we really would like to have got. Did Spann tell you to do this thing?'

'Yes, he was the one who told me to do it.'

Schulz was past the point of no return. But, in that camp office, McKenna still had his riskiest question to frame.

'Which did you shoot, the taller or the shorter officer?'

'The taller. I did not want to.'

McKenna did not wait for the interpreter, who had not re-translated the last two questions into French.

'Squadron Leader Bushell', said McKenna. 'I should like the commandant to hear what you say. You shot Squadron Leader Bushell?'

'Yes', said Schulz. Van Giessen translated the question and answer.

McKenna turned briskly to the commandant. 'I want this man for murder', he said. 'There's nothing worse than that in the calendar. May I take him away?'

The commandant hesitated. McKenna knew that the next step in the form-book would be a telephone call to Baden-Baden and endless delays, possibly stalemate, in clearing the prisoner. As the commandant's hand was moving towards the telephone McKenna brought out two packets of English cigarettes, laid them on the desk, and said, 'My compliments'.

The commandant was delighted. He stood up, shook hands, opened a packet, and lit a cigarette.

'I'd like to get this man back to base as quickly as I can', said McKenna. 'May I take him over?'

'If you're prepared to sign for him I'm prepared to hand him over', said the commandant genially. He called to his administrative officer for a form of receipt. The details were filled in. McKenna signed, and the three officers got Schulz into their car as fast as possible. As they drove out of the gate Warrant Officer Williams said, 'You were boxing clever, sir'. 'No time for admiration yet', said McKenna. 'If the commandant telephones Baden-Baden now they'll play hell about this, and there's still time to set up a road-block. We've to get out of the French zone fast.'

They roared into the town, and up the eastern autobahn. But, even in his urgency to get out of the French zone, McKenna permitted himself one indulgence. He had pinpointed the site of the murders, by the side of the road. Schulz was sitting at his side, and McKenna knew that he was beginning to recognize the terrain. McKenna caught

Schulz giving him an occasional sly glance, and then looking away and staring into the woods. As McKenna approached the murder spot he slowed down, switched the car into neutral, and coasted in to the verge of the road.

He turned to the interpreter, and said, 'Ask Schulz if he would like to take this opportunity of relieving himself, as we have quite a long way to go'.

McKenna was using the exact words, as narrated by Breithaupt, which Spann had spoken to Roger Bushell and Bernard Scheidhauer a few seconds before they were shot. And Schulz recognized them. He stiffened in his seat, thrust his feet under the dashboard, and leaned back as if to resist being dragged out and butchered. 'No. No. No', he said.

'Ask him if he's sure', said McKenna.

'No, no, no.'

'All right', said McKenna. 'But we've a long way to go.' He started the car and shot away towards the border of the American zone.

It took a further day to get to Minden, and McKenna went in early next morning to get a full statement from Schulz. His account did not clash with Breithaupt's except on two points. The officers had been handcuffed, behind their backs, and Schulz had removed the manacles before they got out of the car. As for the shooting, he maintained, despite Breithaupt's clear narrative of Spann's giving a signal which was followed by instantaneous shots, that Spann had fired the first shots at both officers:

'I put the handcuffs on the rear seat of the car and took my pistol out of its holster. I walked round the back of the car, and whilst I was still on the autobahn I could see the two officers standing together, about three or four metres from Dr Spann. At that moment I heard shots fired, and Dr Spann shouting, but I could not tell what he was shouting. I saw both officers falling to the ground and I then fired a single shot at the taller of the officers. I could not be sure if my shot hit, but the two officers fell forward to the ground.

'The smaller one fell face downwards, and the taller one fell sideways and dropped on his right side and slowly turned over on his back. He drew up his legs and made a groaning sound, and I could see that he was in great pain. He did not speak, and I lay down on the grass close to him and, taking careful aim, I shot him through the left side of the head. . . .'

McKenna and Schulz discussed the crime quietly but not dispassionately, in the words that have been given in the beginning of this book. 'I told Dr Spann that what he was asking me to do was wrong', said Schulz. 'All he said was: "Just do as I tell you".'

McKenna took Schulz back to London for full interrogation in the Cage. Their Dakota could not get off the ground, and they had to change into an old Anson. 'It's airworthy', said the pilot, cheerfully. 'As an engineer', said McKenna, 'I beg to inform you that it is clapped out.' They were forced down at Eindhoven, took off again, skimmed over the Channel, and had to make an emergency landing at Manston. McKenna had to take his prisoner to London by a returning excursion train from Margate. There was no room in the carriages and they had to stand in the corridor. Schulz asked McKenna if he would grant him a great favour. He said, 'I want to write to my dear wife'. 'You are asking something quite impossible', said McKenna, 'you must know it is forbidden for you to write.'

'I thought that perhaps you might very kindly take the letter', said Schulz. 'I know that this is the end of the road. I shall have to pay with my own life for what I have done. My wife will never see me again, and I should like to write her a letter.'

McKenna considered. He said, 'I'll permit you to write this letter, provided you don't put in it anything of length about this particular case'. Schulz said he understood. 'I can't give it to your wife to keep', McKenna continued. 'But I will give you my word of honour to take it to her and let her read it, and then she must return it.'

McKenna took off Schulz's handcuffs and made space for him to sit down on the floor of the corridor. He tore a sheet of paper from one of his notebooks, and passed it to him with a pencil and a case to rest the paper on. Schulz wrote the date.

'It's my birthday', he said, and looked up and smiled.

With trippers climbing over him to go to the lavatory, Emil Schulz wrote his letter. He knew that McKenna would need to have it privately translated before he delivered it. The letter ran:

17.8.07—17.8.46

Dear Angela, dear Ingeborg, dear Helga, you dears of mine!

I am already in England now, and, alas, could not say Goodbye to you.

I am here as a prisoner because of carrying out an official order in the spring of 1944.

I never on my own initiative acted against the laws of humanity. Had I not taken part then, I should have gone down at that time. I was on guard duty with Ludwig Weiss, who is in hospital in Hamburg. Ask him!

I'm waiting for justice. I only ask to be treated as I deserve and judged according to my position. In that case, I'll be all right. Do what you can for me. You, dear Angela, have courage and live only for the children. I'll do the same.

The snaps of Ingeborg and Helga are my faithful companions. From them I find a lot of consolation and new strength.

If I did not tell you anything, it was only because I did not want to worry you unduly. It would have been much, much more difficult for me. How easier it would be to suffer death three times in order to prevent all this happening to you and especially to the children. Maybe it will be all right, because I was not and am not a criminal. Always think that, dear, and that I only belong to you and the children. Ask Rudolf Specht to help you in everything you undertake for me. He can help you. I shall write again as soon as I can. Be brave with the children. My regards to my old father, brothers and sisters. They will stand by you. Greetings to you, dear Mother, your suffering goes to my heart, it hurts me very much. Give my regards to my two brothers-in-law who are now in England.

Ever your faithful husband, your daddy and your

Emil.

In Germany McKenna travelled to Frankenholz and called on Frau Schulz. She invited him in and asked if he had news of Emil. McKenna said, 'Yes. He is charged with a very serious crime, and I don't think you are likely to see him again.' She burst into tears. He said, 'I have a letter from him. It was very wrong of me, according to our regulations, to permit this sort of contact, and so, although I can let you read the letter, I am sorry that I cannot leave it with you.' She said he was being very good and kind. He passed over the letter. He made no effort to hurry her. She read it perhaps a dozen times. She handed it back, and McKenna said goodbye. They shook hands. McKenna said, 'I wish you well'. He drove away.

To clear the case, McKenna decided to go to Linz to confirm that Dr Spann really had been killed there. He made the mission coincide with another assault on Panzinger, the adjutant of Müller in Berlin. American Counter-Intelligence had traced his mother to an address in Bavaria. The SIB raided the house, and she said that she had last seen her son Fritz three years previously, and did not know where he was. But a search of the house revealed a pencilled copy of a letter to Panzinger that she finally admitted she had sent only that morning. After further interrogation she gave his address, which was found to be a convent fifteen miles inside Russian-held territory. McKenna asked permission from the Russians to raid the convent, since where one high Nazi was in cover there might well be several more. The Russians replied that he could not bring a party, but he could visit the convent himself if he would meet a Russian liaison officer on the border at a certain time. McKenna attended the rendezvous, but no liaison officer arrived. Later he telephoned, and was told that the officer had been unable to obtain a pass for McKenna, and if he desired to pursue the matter further he should apply in writing to the General of the Russian staff in the central office in Vienna. But when this was reported to London the War Crimes Investigation Unit decreed that Panzinger's body was no longer required and further effort should not be wasted on him.

McKenna took the opportunity to check in Linz on the fate of Spann. In the appropriate register he found an entry: 'The official, doctor, and barrister Leopold Spann, living at . . . [address] died at 1400 hours on 25.4.1945 at Langgasse 13, Linz on the Danube, during an enemy air raid. Cause of death: crushed cranium and crushed bones.'

McKenna knew that Langgasse 13 was the Headquarters of the

Linz Gestapo, and he had heard that fifty other Gestapo officers had been killed from a direct hit during what was one of the last air raids of the war. He was puzzled that Spann had been given no official title in his formal notice of death. But a search through further records provided the answer.

He found a paper which read:

> In the death records of the Kriminal Polizei office at Linz dated 26.4.45 no. 1470/45 K. N 2155, the profession of Dr Leopold Spann, who died in Linz on 25.4.45 was recorded as 'Leader of the Gestapo, Linz'. By order of the undernamed authority of administration it was ordered that this description of profession should be altered to the occupation 'official'.
>
> Signed: The Official of Town Administration

Even in death and defeat, the Gestapo found kindly souls who would cover up for them.

'BIG X'

Squadron Leader Roger Bushell and Lieutenant Bernard Scheidhauer, murdered near Kaiserlauten, 29th March 1944:

Walter Breithaupt in British custody 10.7.1946.
Emil Schulz in British custody 10.8.1946
Leopold Spann killed 25.4.1945.

9 Harry, this must be it

Scharpwinkel sat in a room in a Moscow gaol with Captain Cornish of the Intelligence Corps seated opposite him at a table with a typewriter, and four Russian officers to see fair play. Wing Commander Bowes and Flight Lieutenant Lyon had not, after all, been able to make the trip to Moscow. After six weeks' negotiations the Russians had laid it down that only one man should go, that Scharpwinkel could be interviewed only when German-speaking and English-speaking Russians were present (since Scharpwinkel spoke English well), and that everything Scharpwinkel said should be put down immediately on the typewriter. With all this formality, the British investigator spent three months in Moscow and got only two formal statements from Scharpwinkel.

Captain M. F. Cornish, a member of Colonel Scotland's staff at the London Cage, was well acquainted with the Sagan investigation, and had done much to help Flight Lieutenant Lyon with the exhaustive interrogations at Esterwegen. He was a stocky man with a rugged face, a bespectacled schoolmaster in civilian life, and he had had an extremely adventurous war, which included his own escape from imprisonment and a spell of special operations. As he sat opposite Scharpwinkel, tall but bent and prematurely greying, Cornish knew that the German was playing from strength. The Russians had certified him medically unfit to stand trial before a British war crimes tribunal. Their witnessing officers stopped Cornish from exerting the slightest pressure during interrogation. At one point Scharpwinkel gave an answer that Cornish knew to be wide of the truth. Cornish banged the table, pointed his finger, and said hotly, 'Now look here, Scharpwinkel—' That was as far as he got. The Russians interposed and reprimanded Cornish for intimidating the prisoner. They said he should not talk to him in that tone of voice. This was in autumn 1946, at the height of the Stalin purges by execution and the massive deportation programme to Siberia.

Scharpwinkel's first statement was taken on 31st August 1946. A copy reached Bowes in Rinteln in early September. He underlined one not very conspicuous sentence in it, and sent its content urgently to Lyon, who was at that time in the field with Harrison.

The most mysterious among the deaths of the officers from Sagan —because of the complete lack of information—concerned the two pairs of escapers Lieutenants Hallada Espelid and Nils Fuglesang, of the Royal Norwegian Air Force, and Squadron Leader James Catanach, Royal Australian Air Force, with Flying Officer Arnold Christensen, Royal New Zealand Air Force. Espelid and Fuglesang had been seen on a Berlin railway station, and nothing more was known of them. Catanach and Christensen had not been seen at all by any of their fellow-escapers who survived to give evidence. The cremation urns of all four officers had been returned to Sagan bearing only their names, with no indication of the date or place of death. The only slim indication of where to search for them was the fact that two were Norwegian and one was of Danish origin. The Norwegians could be presumed to have headed north, possibly through the port of Stettin which had been used by the successful Norwegian escapers Jens Muller and Rocky Bergsland. Christensen had been the intelligence expert on Denmark, and would have been expected to make for it. Stettin was now in Polish territory, and the investigating officers were banned from it. Bowes had asked Lyon and Harrison to start from Hamburg and range north on a detailed investigation of crematoria. Harrison had examined so many of these records already in his time that he was often referred to by his wife, who was working at RAF headquarters in Bückeburg, as Herr Crematorium. McKenna at that time was pushing hard all over the country in a search for Dr Venediger, the boss of Bruchardt as Chief in Danzig, but had to drive back to base from Berlin in great pain, and was destined to undergo a surgical operation and a long convalescence.

The sentence in Scharpwinkel's first statement to which Bowes paid especial attention ran:

> From the teleprint, or from another document, I can remember that prisoners who took part in this escape had been captured in the Dresden and Berlin areas and, I think, if I remember rightly, also Königsberg, Danzig, Stettin, Kiel and probably also Munich so that in my opinion the headquarters in the towns mentioned must have received corresponding orders.

In 1946 Könisberg, on the Baltic, was a recent acquisition to Russian territory, called, as now, Kaliningrad. Dresden, Danzig and Stettin were all east of the (Polish) border, and Berlin had been combed as thoroughly as possible. The Munich crime had been exposed. Only Kiel had missed thorough investigation. Lyon and Harrison, who had drawn blanks at Hamburg and Schleswig, were asked to go swiftly to Kiel, and there they turned a page and threw the whole case wide open.

They went to Kiel crematorium. The keeper there had been in his post for many years. He produced the register for 1944. And there, on the date 29th March 1944, were four lines which were completely blank, except for the Roman numerals I, II, III, IV.

'Harry', said Lyon to Harrison. 'This must be it. If you live to be a hundred you'll never have another job like this in the Provost Branch.'

The cremation official not only remembered the incident but produced a logbook which confirmed the dates. He said that at 1830 hours on 29th March 1944 four of the Kiel Gestapo came to the crematorium. They were followed by employees of the undertaker Tischendorf who carried in two open coffins, each containing two corpses. The bodies were clothed in woollen underwear and socks. (It was afterwards established that the Gestapo had sent the blood-stained outer clothing to the cleaners.) The senior Gestapo officer, who organized everything, had four stars on his uniform and must therefore have been a Sturmbannführer or an Obersturmbannführer. The crematorium official gave a description of him. The man merely said, 'Here are four corpses to be cremated'. The official, Arthur Schäfer, asked for authority. The Gestapo leader said, 'Berlin ordered it. I have got no authority.' Schäfer asked for particulars of the dead men, to fill in his official records, and the Gestapo officer said he was providing nothing. The next morning a clerk at the crematorium telephoned the Gestapo to say that they could not possibly cremate bodies without authorization. He was told that it was a Gestapo matter and no normal police authorization was necessary. The clerk did not accept this, and telephoned the Kripo. The Colonel of Police said that the Kripo did not issue permits for the Gestapo, and they wanted nothing to do with the matter. The bodies were cremated, but the clerk persisted in trying to obtain some information for the blank lines in the register. Eventually the Gestapo said that they still refused to disclose the identity of the dead, and the clerk had better put a reference number in roman, I, II, III, IV, as some sort of identification in the register. He added that this was rather a good idea, and they must do it more often. In fact, at a later date two more corpses were sent in and labelled V and VI.

The crematorium official told Lyon and Harrison that the Gestapo officer had said that the four men had been shot by the Gestapo because they were 'agents'. He said that although he did not remember the name of the officer, that could easily be found from the local police records. The Royal Air Force officers went immediately to Wilhelm Tischendorf, the Kiel undertaker, who also remembered the incident. Gestapo officers had come to him at six o'clock in the evening and told him to pick up the bodies of four men who had been shot near the Rote Hahn (the Red Cock, an inn). Tischendorf asked who the victims were. One Gestapo man said, 'French. Shot whilst trying to escape.' He drove away in a car, and the undertaker asked a second officer the same question. He said they were British airmen. Tischendorf asked if they were some of the fifty airmen whose escape he had read about in the papers, and the officer confirmed this. Later, when he had sent out his men to pick up the bodies, one of his drivers told him that the men had been shot in the back. 'I can't remember much more', said Tischendorf. 'My documents were destroyed during air raids in August 1944. I do know that the bills for the transport and two coffin supports were paid by the Gestapo, after several requests for payment.'

The crematorium official had remembered that the 'agents' had been captured by the police in Flensburg, north of Kiel and right on the Danish border. Lyon and Harrison went to Flensburg, where the local police confirmed this and produced a register showing the names of the officers and the fact that they had escaped from a prisoner-of-war camp. They even had photographs of them, which were later valuable in getting the murderers to identify which men they had shot. The police said they had reported the recapture of the men, had held them for about twenty-four hours, and they had then been visited by an SS Sturmbannführer Post, with other Gestapo officers, who said they had been ordered to take over the prisoners and return them personally to their camp. The Flensburg police knew Post, and had no hesitation about complying with his instructions. Post signed a receipt for the take-over of the four officers.

After some thought, the co-operative Flensburg police were able to give the names of all the Gestapo officers who had called on them, and even the name of one of the drivers. Post, they were sure, had escaped at the end of the war, but the rest of the Gestapo officers, though not the drivers, had been arrested, and were kept in the internment camp at Neuengamme, near Schleswig, where they should still be.

Lyon and Harrison drove back to Kiel to register the evidence—formal statements from those they had interviewed, and a photograph of the crematorium register—and collected some supporting statements from the Gestapo typists and the men who had been sent by Tischendorf to collect the bodies: they pointed out the scene of the crime, which was photographed. One undertaker's labourer said that all that had been uttered by the Gestapo when they put the bodies in the coffins was the remark from one man: 'If the Russians were to come they would do the same to us'. Lyon and Harrison then returned to Hamburg, which was the headquarters of a Royal Air Force police district. They telephoned the commandant of the camp at Neuengamme to ensure that the men they were after were still there, and collected RAF Police reinforcements to pick them up. They were after four men: Franz Schmidt, Oskar Schmidt, Walter Jacobs and Hans Kähler. They did not expect to find the drivers concerned, Artur Denkmann and Wilhelm Struve, and they knew that the leader of the murder squad, Johannes Post, was not in custody.

They arrived at Neuengamme with half a dozen police NCOs, identified the four prisoners, and escorted them into trucks for transport for Minden. The four had noted the Royal Air Force uniforms, and as they were being loaded into the trucks Lyon overheard one man say, turning to another, '*Dies sieht schlecht aus*'—'This looks bad.' Since Lyon had made no explanation to them for their removal, but merely established their identities, he thought this remark was significant. The drivers were picked up soon afterwards. Struve was working at the town hall in Pretz. Lyon found Denkmann ill, and consigned him to hospital under guard. Lyon had not mentioned to Struve the precise reason for his arrest, but on the car journey to Minden Struve kept protesting that he had not shot the Royal Air Force officers.

Lyon decided to conduct a formal interrogation of Struve first. It was likely enough that the Gestapo had not confided in their drivers that they were engaged on a journey which would involve the murder of prisoners of war, and it could therefore be presumed that the drivers would co-operate by giving all the information they had in order to save themselves. Struve said that they had been informed that there was to be an execution of enemy agents on whom sentence of death had already been passed. The drivers prepared two cars in Kiel and drove the Gestapo officers—the four in custody and their missing leader, Johannes Post—to Flensburg. They waited while the prisoners were interrogated. They then drove back through Kiel to a point some sixteen kilometres to the south, the inn and hamlet of Rote Hahn. Denkmann, when he was fit to make a statement, confirmed this and made an interesting addition. He was driving the first car, which contained Post, Kähler and Squadron Leader Catanach. Post ordered him to make a diversion, because he had arranged to take his mistress, Marianne Heidt, to the theatre that night, and he thought this business of murder might delay him. He therefore got Denkmann to take the theatre tickets up to Marianne Heidt's apartment so that he should not disappoint her. In the event he was back in time to go to the theatre.

The party reached the murder site, which had already been prospected and chosen. The drivers had been told to park their cars and station themselves about a hundred metres north and south of the entrance to the field where the shooting was scheduled. As it happened, Denkmann arrived first. Post and Kähler took Catanach into the field, and he was shot. When Struve drove up Jacobs and the two Schmidts—who were not related—took Fuglesang, Espelid and Christensen into the field, handcuffed. The three officers almost stumbled over Catanach's body, gave a shout of alarm, and were shot from behind.

Lyon then proceeded to the individual interrogation of the four

Gestapo men. They all insisted that they had had no idea that the men they had shot had been recaptured Royal Air Force officers, but they had been told, and they believed, that they were enemy agents, spies who had been caught in plain clothes. They admitted that they had been recruited for this job by Post and his superior, Friedrich Schmidt—the third Schmidt in the cabal, and, again, no relation. They admitted the journey to Flensburg. But when Lyon produced from the Flensburg police files the photographs and descriptive forms which showed that the four officers were recaptured prisoners of war they denied having seen them, and said that all the release procedures with the Flensburg police had been conducted by Post personally. Lyon asked them if they were in the habit of shooting people out of hand without trial, and their answer was 'Orders are orders. War is war.' They did not rely on any cover that they had shot prisoners who were trying to escape.

They had therefore established a position which it was very difficult to breach. If a court believed that they honestly thought that they were carrying out superior orders to shoot plain-clothes agents the evidence on the Sagan murder charge would be considerably weakened.

Lyon decided on a final effort. He had selected Franz Schmidt as the weakest member of the four. He called him in one afternoon and gave him a long and strong interrogation. Franz Schmidt tripped over the repeat of his story that he had never seen the identity photographs in the Flensburg police station, or interrogated the officers there about their escape—which he had. Lyon pounced, and would not let him go. Franz Schmidt capitulated. He confessed that he had participated in the murder knowing the full facts of it.

It was late October, and darkness had fallen. Lyon sent him to his cell with a pencil and paper so that he could write his own voluntary statement. Lyon dropped in on the commandant of the Minden prison and was sitting in his office when an orderly burst into the room, white in the face. 'Gawd, sir,' he gasped. 'Number Eleven has hung himself.' They ran downstairs to Schmidt's cell at the end of the corridor. Franz Schmidt had taken off his vest and managed to pass the shoulder-piece, twisted like a paper spill, through the iron squares of a ventilator high in the outside wall, and knot it when he retrieved it. He had then tied the vest round his neck, kicked the chair away, and dropped. The chair had been used as a desk for him to write his confession on. The pencil and sheets of paper were scattered on the bed, but he had not reached a point in his statement where he had confessed in writing to the murder.

Lyon lifted Schmidt by the legs, and they cut him down. The commandant sent immediately for a doctor. He came running, and they placed Franz Schmidt with his back across a chair, his head down and his chest arched upwards. The doctor produced a hypodermic syringe and a long needle, and injected straight into the heart, muttering as he worked '*Schlechter Mann, schlechter Mann*'—'Bad man, bad man.' But Franz Schmidt was dead.

On the following days the other three men, shocked into truth by the event, made fairly full statements. Jacobs underwent a religious conversion, which also assisted. But although each now admitted that he knew that the men to be shot were Royal Air Force officers, each maintained one peculiar twist in their story. They had all gone into the field. Post had shot. The other three had shot. But the man making the statement had not shot. Again, as in the case of others, the men were sent to the London Cage where fuller interrogation might sort out their stories.

Lyon still had two major participants to find: Friedrich (Fritz) Schmidt, the Kiel Gestapo Chief who had ordered the killings, and Johannes Post, his second-in-command who had organized them and carried them through. He spent many frustrating weeks on this. When McKenna came back from his convalescence they together raided the house of the parents of Marianne Heidt, Post's mistress, in Kiel. They advanced a little further, but got no firm lead. But they obtained one snapshot of Post and Heidt in skiing costume on a holiday in the Harz Mountains. That in the end was the means by which Post was caught.

Flight Lieutenant Lyon was recalled to the United Kingdom to resume his service in the Metropolitan Police. He made one last effort in the north to trace Post and Schmidt. McKenna was with him, and saw him off on the home journey. One month later, in May 1947, McKenna found that he had a quiet day, and dropped in to the holding prison at Minden to check if there had been any new arrivals. The commandant mentioned that one man had been brought in by another war crimes investigation unit, on suspicion of a war crimes charge. There was as yet no actual charge, and inquiries were still proceeding. The man's name was Johannes Pohlmann, a haulage contractor from Celle. 'I'll have a look at him', said McKenna. 'No. 4 cell', said the commandant.

McKenna went along the ground floor corridor and looked in through the spy-hole of No. 4. A man was sitting on the bed, apparently staring straight at him, and McKenna unconsciously dodged back for a moment until he realized that he could not be seen through the lens. McKenna thought that his face looked familiar. It was big, and in the literal sense brutal, with angry staring eyes. But McKenna could not place him. He went for a stroll in the town, went down to the bridge by the Weser, and he could not get this face out of his mind. Then he brought out his wallet, in which he carried photographs of suspects as well as his loved ones, and he came across the snapshot of Marianne Heidt and her lover in the snow.

He thought: 'It can't be. But it must be.' He hurried back to the prison, and looked through the spyhole again. The man was on his feet now, walking around, once or twice looking at the window, and muttering to himself. McKenna was now certain in his mind that this must be Post.

He went to the telephone and spoke to Group Captain Somerhough, the head of the North Western War Crimes Investigation Unit. He told him what he thought. The group captain was sceptical. McKenna said he was as sure as he could reasonably be. 'You know what I want Post for, sir,' he said. 'It is for murder. You have him in on suspicion of a war crime, but if this is Post, surely he must be released to me, and whatever else he has done can be considered later.' Group Captain Somerhough said, 'By all means go in and see him. If you establish that this is definitely Post, the man you are looking for, we waive all our right to him. You press on from there, and keep me in the picture.'

McKenna called a guard to unlock the cell, and went in. 'What is your name?' he asked. 'You already know', said the man. 'It is Pohlmann.' 'Where are you from?' 'Celle, a haulage contractor.' 'Tell me about your work', McKenna invited, and the man spoke in detail for some time.

McKenna asked a number of minor questions, to let the man establish his identity. Then he said:

'I don't believe you are telling me the truth. I believe you are nothing but a liar. I think your name is Johannes Post, and you were Sturmbannführer SS in the Gestapo at Kiel in March 1944, and your boss was Fritz Schmidt.'

The man strongly denied this.

'Well, I have a photograph of you as Post,' McKenna said, and he showed the snapshot of Post and Marianne Heidt.

'Where did you get that?'

'There is no reason why I should tell you.'

'Well, that's me. I am Post.'

'You know all about the Kiel murders?'

'Naturally. I was in command.'

'I'll come back and talk to you later.'

McKenna went to the telephone and spoke to Group Captain Somerhough. Then he rang Bowes, who was extravagantly delighted. 'You're almost bursting into song', said McKenna. 'I'm almost dancing a jig', said Bowes. 'Well, I'm going back to get a statement', McKenna said.

He fetched an interpreter and went back into the cell. Post seemed almost drunk with potentiality, as if he relished, after over two years, the chance to give a full account of what he had done. He described the operation in detail, expressed no regret, and volunteered the information that this was only an item in a long line of killings that he had carried out for the glory of the Führer. But when it came to writing a statement, he was remarkably reticent, and even omitted the fact that he knew that the men whom he was to shoot were Royal Air Force officers.

> In March 1944 [he wrote] I was ordered by my former chief, SS Sturmbannführer Fritz Schmidt, to transfer four male persons from Flensburg to Neumünster via Kiel. I was told that these four individuals were foreign agents who had escaped and had been sentenced to death. On the pretext that they had attempted an escape, they were to be shot at a place which had been exactly indicated. My objections were refuted with a warning that refusal would result in immediate arrest, transfer to a concentration camp, and execution by shooting, as the order was definite and originating from Oberstgruppenführer Müller of Amt IV, Berlin. I then carried the order out. The above statement is true.
>
> Signed: Johannes Post

It was therefore left to Post's flamboyant evidence at his trial for the full nature of his conduct, and of his character, to be revealed:

'On the 29th of March 1944 SS Sturmbannführer Fritz Schmidt called me into his office and said I should keep myself in readiness to take over some prisoners, and he would like to know a suitable place on the road to Neumünster where four men could be shot. I said I did not know the road very well. He said, "All right, we'll drive out and look". We stopped at a bend before the Rote Hahn, he went through a gate into a meadow, and he said, "This is the place where the men will be shot. Remember it."

'We drove back. SS Sturmbannführer Schmidt called me into his office with SS Leutnant Oskar Schmidt, SS Sergeant-Major Franz Schmidt—I think he hanged himself in Minden—the administrative officer Kähler, SS Staff Sergeant Walter Jacobs, and the drivers Struve and Denkmann.

'SS Sturmbannführer Schmidt had a teleprint message in his hand. He said, "I have to acquaint you with a top-secret matter. It is an order from the Führer. Four men who are at our disposal at the Kripo in Flensburg are to be shot at the place determined by me. They are supposed to be English officers. They have been condemned to death. They are agents who have been proved guilty of attempted sabotage and espionage who, however, succeeded in escaping once again and have now been arrested when trying to cross the frontier into Denmark."

'Turning to me, he said, "Post, you will go to Kriminalkommissar Schneider in Flensburg. He has already received instructions from Berlin. You will interrogate these men briefly, but it need not be expected that they will make any further statements. Since they are violent persons, they will be handcuffed with their hands behind their backs. You will leave for Neumünster and shoot them on the spot previously indicated. After the shooting you will inform an undertaker, who will take the bodies to the crematorium. SS Leutnant Schmidt will see that the cremation is carried out and the death certificate signed.

' "For firing, a service pistol of calibre 7·65 will be used, shot into the heart in between the shoulder blades. A rifle will be taken along in case, contrary to expectations, an attempt to escape should be made and the range of the pistols is exceeded."

'Turning to Sergeant-Major Schmidt, he said, "Get the handcuffs issued, four pairs".

'Turning to Kähler, he said, 'Get a rifle and ammunition. The drivers will if necessary seal off the road in case curious persons want to come along and watch."

'Turning to me, he said, "Post, I make you responsible. You are in charge of the party."

'Turning to the others, he said, "The orders of SS Major Post will be complied with explicitly. As I have already said, this is an order of the Führer. It will be carried out as I have told you. Any lack of discipline in carrying it out will be severely punished. This refers to the pledge of silence, too. If anyone offends against the pledge of silence or in any other way against the orders given he will have to reckon with immediate arrest and his being handed over to a concentration camp for special treatment, death by shooting. I will now take your oaths to say that you will carry out the order and that you will remain silent towards everyone. Have you any questions?" '

Post described how he had taken over the officers, interrogated them, and put them handcuffed into the cars.

'I had a short stop in Kiel. I had bought theatre tickets for that day. Since, in view of the instructions I had received, I was not able and did not want to go to the theatre, I had the ticket given to an acquaintance so that it did not become invalid.

'We got to the scene of the shooting between 1630 and 1700 hours. The other car was a few minutes later. I got out with Catanach and Kähler. I told Denkmann that we intended to relieve ourselves, and he said to Kähler, "You will have to take the prisoner's handcuffs off". Kähler took them off. While he was doing so I told Catanach that he would be shot according to orders. Kähler took his pistol out of his pocket and recocked it. This resulted in a stoppage, because there were two rounds in the breech at the same time. I saw that he was very nervous, and excitedly making efforts to get his pistol straightened out. During this a shot went off from his pistol. In view of these circumstances I feared that Kähler might miss if he fired, so I took my pistol out of the holster and shot Catanach through the heart as ordered.

'The second car came immediately. The three other officials came on to the meadow with the three prisoners. The prisoners were handcuffed. Suddenly one of them let out a shout. I assume he saw Catanach lying there, and, understandably, the prisoners became excited. The one on the right made a dash to the right. Franz Schmidt fired. The other two officials shot immediately afterwards. The prisoner who had been shot by Oskar Schmidt showed some slight signs of life. In order not to let him suffer any more pain I tore the rifle from Kähler's hand and administered the coup de grâce. These prisoners had not been informed that they were to be shot, because there was no time.'

Post had, in fact, through the separation of the victims into two cars, been baulked from enjoying one of his keenest pleasures. Because he did not travel with Arnold Christensen, Hallada Espelid and Nils Fuglesang, he had not been able to inform them in advance that they were to be shot and to savour their reactions. Usually, as he had told McKenna in a moment of euphoric frankness,[1] he liked to give this news many hours before the shooting, announcing what he called the *Himmelsfarht* with the bland assurance to his victims that they would appreciate the time he gave them to prepare to meet their God. But he had fully savoured the impact of his notification to James Catanach. They were driving through Kiel towards the field of execution. Post urbanely pointed out some of the landmarks. He stopped the car at a convenient spot and identified the principal sights. Catanach observed in a friendly fashion that he knew some of them quite well, since he had been engaged in combat operations over Kiel. Post continued chatting for some time, and then said:

'We must get on. I have to shoot you.'

Catanach did not comprehend what he had heard. 'What did you say?' he queried. Post affirmed:

'I am going to shoot you.'

Catanach smiled at the tasteless joke. 'Do you mind?' he said. 'Another time. I have an appointment in the cooler at Stalag Luft III. I've done nothing wrong except go under the wire. You can't shoot me.'

'Those are my orders', said Post, searching Catanach's face keenly.

The Australian did not reply. The car was ordered on, with the diversion through Kiel town that Post required. The car stopped at the apartment of Marianne Heidt, and Post sent the driver Denkmann upstairs with the theatre ticket. In the parked car Post had leisure again to study the face of the silent squadron leader. When they drove on, and finally came to the field, he knew that Catanach was no longer in any doubt. In the middle of the field the party stopped, and Post again said:

'I have orders to shoot you.'

Squadron Leader Catanach merely asked:

'Why?'

Of all the evidence given in the Hamburg courtroom over fifty days of trial, the account of the Kiel killings, more than any other narrative, caused the clearest response of shock in the German spectators who were listening.

Fritz Schmidt was not yet on trial. McKenna sought him con-

[1]See pp. 10–11.

stantly. He traced Schmidt's mother to a hillside cottage by the Bodensee. She was seventy-two, a senile, happy woman. She said that Fritz had come to see her three weeks ago, and had said goodbye, perhaps for ever, but if he did come back she would be sure to let the Herr Major know.

It was another twenty-one years before Fritz Schmidt was sentenced.

KIEL

Squadron Leader James Catanach DFC, Flying Officer Arnold Christensen, Lieutenants Hallada Espelid and Nils Fuglesang, murdered near Kiel, 29th March 1944:

Oskar Schmidt in British custody 6.10.1946.
Hans Kähler in British custody 6.10.1946.
Walter Jacobs in British custody 6.10.1946.
Franz Schmidt, suicide 27.10.1946.
Wilhelm Struve in British custody 8.10.1946.
Artur Denkmann in British custody 20.10.1946
Johannes Post in British custody 19.5.1947.
Friedrich (Fritz) Schmidt: URGENTLY WANTED.

Flight Lieutenant Lyon spent the greater part of the winter of 1946–7 in an intensive search for Post and Fritz Schmidt. He recalled: 'After we had completed the interrogation of the Kiel Gestapo and taken their statements, all the documents were handed over to the Judge Advocate General's department, and I turned back towards Hamburg, Schleswig-Holstein, Kiel and Flensburg and up into Denmark in an effort to find some trace of Johannes Post or Fritz Schmidt. I believe this was the most bitter winter of the century. Fuel for heating was almost non-existent, and the undernourished Germans were dying like flies. In Hamburg the authorities constructed what they called heating halls where people could go to warm up. Between Christmas 1946 and the middle of March 1947 the temperature in Germany never rose above zero. A very great number of leads were followed up, based on information obtained from the Kiel Gestapo prisoners, from the Gestapo members who had been incarcerated at Esterwegen, and from some solid pointers provided by Dr Hans Merten, of the Kripo department of RSHA Berlin, whom I had released from Esterwegen and who was now living with his family in Kiel.

'In spite of the most appalling weather—and my only transport was an open jeep—most of these leads were followed right through. I went up as far as Copenhagen two or three times, where I was assisted very ably by a Danish police officer named, believe it or not, Hans Christian Andersen. He told me that there were still some German prisoners in custody, who might possibly be of some assistance, in Aalborg, near the northern tip of Denmark. I drove there from Copenhagen, crossing by the ferry to Aarhus, and driving off in a snowstorm just as dusk was falling. I shall never forget that drive. Although there was only one main road to Aalborg, it became almost untraceable. The snowstorm increased until it was something out of Scott of the Antarctic. *The road was utterly deserted, and I do not remember passing or being passed by any other vehicle the whole way. The surrounding landscape appeared utterly desolate. The surface of the road was solid ice, and the snow was beginning to deepen on it. To top everything, well before the halfway mark the windscreen wiper packed up and I was forced to lower the windscreen. The lights on the jeep were not too good, and it was extremely difficult to make out where the roadway ended and the ditches and fields at the side began. I remember thinking to myself: "Dickie, my boy, if you ditch this jeep you're bloody well going to freeze to death". I should, of course, have found a*

farmhouse, asked for shelter, and sat the storm out. But, being young and foolish, I pressed on my slithering way and finished up frozen stiff in Aalborg. I saw about ten Germans there, but they were able to provide nothing of value. Back in Copenhagen, Hans Christian Andersen had dug up a few more German internees who he thought might be valuable. I saw them all, but nothing of any use was obtained. Andersen also introduced me to a most charming blonde actress and, after the rigours of the winter and an accumulation of unclaimed leave, this meeting resulted in my return being delayed rather longer than had been originally scheduled. . . .'

10 The prisoners showed considerable calm

Detectives declare cases cleared when there is nothing more that they can do about them. The file on the murders of the twenty-nine officers from Stalag Luft III who were recaptured or transported within the Breslau Military District was closed in the sense that the officers of the law knew much of what had happened. But there was no bar on this earth where most of the offenders could stand. The names of some men whose fate was uncertain were kept in a handy Pending index. The amount of time spent by the Special Investigation Branch in investigating these murders was more than proportionate to their number, and to the number of men whom the Judge Advocate eventually charged—a total of two, and the head of neither was offered to the SIB on a platter. Sometimes it takes longer to prove that a man is dead than to find him alive.

Through the first twenty-one months of active investigation a list had been built up—and whittled away as deaths were reliably confirmed—of those members of the Breslau Gestapo who could most likely have served in a murder squad: if Scharpwinkel had recruited a murder squad. That doubt was resolved by Scharpwinkel himself in his Moscow interviews with Captain Cornish. He said he had appointed Kriminalobersekretär Lux to command a gang. With a perverseness which could be better understood by the fact that he had a safe refuge in Moscow, Scharpwinkel refused to name the members positively, except two,[1] but he mentioned nine of Cornish's suspects who, he said, were not in the murder squad.[2]

The outstanding feature of the Breslau case, in which it differed

[1]The names and subsequent fate of the denounced killers are recorded in Appendix V, The Accused.

[2]Among those whom Scharpwinkel excluded was Erwin Wieczorek, who was charged with being concerned in the killing of Flight Lieutenants Kiewnarski and Wernham, and Flying Officers Pawluk and Skanzikas; was found guilty and sentenced to death; and whose sentence was quashed on review.

from the organization of all the other murders, was that the Criminal Police were actively co-opted into the conspiracy. Breslau was comparatively near Berlin, 180 miles, but not a very convenient distance in wartime Germany, when the journey generally entailed an all-night train or a military aircraft. Since there were so many killings that had to be done there, the head of the Breslau Kripo, as well as of the Gestapo, was summoned to RSHA, the security headquarters in Berlin, for conferences intended to speed and smooth the operation.

The Breslau Kripo Chief was Max Wielen, in 1944 a 62-year-old professional police officer, and he had been in British custody since his capture near Cologne before the capitulation. Though Wielen had often been asked questions, he had never been requested to write a formal statement of what had happened until there was a rival statement which would give ground for testing and interrogating him. This occurred in October 1946, when the two statements made by Scharpwinkel in Moscow became available. Clearly Scharpwinkel had been slyly unloading much of his own responsibility on to Wielen in the account he gave to Cornish, and this had the useful effect of provoking Wielen into an angry statement which exaggerated his own innocence in areas which an experienced investigator could determine. Nothing was shiningly clear in the murky Breslau case, where, unlike the situation in many others of the cases, there was no chance of the clash of confrontation producing the spark of truth. What did come through was that, although the Kripo in Breslau was on as bad terms with the Gestapo as in most other areas in Germany, nevertheless Wielen of the Kripo *was* conscripted by Berlin into the conspiracy, *was* given access to confidential planning that elsewhere was totally barred to Kripo cognizance, *was* an integral part of the Berlin–Breslau pyramid. His statement therefore had to be read as not the whole truth, but less self-incriminating, using all the expertise of an old professional.

Wielen recounted how, as the officer responsible, he had instituted the general alarm and then the *Grossfahndung* after receiving news of the break-out from Sagan. Absalon and Brünner began their investigations at the camp. Wielen was summoned by General Nebe to go to Berlin, and he went expecting to be dismissed the service for not having prevented the escape. Nebe, however, did not reproach him, but told him that Hitler was very angry and had ordered shooting. 'He wanted to show me an order from the highest authority so that, when the Gestapo approached the Criminal Police to name the prisoners and their locations, the Kripo would raise no objection. He gave me to read a teleprint signed by Kaltenbrunner which read: "On the personal command of the Führer, reference the Sagan escape affair, more than half of the recaptured English officers will be shot. The Gestapo will receive the appropriate orders from Gruppenführer Müller. Everything is to be avoided which might bring to light the action of the Gestapo."

'After quickly reading through the order and returning it, I protested impulsively with the words that the shooting was first of all contrary to the Geneva Convention and contrary to the laws of war, but, on the other hand, could not be kept a secret for ever, and would result in reprisals against German flying officers in British camps.

'I said, "I decline to accept responsibility". Nebe, who looked extremely tired, and was obviously suffering from very severe emotional strain, replied that I would not assume any responsibility, as the Gestapo would receive direct orders from above, and therefore would act on their own responsibility. Furthermore, nothing could be done against a Führer Order, and if the Kripo raised difficulties I should have to bear the consequences—SS court martial and shooting.'

Wielen went back to Breslau and asked Scharpwinkel if he had yet received the orders. Scharpwinkel said he had not, but when Wielen explained the Führer Order he said, 'I'll do this personally, I'll do this personally'. Later that day Scharpwinkel telephoned to say that he had now received his orders from Müller.

Wielen said he received a 'decree' from Amt V, Berlin—that is, Nebe—containing a copy for information of the list of officers who were to be shot by the Gestapo. The relevant Gestapo offices throughout Germany received their instructions from Müller. 'I presume that this general order also said that the corpses were to be cremated and the urns were to be sent to the Kripo Headquarters in Breslau. The Kripo in Breslau only received an order from Nebe to collect the urns on arrival and to send them to the prisoner-of-war camp at Sagan. At the same time a letter arrived from Amt V which was to be sent to the camp at the finish, and which said that the officers had been shot after a renewed escape or when offering resistance. The camp had to make the text of this known to all prisoners of war.'

In this passage Wielen was still smarting under the acute embarrassment he had suffered by being made personally responsible for the storage of the urns of the cremated officers as they gradually came back from the Gestapo outposts—a gratuitous involvement of him in the conspiracy. Eventually he had to clear out the contents of the bookcases in his office and store the urns on the shelves. He lived with them for some weeks, and put up yellow curtains to hide them.

Many weeks later Nebe telephoned Wielen and told him to come with Scharpwinkel, in Scharpwinkel's car, for a conference in Berlin. 'Nebe told me that he had been reproached by Müller because the Kripo had not put the recaptured prisoners into separate cells, and had also carried out transfers, so that the selection of certain officers by the Gestapo could not have been done without the remaining officers noticing.' This error, of course, had been of undoubted value to the SIB investigators because it had enabled the survivors of the massacre to give circumstantial reports of the treatment and removal of the shot officers which had been the only source of the SIB's reconstruction of the progression of events and the identification of the officers in the separate batches taken out to be shot.

At this point in the conference there was a prolonged interruption because of a succession of air raids. During one lull they went out of the shelter and found that Scharpwinkel's car had been buried by fallen masonry. They sawed away the wreckage and dug out the car, which was battered but still usable. Wielen in his statement almost certainly exaggerated the time he himself took in dealing with this incident, because he said that in the meantime there was a further conference which Scharpwinkel attended, but he arrived only as it was closing. The second half of the conference was in fact what was called the 'whitewash conference' which discussed the measures to be taken to hoodwink an international commission into the Sagan murders which was now fully expected. Wielen was stretching himself to take peculiar pains to establish that he was not present at this whitewash conference, for reasons which are difficult to perceive, since he had admitted so much involvement previously.

Clearly there was great tension between Wielen and Scharpwinkel, which was resolved in October 1944, when Scharpwinkel got himself appointed Security Police Commander in Breslau, at last outranking Wielen, who was posted to Cologne—to the great good fortune of the SIB, for his subsequent capture ensured that there was one available live witness of the events in Berlin and Breslau: though the fact that Wielen was unique enabled him to trim his story without refutation.

Scharpwinkel had done his best from his cell in Moscow. Wielen was shown his statement, and responded angrily: 'It is ridiculous to suppose that I expressed to Scharpwinkel my displeasure at the fact that the Gestapo, and not the Kripo, was to carry out the executions. I thanked God that the Kripo had not received the order, and I made the clear comment to my wife: "I would not have been able to do this".

'The Gestapo and Kripo had completely different duties. Executions were only carried out by the Gestapo. In this case, as I can now clearly see, the supposedly correct Kripo was used by Himmler or Kaltenbrunner to a certain extent as a screen behind which the gruesome deed of the Gestapo was to remain secret.'

Wielen declared, probably with truth, that Scharpwinkel had told him nothing about how the shootings had been carried out. The Special Investigation Branch slowly obtained eye-witness accounts of most of them.

The first was the shooting at Halbau of Squadron Leader Cross, Flight Lieutenants Casey, Leigh and Wiley, and Flying Officers Hake and Pohe, who were later cremated at Görlitz. Scharpwinkel told Cornish:

'I appointed Lux as the detachment leader throughout. I arrived at Görlitz with the detachment. Besides Lux, the detachment included Knappe and Pattke. I do not know the names of the others. There were one or two, possibly Kiske. Probably Läuffer and

Wieczorek, who accompanied me on the day in question were present. My driver was Schröder. The British were brought to the headquarters. As I speak English, I put one or two questions to the prisoners while they were being interrogated: were they married? had they children? etc. Lux explained to the prisoners that by order of the Supreme Military Commander they had been sentenced to death. Then we drove away. When the Reichsautobahn was reached the summary shootings were carried out. Everybody got out. The prisoners were placed in position. It was revealed to them that the sentence was about to be carried out. The prisoners showed considerable calm, which surprised me very much. The six prisoners stood next to one another in the wood. Lux gave the order to fire and the detachment fired. Lux shot with them. By the second salvo the prisoners were dead.

'In my opinion Lux's detachment carried out twenty-six or twenty-seven shootings. As far as I know, all these shootings were, without exception, carried out in the Breslau area at a short distance from places where there were crematoria. Only in the Görlitz case was I personally present at the shooting. I did not take part in the shooting, I was merely an observer.'

One of the Germans present whom Scharpwinkel did not mention was Kriminalinspektor Richard Max Hänsel, in charge of the Gestapo sub-office at Görlitz, who was taken along as a local man who knew the road and could arrange the subsequent cremations at Görlitz more easily. He identified as members of the party Oberregierungsrat Scharpwinkel, Kriminalrat Wieczorek, Kriminalrat Dankert, Kriminalkommissar Läuffer, Kriminalinspektor Hampel and Kriminalobersekretär Lux. Robert Schröder, Scharpwinkel's driver, who was not picked up until four years after the crime, included in the murder gang Lux, Knappe, Pattke, Lang and Kreuzer, but also said that Dr Absalon was present—the first sworn evidence of what had long been suspected, that Absalon had not only investigated the escape from Stalag Luft III but had participated in the shootings. Hänsel described how the killings had taken place in full daylight, how the officers had been marshalled and kept standing in the road for five minutes, and were then ordered by Scharpwinkel to move off into the trees. Hänsel said he did not accompany them. He went back to his car to get a sandwich from his briefcase, because the convoy had moved off without giving him time for lunch. As he was chewing his bread and butter he heard the shots, which he said came from two sub-machine-guns only, one of them fired by Lux. He ran up into the wood and saw the sprawling bodies of the dead officers.

Hänsel said he heard Lux say to his squad, 'Tomorrow, or the day after, we'll be going to Hirschberg'. In the SIB reconstruction of the timings of the shootings by the Breslau Gestapo the murders of Flight Lieutenants Kiewnarski and Wernham, Flying Officer Pawluk and Pilot Officer Skanzikas, who had been imprisoned at

Hirschberg after recapture, had taken place earlier than those from Görlitz, and this was never satisfactorily cleared up. Wieczorek, who admitted he was present but said he did not shoot, could not confirm a date. But he was certain that Scharpwinkel had been present, although Scharpwinkel had told Cornish that he had attended only one set of murders.

Wieczorek said the party left Hirschberg, going towards Sagan, in four cars with one prisoner, two officials and a driver in each. It was dark, well past six o'clock on a March night. Scharpwinkel was in the leading car of the convoy, and apparently instructed his driver to fake a breakdown. The car slowed and stopped, and the driver began to tinker with the engine. Scharpwinkel came along the convoy, shouting that there was a breakdown and everyone was to leave his car, bringing the prisoners between the second and third cars. Wieczorek said he went to the first car and watched the driver working, and after ten minutes the car was in order.

'Quite suddenly we heard some very loud shouting and exclamations, and several shots were fired. We could not see anything because the headlights of the car behind were blinding us. But we saw an amount of movement between the headlamps of the third car and the back of the second car. With the two drivers I went to the spot where the shots were being fired. The officials were running around excitedly. I saw a number of officials running around on the field adjoining the road, and they were shining torches on dark shadows which were lying in the field. The last car turned round and set off at great speed towards Hirschberg. I heard somebody report to Scharpwinkel: "They are all dead".'

Robert Schröder, the driver to Scharpwinkel, was the eye-witness to the shooting of the group of ten officers: Flight Lieutenants Evans, Hall, Humphreys, Langford, McGill and Swain, and Flying Officers Birkland, Kolanowski, Stewart and Valenta. Again he said that Scharpwinkel and Absalon were in the party, with Läuffer, Lux, Knappe, Pattke, Lang and Kreuzer. All the ten prisoners were in a lorry.

'It was the Sagan road. About halfway there was a halt to let the prisoners and the guards relieve themselves and also warm themselves up a bit. It was cold and freezing. The lorry stood about forty metres behind me. I was sitting alone in the car when I suddenly heard shouts followed immediately by a mad firing of machine pistols. I jumped out of the car and ran to the rear. Behind the lorry lay the prisoners scattered on the ground. Some of them were right on the road, others were on a slope nearby, but they were all close together. When I had asked one of the officials what had happened, he said that some of the fellows had tried to escape and that they had all caught it.'

No one was ever found who could give any first-hand account of the deaths of the six companions who were last seen alive on 6th April: Flight Lieutenants Grisman, Gunn, Milford and J. F.

Williams, Flying Officer Street, and Lieutenant McGarr; nor of the isolated deaths, also associated with Breslau because of the inscription on their urns, of Flight Lieutenant Long, Flying Officer Krol and Flying Officer Tobolski.

Wing Commander Bowes still hoped that the extradition of Dr Scharpwinkel from Moscow could be arranged, so that a full interrogation could be carried out. In early 1947 the Russians made a surprising offer. They said the British could have Scharpwinkel if in exchange they would trace a certain Baron von Walter and hand him to the Russians. Bowes quickly found Baron von Walter, who was now heading his own small industrial plant in Solingen, near Cologne. He had been a member of the German Embassy in Moscow just before the severance of diplomatic relations and the German advance into Russia in 1941, and it was apparently for some reason connected with these duties that the Russians wanted him. Bowes arrested him and brought him in to the London Cage, although the baron had previously passed a denazification court. The British Foreign Office then made repeated applications to Moscow for particulars of the war crime which von Walter was alleged to have committed. 'We cannot authorize the handing over of anyone', the Foreign Office instructed the British Ambassador, 'against whom a prima facie case of a war crime does not exist'. The Russian authorities continued to disregard all requests for further information, and in May McKenna escorted von Walter back to his home and family, which he had never expected to see again.

McKenna then heard that the Russians had applied for the extradition of Anton Kaindl. Kaindl was undoubtedly a war criminal, with a black record based on far more than prima facie allegations. He had been commandant of the concentration camp at Sachsenhausen/Oranienberg, where many thousands had been exterminated, including a vast number of Russian prisoners. McKenna suggested that Kaindl should be handed over only in exchange for Scharpwinkel. The Foreign Office said austerely, 'We do not trade in human flesh'. There was enough evidence against Kaindl, and they were going to hand him over without conditions. McKenna could only mutter quietly to himself. Kaindl was eventually convicted of a multitude of atrocities and sentenced to hard labour for life in Siberia, the Russians having recently abolished capital punishment in peacetime. Kaindl was reported dead shortly afterwards.

Nothing about the inquiry into the Breslau murders was spectacular. Patient investigation uncovered names among the murder squad. Constant interrogation disclosed new cover-names and false identities of many people on the run, who were eventually found—whatever else they were running from—not to have Sagan on their consciences. The most characteristic, true *detection* was that, through persistently probing the cotton-wool of diplomatic obscurantism, and through annoying many good people who preferred not to be disturbed over matters so trifling as fifty deaths, *Scharpwinkel was found.*

BRESLAU

Within the Breslau Military District:

Killed at Halbau, 31st March 1944: Squadron Leader Ian Cross, Flight Lieutenants Michael Casey, Thomas Leigh and George Wiley, Flying Officers Albert Hake and John Pohe.

Killed at Hirschberg, ?30th March 1944: Flight Lieutenants Antoni Kiewnarski and James Wernham, Flying Officer Kazimierz Pawluk and Pilot Officer Sotiris Skanzikas.

Killed between Görlitz and Sagan, 1st April 1944: Flight Lieutenants Brian Evans, Charles Hall, Edgar Humphreys, Patrick Langford, George McGill and Cyril Swain, Flying Officers Henry Birkland, Wlodzimierz Kolanowski, Robert Stewart and Ernst Valenta.

Killed at a place unknown on or after 6th April 1944: Flight Lieutenants William Grisman, Alastair Gunn, Harold Milford, John F. Williams, Flying Officer Denys Street, Lieutenant Clement McGarr.

Killed at a place unknown on or after 2nd April 1944: Flying Officer Pawel Tobolski.

Killed at a place unknown on or after 12th April 1944: Flying Officer Stanislaw Krol.

Killed at a place unknown on or after 13th April 1944: Flight Lieutenant James Long.

Involved in the general conspiracy at Breslau:

Max Wielen in British custody 26.4.1945.
SS Standartenführer Seetzen, suicide 28.9.1945.
Ernst Schmauser in Russian custody.

Identified in the Breslau Murder Squad:

Wilhelm Scharpwinkel in Russian custody.
Gunther Absalon in Russian custody.
Richard Hänsel in British custody 20.6.1946.
Lux killed 1944.
Knappe killed 1944.
Walter Pattke: WANTED.
Paul Kiske killed 1944.
Läuffer, ?suicide 1945.
Erwin Wieczorek in British custody 28.6.1947.
Robert Schröder in British custody 24.5.1948.
Dankert: WANTED.
Walter Hampel in British custody 1.9.1948.
Lang: WANTED.
Kreuzer: WANTED.
Prosse died 1944.
Kuhnel killed 1944.

11 Thou shalt not kill on Good Friday

It was only a rain-blotted notice on the board at Sagan that gave any official assurance of the death of Flying Officer Anthony Hayter, and the fact that it was copied into official communiqués and passed to next of kin. One urn among the fifty had been returned to Stalag Luft III with no inscription at all as to name or place or date. Tony Hayter had been reported by the Gestapo as shot, and it had to be assumed that the urn was his. But there was no location for investigators to concentrate on. Any details about his death had to emerge from general inquiries.

No leads at all were given in the first fifteen months of the operation in Germany. Then a routine re-examination of Walter Herberg occurred. Herberg was the man who had been included in the death squad for Dennis Cochran at Karlsruhe because he could talk better than the others and smooth the Gestapo path in areas where State officials still demanded law and authorization. He was being reinterrogated, not to squeeze some vital admission out of him, but because people who had been through a memorable experience often remembered other details about it when they were asked to repeat the narrative.

Herberg had been taken back over his trip to Berlin. This was the occasion when Muller had complained bitterly that all the Gestapo branches had reported in the same strain, that their man had attempted to escape after being allowed out of the car to relieve himself. It was a dubious criticism, since there was some evidence, although all the incriminating teleprints from Berlin had been destroyed, that this is exactly what the RSHA had recommended in many cases—that the crime should be committed *während einer Pinkelpause*. Herberg remembered that there had been other Gestapo officers in the ante-room on the same errand, and one of these had been Kriminalsekretär Heinrich Hilker of the Strasbourg Gestapo.

Strasbourg therefore became a focal point of investigation. Several former Gestapo staff were found and interviewed. Hilker's photograph and dossier-card became available. His wife was visited, and said she did not know where he was, but was thought to be lying. A censorship on her mail was co-operatively imposed by the American Counter-Intelligence people in Karlsruhe. Flight Lieutenant Harrison searched the records of the Strasbourg crematorium without result. Then he discovered the whereabouts of the Strasbourg Gestapo's chief executioner. This man, Obersturmführer Julius Gehrum, was held in a French camp for charges relating to twenty murders. Gehrum told Harrison that he was indeed the executioner for the Strasbourg Gestapo. If orders had been issued for the shooting of any person in Strasbourg they would have come to him. He had no knowledge of the shooting of a recaptured prisoner of war of Hayter's description, and therefore he sincerely believed it had not occurred in Strasbourg. He added that since he was already being held for so many murders, all of which he had confessed to, another one would not have made any difference. 'If I had done this one', he said, 'I'd be very happy to give you a full confession. But I can't tell a lie.'

This interview damped down belief in Hilker's involvement, but he was still sought. Many people knew Hilker, and some had last seen him in Heidelberg in February 1945, wounded in the left shoulder. Later he had been seen by others, after the capitulation, staying with a family in Karlsruhe, still suffering from his shoulder wound, and resting before setting out to find his wife.

At the end of April the Judge Advocate General's office in London came into possession of a detailed report on the arrest of Hayter, which again swung the search strongly into Strasbourg. The document had been found, just after the liberation, by a French lieutenant who had been searching the archives of the gendarmerie at Zillisheim, but it had taken nearly two years to reach London. It gave a full report saying that Flying Officer Anthony Hayter had been stopped by three Home Guards, who were named, on the road between Mulhausen and Altkirch. His papers were checked. It was noticed that he was a foreigner. His papers said that he was a Dane. The Home Guards had orders to take in every foreigner to the Zillisheim detachment headquarters. A sergeant there thought Hayter's pass was false, because of the differing colours of several of the office stamps, which were supposed to have been put on in Leipzig, but on one of the stamps the name of the city was spelt Leipsich. Hayter was challenged, and then admitted his identity. He was arrested and taken to Mulhausen. The French had now forwarded this information to ascertain if Hayter was still alive so that they could get from him more precise information on what had happened after his arrest.

The full lists of the Strasbourg Gestapo were then studied. The head of the office, Dr Alfred Schimmel, had been interviewed already by Flight Lieutenant Harrison, who had been informed by Schimmel that he had been posted away from Strasbourg in May 1943. Flight Sergeant Daniel, who had now got hold of Schimmel's personal file, went to Dachau, where he was in American custody, and after reinterrogation gained the admission that Schimmel had been in Strasbourg until May 1944, when he was sent to Oslo. Schimmel said that the reason why he had lied before, and made false entries in his papers to support his story, was that he was afraid of being accused of Gestapo mass shootings of paratroopers, which he had had nothing to do with.

Schimmel's new statement was that, while he was in charge o the Strasbourg Gestapo, he had been called to Berlin in March 1944. On his return he was told that Hilker had gone away to transfer to Breslau a man who had been caught on the frontier during the *Grossfahndung*. When Hilker returned Schimmel was dissatisfied with the answers to his questions, and began to suspect that Hilker had shot the man he was supposed to escort. This suspicion was finally confirmed when he consulted an SS Obersturmbannführer who was his superior in the military area. Hilker then said that the prisoner had been shot whilst trying to escape. Schimmel strongly denied to Daniel that he had had anything to do with it, or that he knew anything about a teleprint order from Berlin giving instructions for this shooting. As for Hilker's whereabouts now, he knew that he had false identity papers making him seven years younger and describing his trade as furniture worker.

More of the SIB team were thrown into the Strasbourg area. Warrant Officer Williams finally got a statement from a former Gestapo official, Rudolf Peters, testifying that Hayter had been taken to Strasbourg and interrogated by Schimmel and a Kriminalkommissar called Dissner and by Peters himself. He said that Hayter had given away no information, and had later been taken away in a closed car by Dissner and Hilker.

Harrison and Williams made a renewed search in crematoria in Strasbourg and Baden-Baden but found nothing. They went to the concentration camp at Natzweiler, but all records had been destroyed.

The time had come for a strong reinterrogation of Dr Alfred Schimmel. He was handed over by the Americans, and at last he extended his story. He was a 41-year-old, short, balding lawyer whose mild appearance was enhanced by his large spectacles.

He said he came back to Strasbourg on 6th April 1944 and heard about the recapture of a prisoner. He told his men to take Hayter away and hand him over to the Wehrmacht. But he was told by his opposite number in the Kripo that he had already received teleprint instructions from Nebe to hand Hayter over to the Gestapo. Schimmel said he was uneasy. He took Hayter into his room, talked to him over a cigarette, and in his presence tried to ring his superior, Dr Isselhorst, for instructions. Isselhorst was out to lunch, so Schimmel went too. When he returned he found a teleprint order from Müller ordering the shooting.

Schimmel said he put through an urgent telephone call to Müller.

'Müller said he had made himself perfectly clear, and there was nothing to be doubtful about. I gave him to understand that one must have the most serious qualms about carrying out this order because of the far-reaching consequences.

'Müller said, "Schimmel, I know you as a man whose attitude is all too soft. Either you carry out this order or you can expect to be arrested and shot for refusing to carry out an order and for betraying a State secret." I consulted Dr Isselhorst, although my instructions forbade me to, and I mentioned the possibility of reprisals. Isselhorst suggested I should do it on the way to Natzweiler, and have the body cremated there. He asked me who would be in charge. I said, "Perhaps Dissner and Hilker". He said, "Good. I agree." '

Schimmel told Squadron Leader McKenna that he thought he might get out of it by taking Hayter personally to the Swiss border and letting him wander away. 'Then I should have escaped into Switzerland myself', he said. 'But I was afraid of the consequences on my family.

'There was a further realization,' he told McKenna, 'and that was the worst of all. Müller's order was to shoot the man on the following day. That was Good Friday, the holiest day of the year. I could not have this man killed on Good Friday. I could not go to church knowing that that was happening.'

'How did you resolve that?' asked McKenna.

'I had him shot on Maundy Thursday. I called Dissner and Hilker and said they had to do the job fast that night.'

Dissner returned to Schimmel with his report on the morrow. He said that he and Hilker had stopped the car near Natzweiler camp, at a turning in a wood about a kilometre away. Dissner took the prisoner on to the roadside to relieve himself. He kept Hayter in conversation, while Hilker came up behind and shot him in the temple. Death was instantaneous, and they took the body to the concentration camp and asked for the urn to be returned.

Hilker evaded the attention of the Royal Air Force and the German police until 1966. He was charged with the murder of Flying Officer Hayter, and acquitted just in time for Christmas. Dissner was arrested by the RAF in Hamburg on 11th May 1948 under a false name. He was taken to the holding prison in Minden. Before he could be interrogated he tore a strip from his blanket, twisted it, and hanged himself in his cell in the dawn.

Flying Officer Anthony Hayter, killed near Natzweiler on 6 April 1944.

Wing Commander Bowes was able to complete the main entries in his account rendered of the Stalag Luft III murderers when Dr Alfred Schimmel was handed over by the Americans in Dachau and placed in RAF custody in May 1947. There were a number of adjustments to make through the following years, and the record finally read:

Alfred Schimmel in British custody 1.5.1947, executed 27.2.1948.
Max Dissner suicide 11.5.1948.
Heinrich Hilker: WANTED. *Traced and charged by the West German Prosecutor, and case dismissed 23.12.1966; died 11.4.1968.*
Erich Isselhorst executed on other charges 1947.

On 7th and 10th June 1947 eighteen prisoners were flown from London to Buckeburg to stand trial in Hamburg. Highest-priority security was ordered, as the prisoners were considered both dangerous and suicidal. A legal ruling was given that as the prisoners were charged with war crimes they were not subject to the Geneva Convention, and therefore could be tied or manacled to their seats. Each prisoner was tied into his seat with rope, and his escort was provided with a knife to cut the rope for quick release in the case of accident.

12 It was not an atmosphere for heroes to live in

There were two trials in the case of the Stalag Luft III murders. Reinhold Bruchardt, of the Danzig Gestapo, having refused to confess after being beaten up in the Minden jail, hung out resolutely and almost endured. For there was no corroborative evidence available for a year after his arrest. Then the SIB, who had been ruthlessly searching for them, picked up two drivers who had worked for the Danzig Gestapo. One of them was Dr Venediger's chauffeur, and both of them had witnessed the shootings and were clear that Bruchardt had taken part. Standing with Bruchardt in the second trial, which lasted twenty days from 11th October to 6th November 1948, were Erwin Wieczorek, Scharpwinkel's deputy at Breslau, who, once named by Scharpwinkel, had eventually been found in an American camp, and Max Richard Hänsel, on whom the Judge Advocate General thought there was insufficient evidence in 1947.

The first trial began on 1st July 1947 and lasted fifty full days. It was held before No. 1 War Crimes Court in the Curio Haus, Hamburg. There were eighteen defendants. Space had been left for Scharpwinkel, but the Russians said he was unfit to travel.

Two main charges were laid against all the accused:

1. Committing a war crime in that you at divers places in Germany and German-occupied territory between 25th March 1944 and 13th April 1944 were concerned together and with SS Gruppenführer Müller and SS Gruppenführer Nebe and other persons known and unknown in the killing in violations of the laws and usages of war of prisoners of war who had escaped from Stalag Luft III.

2. Committing a war crime in that you in divers places in Germany and German-occupied territory between 25th March 1944 and 13th April 1944 aided and abetted SS Gruppenführer Müller and SS Gruppenführer Nebe and each other and other persons known and unknown in carrying out orders which were

contrary to the laws and usages of war—namely, orders to kill prisoners of war who had escaped from Stalag Luft III.

These were the only charges against Max Wielen. The others were charges of individual murder. The third charge (against Emil Schulz and Walter Breithaupt) was:

> Committing a war crime in that you between Homburg and Kaiserslautern, Germany, on or about 29th March 1944, when members of the Saarbrücken Gestapo, in violation of the laws and usages of war were concerned in the killing of Squadron Leader R. J. Bushell and Pilot Officer B. M. W. Scheidhauer, both of the Royal Air Force, prisoners of war.

Similar charges were brought against Alfred Schimmel for the killing of Flight Lieutenant A. R. H. Hayter;

Josef Gmeiner, Walter Herberg, Otto Preiss and Heinrich Boschert for the killing of Flying Officer D. H. Cochran;

Emil Weil, Eduard Geith and Johann Schneider for the killing of Lieutenant J. R. Stevens and Lieutenant J. S. Gouws;

Johannes Post, Hans Kähler and Artur Denkmann for the killing of Squadron Leader J. Catanach DFC, Pilot Officer H. Espelid, Flight Lieutenant A. G. Christensen, and Pilot Officer N. Fuglesang;

Oskar Schmidt, Walter Jacobs and Wilhelm Struve for the killing of Pilot Officer H. Espelid, Flight Lieutenant A. G. Christensen and Pilot Officer N. Fuglesang; and

Erich Zacharias for the killing of Flying Officer G. A. Kidder and Squadron Leader T. G. Kirby-Green.

All the accused pleaded Not Guilty to all charges.

It was a hard-fought trial, although there were statements admitting implication from every defendant, and their evidence did not confute this later. There was great concern with the issues of obedience to orders, of behaviour to be construed as mitigation of action, and of claims that statements had been extorted by brutal interrogation.

Schimmel called two priests, one the secretary of the Archbishop in Munich, to say that he had softened the traditional attitude of the Gestapo towards the Church. 'I would even go so far as to say that Schimmel was prepared to infringe the laws if he did not think they were just.' When the witness had been arrested, but later released, 'Schimmel congratulated me almost with tears in his eyes'.

The Judge Advocate, Mr C. L. Stirling, CBE, KC, observed that the charge against Schimmel was that he arranged for a British officer to be very brutally murdered, and that the tears in his eyes were irrelevant. 'This witness can only say that this defendant was a kind and friendly man with a disposition not to obey his superiors but help the Church. I would have considered it was the most dangerous type of evidence to call.'

The Prosecutor, Colonel R. C. Halse, OBE, asked the witness:

'Monseigneur, what your evidence amounts to is that there were many occasions when Schimmel was prepared to disobey orders from superiors in order to help the Church, is that right?'

Monseigneur Thelhaber: 'That is so.'

The Judge Advocate asked Schimmel: 'Why did you not carry out this killing yourself? That would have made one less person in the secret, would it not?'

Schimmel: 'No, I could not do this.'

Judge Advocate: 'What, you could not kill a man, do you mean?'

Schimmel: 'Yes, that is what I mean.'

Judge Advocate: 'And you salved your conscience by making another man do it, is that it?'

Schimmel: 'The execution of this order was just as difficult for me as passing on the order to another official.'

Judge Advocate: 'Let us be sensible, Schimmel, it is no use talking nonsense. I will start again. Why did you not carry out this order yourself?'

Schimmel: 'I could not have done it personally myself.'

Judge Advocate: 'And therefore you passed it on to somebody else?'

Schimmel: 'I had to give the order to someone.'

In the main there was little rough-riding of witnesses. Occasionally a bubble or two was pricked. Boschert admitted that he and Gmeiner were also involved in charges of sending six Englishwomen to concentration camps to be killed. Colonel Halse suggested that Boschert had probably been given the duty as Gmeiner's adjutant because he was the biggest thug. 'You agree that the Gestapo were a lot of thugs, do you not?'

Boschert: 'I never regarded myself as one of them.'

Colonel Halse: 'How long do you have to be in the Gestapo before you become one of them? You were there since 1938.'

Boschert: 'I was a member of the Gestapo from the first day I joined it.'

Colonel Halse: 'And you considered yourself a member of the Gestapo, and you strutted round Karlsruhe in the Gestapo uniform, and you were proud of your uniform at that time, were you not?'

Boschert: 'Yes.'

Colonel Halse: 'It is only when you lose the war that you become a timid little mouse, running away when you hear a shot fired, and driving away.'

But there was gentleness towards a man like Denkmann, the driver at Kiel, who tried to go into the witness box to make an unsworn statement, clearly influenced by sickness—he had a tumour on the gall-bladder—and by mental strain and confusion. The Judge Advocate told him:

'You have only to sit in the witness box and listen to the questions. We will all treat you very kindly, and the Prosecutor will ask you questions in the most proper way so that you will not in any way have your nerves worried. So just keep calm. We will treat you very specially, because we see that you are a sick man. Is that clear?'

Great play was made from time to time of the intimidating fear felt by the defendants that their wives and children would be shot if they refused to obey an order. The Judge Advocate asked a police witness: 'Are you prepared to swear that you have ever heard of any wife being killed or any child?'

'No, I do not know,' was the answer. 'I know only about arrests.'

Gmeiner said, 'To refuse to obey the order and to inform Berlin that the unit was not prepared to carry out the order would have had the result of immediate arrest and a subsequent condemnation by an SS and police court.'

Jacobs said, 'At the very worst I undertook a killing, not a murder, by order of the Leader of the State. What happened was against my wishes, but I was in no position to alter the situation in any way. If I am told that, should I disobey the order, I should have to prepare to face my death and my family would also be held responsible, I do not think that any man would have refused to carry out the order under those conditions.'

Post, who had proudly detailed all his Party decorations (after a modest query, 'Do you want to know all of them or just one or two?'), expanded on the legal subtleties: 'My attitude is quite clear. If I receive an order as I received it then—that is, if I had been told that by order of the Führer four British prisoners are to be shot—this would be a violation of international law, but for the officer who carried it out it would be an entirely legal action. I will prove this. We live [*sic*] in an authoritarian state headed by a Leader, and there can be no doubt that an order given by an authoritarian Head of State is law.'

Dr Meyer Labastille, the principal counsel for the defence, said in his general speech of mitigation:

'It was not an atmosphere for heroes to live in.'

Yet there had been one outstanding contradiction to this theme from an old German. Colonel von Lindeiner-Wildau, the 66-year-old commandant of Stalag Luft III, a veteran of the first war and bearing many wounds, was called as a witness for the defence. A defence counsel drew from him that he had warned the Senior British Officer at Sagan to discourage escapes. He was asked if he had reason to believe that officers who escaped would be in danger. He replied that he had no direct information but during previous months he had become uneasy about their possible fate, and had thought it right to give this warning to the Senior British Officer. The defence counsel reminded him that, as a German officer, he had given an oath of unquestioning obedience to Hitler.

'In view of this, what would you have done if you had received the order to shoot these officers yourself?'

The colonel looked down from the witness stand at the defence counsel as if he were something unclean.

'I should have put a bullet through my head', he said.

The only man who refused to put in any plea in mitigation was Johannes Post. He was tempted by his Counsel to recount a good deed said to have been done in his life, which it had been thought he would advance. He declined.

'You have heard', said his Counsel, 'and you have also seen several affidavits which almost every accused person has put into this court. Why did you refuse to give me permission that I should do the same for you?'

'I do not wish to do it, and I do not understand it at all.'

'Why do you not wish to do it?'

'Because I could not have been a National Socialist for many years, and suddenly put in affidavits from Communists or Jews or Freethinkers.'

The verdict of the court was that Max Wielen, but not the others, was guilty of the first two charges of conspiracy and aid to Müller and Nebe. He was sentenced to life imprisonment.

All the others were found guilty of the separate charges against them. Schulz, Schimmel, Gmeiner, Herberg, Preiss, Boschert, Weil, Geith, Schneider, Post, Kähler, Schmidt, Jacobs and Zacharias were sentenced to suffer death by being hanged. Breithaupt was sentenced to imprisonment for life. Denkmann and Struve were sentenced to imprisonment for ten years. On review, Boschert's sentence was varied to life imprisonment. The rest of those sentenced to death were hanged in Hameln Gaol on 27th February 1948.

In the second trial, in November 1948, Hänsel was found not guilty. Wieczorek was found guilty and sentenced to death, but the verdict was quashed on review. Bruchardt was found guilty and sentenced to death: but the British Government had carried through Parliament the suspension of the death sentence for an experimental period, and the policy was also applied in Germany. Bruchardt's sentence was varied to life imprisonment. His stubborn silence over nearly two years had saved his life. His statement that the murders had been committed by a Ukrainian execution squad was finally refuted when Reimer and Bontenbroich, driver-mechanics to Venediger and Bruchardt, swore to having driven them to Gross Trampken, a wood near Danzig, where the four officers were shot.

The Special Investigation Unit had not closed the file on Stalag Luft III.

Squadron Leader McKenna had distributed thousands of photosheets of thirty-eight men still on his wanted list to the British, American and French occupation zones and to the German Civil Police. It was not suggested that all the men sought were guilty, but that they could provide helpful information. Many were traced, interviewed and released.

On 1st January 1948 McKenna went back to the Blackpool Borough Police, and on the same day he was awarded the OBE in the New Year Honours. Wing Commander Bowes, who stayed on as a regular officer, also received the OBE in the Birthday Honours List. Sergeant Stuart Greet was awarded the MBE.

On 3rd February 1948 Hans Ziegler, once Chief of the Zlín Gestapo, who had been arrested and brought to the London Cage, committed suicide there by cutting his throat.

In May 1948 Absalon was reported to have died in a Russian prison camp. Scharpwinkel had been reported to have died in a Russian prison on 17th October 1947.

On 11th May 1948 Dissner was arrested and committed suicide. Weyland of Reichenberg was located inside the Russian zone, and stayed there secure. Asal, sought as a supposed member of the Danzig murder squad of Dr Venediger, was located in the French zone, subsequently handed over, and released after interrogation. Weissman of Reichenberg was also located in the French zone, but was not transferred.

In July 1948 Sergeant Heron of the SIB arrested two Danzig drivers, Reimer and Bontenbroich, just in time to secure a conviction against Bruchardt.

In August and September Heron arrested four men suspected to have been in Scharpwinkel's Breslau murder gang.

In October 1948 a censorship of the mail addressed to the family of Dr Venediger was intensified.

On 17th November 1948 Wing Commander Bowes wrote to the Provost Marshal:

> It has been announced by the Cabinet that no further trials of war criminals will take place. In the particular case of the Stalag Luft III crime it would be a grave miscarriage of justice to allow these men to go free merely because, so far, they have been able to escape arrest whilst men less guilty have been executed. It is suggested that authority be sought to enable Judge Advocate General War Crimes to prosecute any of these prisoners in the event of their being arrested at some future date.

In March 1950 Wing Commander Bowes brought the attention of the Provost Marshal to the fact that Oskar Schäfer, former Chief of the Gestapo at Munich, had been acquitted by a German court on charges of the killing of East European slave labourers, but had not been charged with the murders of Lieutenants Gouws and Stevens of the South African Air Force. The Special Investigation Branch of the Royal Air Force traced the freed man to the British zone, and Bowes applied fresh pressure for further charges, which were not levelled. The matter was not abandoned, even by the German Prosecutor, but after eighteen years, on 11th December 1968, the Munich Court finally threw out the case, although there had been clear evidence at the original trial that Schäfer had not only ordered and planned the murders of Lieutenants Gouws and

Stevens but had ordered the erasure of the records. The men who gave this evidence originally had, of course, long been hanged.

In September 1954 Dr Günther Venediger, who had slipped out of the Russian zone in 1952, was acquitted before a German court on charges of being concerned with the murder of the four Royal Air Force officers at Danzig. Bowes launched a cascade of indignant letters, and, not necessarily because of this, the prosecution appealed. The case was fought through the courts until 17th December 1957, when Dr Venediger was confirmed in a sentence of two years' imprisonment, the lenient punishment being judicially ascribed to the fact that he had not recognized the 'low level' of the superior orders he claimed to have been obeying.

In December 1966 Heinrich Hilker, who had been charged with firing the actual bullet which killed Tony Hayter, on the orders of Schimmel (hanged by Pierrepoint) and Dissner (hanged by himself), was acquitted. He died in 1968.

In January 1967 Fritz Schmidt, the former Gestapo chief of Kiel, was tried before a German court for the murder of the four RAF officers caught at Flensburg. He pleaded superior orders, and delayed the outcome of his trial. In May 1968 he was sentenced to two years' imprisonment.

The members of the Special Investigation Branch team which had carried through the Stalag Luft III inquiry were growing old, and some of them were dying. They had been responsible for some hundred thousand interrogations and the physical arrest of twenty-six persons who were charged with murder, or would have been charged if they had not committed suicide. They established the names of all the murderers of all the fifty Allied officers, and the guilt of those German military leaders who were condemned at Nuremberg by a court which, for the first time in history, was declared competent to try and to punish transgressions of international law. Of the seventy-two men denounced by the Royal Air Force Special Investigation Branch as war criminals deserving indictment for killing and conspiracy to kill, contrary to the laws and usages of war,

21 were executed (some for crimes other than the Sagan murders);
17 were imprisoned;
11 committed suicide;
7 were untraced, of whom 4 were presumed killed;
6 were killed in wartime;
5 were arrested, but for political reasons a charge was not proceeded with;
1 was arrested, not prosecuted, but used as a material witness;
3 were acquitted, or the sentence quashed on review;
1 remained in successful refuge in eastern Germany.

But the resounding achievement of the Special Investigation

Branch team was the moral victory. They solved a crime which was in fact thirteen crimes. They enforced international law, which had been derided, and by that example they issue today a warning to present law-breakers that international law may yet be enforced tomorrow. They kept a politician's promise and re-established a principle which many had considered expendable. In view of that notable national and international consummation, which was later undeservedly ignored in the histories, this author cannot accept the claim made in a letter to him by the Earl of Avon—who originally pledged 'exemplary justice'—that publication of this book so long after the events it describes was undesirable since it would tend to reopen old wounds.

The Stalag Luft III case was the only major war crime ever entrusted to a separate arm of the Service, undiluted with 'specialists' from other Services. The Special Investigation Branch men who completed the case were a very small, very independent, and remarkably dedicated team. Their dedication showed then, and shines through now. Thirty years later Flight Lieutenant Courtney said:

'They left it to us. They picked us, if I may say so humbly, as chaps who would do our best, not out of sinister revenge, but out of a desire to clear it up and with some sense of the absolute in justice. I'm an older man now, and I like to think that that was my ambition.'

Following the formal constitution of a separate Provost Branch of the Royal Air Force on 1st July 1950, King George VI approved the above badge and motto of the Provost Branch and the Royal Air Force Police. The griffin is the heraldic symbol of guardianship. The motto declares 'Let Justice Be Done'.

Appendix I
The victims

Flying Officer Henry J. Birkland, Royal Canadian Air Force, born at Winnipeg 16th August 1917. Prisoner of war 6th November 1941. Was involved in an unsuccessful mass escape from Sagan in June 1943. A strenuous worker in the tunnel 'Harry'. Led a party of walkers, 'the hard-arsers', in the March 1944 escape. Recaptured in the Sagan area, transferred to Görlitz. Last seen alive 31st March 1944. Cremated at Liegnitz.

Flight Lieutenant E. Gordon Brettell, Royal Air Force, born at Chertsey 19th March 1915. Prisoner of war 26th September 1942. Escaped unsuccessfully in 1943. Became an expert forger. Recaptured at Schneidemühl and handed over to the Danzig Gestapo. Died 29th March 1944. Cremated at Danzig.

Flight Lieutenant Lester J. Bull, Royal Air Force, born at Godalming 7th November 1916. Prisoner of war 5th November 1941. He broke through the last yards of the tunnel on 24th March 1944 and controlled the exit. Recaptured in the Reichenberg area. Died 29th March 1944. Cremated at Brüx.

Squadron Leader Roger J. Bushell, Royal Air Force, born in the Transvaal 30th August 1910. Prisoner of war 23rd May 1940. The veteran principal organizer of the escape. Recaptured at Saarbrücken. Died 29th March 1944. Cremated at Saarbrücken.

Flight Lieutenant Michael J. Casey, Royal Air Force, born at Allahabad 19th February 1918. Was in charge of filing and concealing forged documents. Prisoner of war 16th October 1939. Recaptured in the Görlitz area. Died 31st March 1944. Cremated at Görlitz.

Squadron Leader James Catanach, DFC, Royal Australian Air Force, born at Melbourne 28th November 1921. Prisoner of war 5th September 1942. Recaptured at Flensburg. Died 29th March 1944. Cremated at Kiel.

Flying Officer Arnold G. Christensen, Royal New Zealand Air Force, born 8th April 1922. Prisoner of war 20th August 1942. Intelligence expert on Denmark. Recaptured at Flensburg. Died 29th March 1944. Cremated at Kiel.

Flying Officer Dennis H. Cochran, Royal Air Force, born at Clapton 13th August 1921. Prisoner of war 9th November 1942. Made a previous escape. Recaptured at Lörrach. Died 31st March 1944. Cremated at Natzweiler.

Squadron Leader Ian E. K. P. Cross, Royal Air Force, born Hampshire 4th April 1918. Prisoner of war 12 February 1942. Had escaped previously. Recaptured Görlitz area. Died 31st March 1944. Cremated at Görlitz.

Lieutenant Hallada Espelid, Royal Norwegian Air Force, born Bergen 6th October 1920. Prisoner of war 27th August 1942. Recaptured at Flensburg. Died 29th March 1944. Cremated at Kiel.

Flight Lieutenant Brian H. Evans, Royal Air Force, born in Devon 14th February 1920. Recaptured at Halbau. Last seen alive 31st March 1944. Cremated at Liegnitz.

Lieutenant Nils Fuglesang, Royal Norwegian Air Force, prisoner of war 2nd May 1943. Recaptured at Flensburg. Died 29th March 1944. Cremated at Kiel.

Lieutenant Johannes S. Gouws, South African Air Force, born Bultfontein 13th August 1919. Prisoner of war 9th April 1942. Recaptured at Lindau. Died 29th March 1944. Cremated at Munich.

Flight Lieutenant William J. Grisman, Royal Air Force, born at Hereford 30th August 1914. Recaptured in Görlitz area. Last seen alive 6th April 1944. Cremated at Breslau.

Flight Lieutenant Alastair D. M. Gunn, Royal Air Force, born at Auchterarder 27th September 1919. Prisoner of war 5th March 1942. Recaptured in Görlitz area. Last seen alive 6 April 1944. Cremated at Breslau.

Flight Lieutenant Albert H. Hake, Royal Australian Air Force, born at Sydney 30th June 1916. Prisoner of war 4th April 1942. Compass-maker and forger. Recaptured Görlitz area. Died 31st March 1944. Cremated at Görlitz.

Flight Lieutenant Charles P. Hall, Royal Air Force, born at Birmingham 25th July 1918. Prisoner of war 28th December 1941. Ran the passport photography studio. Recaptured Sagan area. Died 30th March 1944. Cremated at Liegnitz.

Flight Lieutenant Anthony R. H. Hayter, Royal Air Force, born at Farnborough 20th May 1920. Prisoner of war 24th April 1942. Recaptured near Mulhouse. Died 6th April 1944. Cremated at Natzweiler.

Flight Lieutenant Edgar S. Humphreys, Royal Air Force, born at Exmouth 5th December 1914. Prisoner of war 20th December 1940. Recaptured Sagan area. Last seen alive 31st March 1944. Cremated at Liegnitz.

Flying Officer Gordon A. Kidder, Royal Canadian Air Force, born at Ontario 9th December 1914. Prisoner of war 13th October 1942. Recaptured near Zlín. Died 29th March 1944. Cremated at Mährisch Ostrau.

Flight Lieutenant Reginald V. Kierath, Royal Australian Air Force, born at Narrowmine 20th February 1915. Prisoner of war 23rd April 1943. Recaptured in Reichenberg area. Died 29th March 1944. Cremated at Brüx.

Flight Lieutenant Antoni Kiewnarski, Royal Air Force, Polish nationality, born at Moscow 26th January 1899. Prisoner of war 28th August 1942. Recaptured at Hirschberg. Died 31st March 1944. Place of cremation unknown.

Squadron Leader Thomas G. Kirby-Green, Royal Air Force, born in Nyasaland 28th February 1918. Prisoner of war 16th October 1941. In Command 'Duty Pilot' scheme and security. Former C.O. Czech Training Squadron. Recaptured near Zlín. Died 29th March 1944. Cremated at Mährisch Ostrau.

Flying Officer A. Wlodzimierz Kolanowski, Royal Air Force, Polish nationality, born 11th August 1913. Prisoner of war 8th November 1941. Recaptured Sagan area. Last seen alive 31st March 1944. Cremated at Liegnitz.

Flying Officer Stanislaw Z. Krol, Royal Air Force, Polish nationality, born Krakau (Cracow) 22nd March 1916. Had made a previous escape. Recaptured at Oels. Last seen alive 12th April 1944. Cremated at Breslau.

Flight Lieutenant Patrick W. Langford, Royal Canadian Air Force. Born Edmonton, Alberta, 4th November 1919. Prisoner of war 29th July 1942. In charge of trapdoor entrance to tunnel. Recaptured Görlitz area. Last seen alive 31st March 1944. Cremated at Liegnitz.

Flight Lieutenant Thomas B. Leigh, Royal Air Force, born at Sydney, Australia 11th February 1919. Prisoner of war 6th August 1941. Recaptured in Görlitz area. Died 31st March 1944. Cremated at Görlitz.

Flight Lieutenant James L. R. Long, Royal Air Force, born at Bournemouth 21st February 1915. Prisoner of war 28th March 1941. Recaptured in Sagan area. Last seen alive 12th April 1944. Cremated at Breslau.

Flight Lieutenant Romas Marcinkus, Royal Air Force, Lithuanian nationality, born Georgenburg 22nd July 1910. Recaptured at Schneidemühl. Died 29th March 1944. Cremated at Danzig.

Lieutenant Clement A. N. McGarr, South African Air Force, born at Johannesburg 24th November 1917. Prisoner of war 6th October 1941. Led one shift of tunnellers. Recaptured in Sagan area. Last seen alive 6th April 1944. Cremated at Breslau.

Flight Lieutenant George E. McGill, Royal Canadian Air Force, born at Toronto 14th April 1918. Prisoner of war 10th January 1942. Led the other shift of tunnellers. Recaptured in Sagan area. Last seen alive 31st March 1944. Cremated at Liegnitz.

Flight Lieutenant Harold J. Milford, Royal Air Force, born at London 16th August 1914. Prisoner of war 22nd September 1942. Recaptured in Sagan area. Last seen alive 6th April 1944. Cremated at Breslau.

Flying Officer Jerzy T. Mondschein, Royal Air Force, Polish nationality. born Warsaw 18th March 1909. Prisoner of war 8th November 1941. Recaptured Reichenberg area at head of a party of train-travellers. Died 29th March 1944. Cremated at Brüx.

Flying Officer Kazimierz Pawluk, Royal Air Force, Polish nationality, born at Warsaw 1st July 1906. Prisoner of war 28th March 1940. Recaptured at Hirschberg. Last seen alive 31st March. Place of cremation not known.

Flight Lieutenant Henri A. Picard, Croix de Guerre, Royal Air Force, Belgian nationality, born at Brussels 17th April 1916. Prisoner of war 2nd September 1942. Recaptured at Schneidemühl. Died 29th March 1944. Cremated at Danzig.

Flying Officer John (Porokoru Patapu) Pohe, Royal New Zealand Air Force, born at Wanganui 10th December 1914. Prisoner of war 24th September 1943. Recaptured Görlitz area. Died 31st March 1944. Cremated at Görlitz.

Lieutenant Bernard W. M. Scheidhauer, Free French Air Force, born at Landau 28th August 1921. Prisoner of war 18th November 1942. Recaptured at Saarbrücken. Died 29th March 1944. Cremated at Saarbrücken.

Pilot Officer Sotiris Skanzikas, Royal Hellenic Air Force, born 6th August 1921. Prisoner of war 23rd July 1943. Recaptured at Hirschberg. Died 30th March 1944. Place of cremation not known.

Lieutenant Rupert J. Stevens, South African Air Force,

born at London 21st February 1919. Prisoner of war 14th November 1941. Recaptured at Rosenheim. Died 29th March 1944. Cremated at Munich.

Flying Officer Robert C. Stewart, Royal Air Force, born at London 7th July 1911. Prisoner of war 27th April 1943. Recaptured in Sagan area. Last seen alive 31st March 1944. Cremated at Liegnitz.

Flying Officer John G. Stower, Royal Air Force, born in Argentina 15th September 1916. Prisoner of war 16th November 1942. Was in previous mass escape from Sagan. Recaptured in Reichenberg area. Died 31st March 1944. Place of cremation not known.

Flying Officer Denys O. Street, Royal Air Force, born at London 1st April 1922. Prisoner of war 30th March 1943. Recaptured in Sagan area. Last seen alive 6th April 1944. Cremated at Breslau.

Flight Lieutenant Cyril D. Swain, Royal Air Force, born in Shropshire 15th December 1911. Prisoner of war 29th November 1940. Recaptured Görlitz area. Last seen alive 31st March 1944. Cremated at Liegnitz.

Flying Officer Pawel Tobolski, Royal Air Force, Polish nationality, born 21st March 1906. Prisoner of war 26th June 1942. Recaptured at Stettin. Last seen alive 2nd April 1944. Cremated at Breslau.

Flight Lieutenant Ernst Valenta, Royal Air Force, Czechoslovak nationality, born 25th October 1912. Prisoner of war 6th February 1941. Recaptured Görlitz area. Last seen alive 31st March 1944. Cremated at Liegnitz.

Flight Lieutenant Gilbert W. Walenn, Royal Air Force, born at London 24th February 1916. Prisoner of war 11th September 1941. Headed the forgery department. Recaptured at Schneidemühl. Died 29th March 1944. Cremated at Danzig.

Flight Lieutenant James C. Wernham, Royal Canadian Air Force, born at Gourock, Scotland, 15th January 1917.

Prisoner of war 9th June 1942. Recaptured at Hirschberg. Died 30th March 1944. Place of cremation not known.

Flight Lieutenant George W. Wiley, Royal Canadian Air Force, born 24th January 1922. Prisoner of war 12th March 1943. Recaptured in Görlitz area. Died 31st March 1944. Cremated at Görlitz.

Squadron Leader John E. A. Williams, Royal Australian Air Force, born 6th May 1919. Prisoner of war 31st October 1942. Head of carpentry department for the tunnel. Recaptrued in Reichenberg area. Died 29th March 1944. Cremated at Brüx.

Flight Lieutenant John F. Williams, Royal Air Force, born at London 7th July 1917. Prisoner of war 27th April 1942. Recaptured in Sagan area. Last seen alive 6th April 1944. Cremated at Breslau.

Appendix II

Statements of the British Secretary for Foreign Affairs

The Right Honourable Anthony Eden, MC, MP, to the House of Commons on 19th May 1944:

I deeply regret to have to tell the House that H.M. Government have received information from the Protecting Power that 47 officers of the RAF, Dominion and Allied air forces have been shot by the Germans after a mass escape from Stalag Luft III. According to the information given to a representative of the Protecting Power by the German authorities in the course of a routine visit to this camp on April 17, 76 officers had escaped from Stalag Luft III on March 22 [*actually 24*]. Of these, 15 had been recaptured, 14 were still at large, and 47 had been shot, some while resisting arrest and some in the course of a new attempt to escape after capture. H.M. Government are profoundly shocked at this news, and have urgently requested the Protecting Power to demand from the German Government a full and immediate report of the circumstances in which these men met their death, and an explanation of its failure to report the facts at once to the Protecting Power. The names of the officers shot (25 British, 6 Canadian, 3 Australian, 2 New Zealand, 3 South African, 4 Polish, 2 Norwegian, 1 French and 1 Greek) were furnished to the representative of the Protecting Power on the occasion of his visit, and the next-of-kin have been informed.

The Right Honourable Anthony Eden to the House of Commons on 23 June 1944:

. . . In my previous statement I told the House that 47 British and Allied air force officers had been shot as a result of an escape from this camp. . . . We have now received an official communication on the matter from the German Government. This states that 50 officers have been shot, and not 47, as previously stated. . . . The Note adds that during March there were a number of mass escapes of prisoners of war from camps throughout Germany, involving several thousand persons; that these escapes were systematically prepared, partly by the General Staffs of the Allies; and that they had both political and military objectives. This situation is stated to have endangered public security in Germany. In order to repress these undertakings, specially severe orders were given to pursue at all costs all prisoners who failed to halt upon challenge, or offered resistance, or made renewed attempts to escape after capture, and to make use of weapons until the prisoners had been deprived of all possibility of resistance or further escape. The Note states that all prisoners who escaped in March, except for about 100, the search for whom is continuing, were recaptured, but that weapons had to be used against some of the rest, including 50 from Stalag Luft III. It is also stated that the ashes of 28 of the 50 officers reported to have been shot have been taken to the camp. . . .

The German Note states that a final communication giving further details will be forthcoming, but H.M. Government feel obliged to declare at once that the explanation now put forward by the German Government is in fact the confession of an odious crime against the laws and conventions of war. I would draw the attention of the House to the following facts: (1) no orders have at any time been given to British prisoners of war to take part, in the event of their escape, in any subversive action as is alleged in the German Note; (2) all these officers knew the futility of attempting any resistance if they were recaptured; (3) as to the possibility of a renewed attempt to escape, we know now that owing to physical exhaustion and ill-treatment at Görlitz they were incapable of any such attempt; (4) whether these officers escaped in small or large numbers there can be no justification for the German authorities executing them. We know, however, that during the original escape the officers were in pairs, and that when last seen after leaving Görlitz prison they were in comparatively small numbers handcuffed and under heavy guard; (5) and most significant, there were no wounded, as would have been inevitable if the shootings had taken place during an attempt to resist capture; (6) the German statement omits all reference to Görlitz and contains no account of the circumstances which led to the death of any single officer; finally, the ashes of 28 of the escaped prisoners have now been returned to Stalag Luft III, although the Germans had previously refused to send back the bodies for burial. This is the only occasion known to H.M. Government or the Protecting Power upon which any prisoner of war who has died during captivity has been cremated.

It is abundantly clear that none of these officers met his death in the course of making his escape from Stalag Luft III or while resisting capture. The Gestapo's contention that the wearing of civilian clothes by an escaping prisoner of war deprives him of the protection of the Prisoners of War Convention is entirely without foundation in international law and practice. From these facts there is, in H.M. Government's view, only one possible conclusion. These prisoners of war were murdered at some undefined place or places after their removal from the Gestapo prison at Görlitz, at some date or dates unknown. H.M. Government must therefore record their solemn protest against these cold-blooded acts of butchery. They will never cease in their efforts to collect the evidence to identify all those responsible. They are firmly resolved that these foul criminals shall be tracked down to the last man, wherever they may take refuge. When the war is over they will be brought to exemplary justice.

Appendix III

The Royal Air Force Special Investigation Branch team

Wing Commander Wilfred Bowes, OBE
Squadron Leader Francis P. McKenna, OBE
Flight Lieutenant (later Squadron Leader) Arthur R. Lyon
Flight Lieutenant Stephen H. Courtney
Flight Lieutenant Harold E. Harrison
(Temporarily attached: Squadron Leader William O. Thomas
Flying Officer David H. Walker)

NCOs and Interpreters (rarely more than half a dozen at one time)

Warrant Officer H. J. Williams

Flight Sergeants
R. M. Daniel
W. J. Hicks
A. G. Maynard
R. Heron
James
Newnham
J. H. Mills

Sergeants
S. B. Greet, MBE
G. A. Townley
J. Brocksom
F. W. Fox
Butler
A. Harrison

Netherlands Military Liaison Mission

Flying Officer Jan Vreugdenheel

Flight Sergeant R. Rosenfeld

Sergeants
B. Tollenaar
C. M. Wannemakers
P. Linssen
A. Salomons
J. Van Giessen
J. P. Kneppers
R. Van Hes
W. Smit
Van der Heyden
A. J. Tessler
Richter
J. W. L. Venselaar
Van der Meer

Appendix IV
The guilty Chain of Command

Hitler

Keitel (Supreme Command)

Himmler (Security)

Göring (Luftwaffe and enemy Air Forces prisoners of war)

Kaltenbrunner (RSHA Berlin)

Nebe (Kripo, RSHA)

Wielen (Kripo, Breslau)

Müller (Gestapo, RSHA)

Scharpwinkel (Gestapo, Breslau)

Gestapo offices at:

Zlín (Ziegler)	**Reichenberg** (Baatz)	**Munich** (Schäfer)	**Saarbrücken** (Spann)
Kiel (Fritz Schmidt)	**Karlsruhe** (Gmeiner)	**Danzig** (Venediger)	**Strasbourg** (Schimmel)

Appendix V

The accused

(in order of seniority)

Including those denounced, but not formally charged because of their death or disappearance.

Hitler, Adolf suicide by shooting 30th April 1945

Göring, Hermann suicide by poison 16th October 1946.

Keitel, Wilhelm executed at Nuremberg 16th October 1946.

Himmler, Heinrich suicide by poison 23rd May 1945.

Kaltenbrunner, Ernst executed at Nuremberg, 16th October 1946.

Müller, Heinrich reported suicide in Berlin, date unknown.

Nebe, Artur executed by Gestapo February 1945.

Breslau

Scharpwinkel, Wilhelm died in prison in Russia 17th October 1947.

Wielen, Max sentenced to life imprisonment 3rd September 1947.

Absalon, Günther died in prison in Russia May 1948.

Lux killed at Breslau.

Wieczorek, Erwin sentenced to death 6th November 1948; sentence quashed on review.

Seetzen suicide by poison 28th September 1945.

Hänsel, Richard acquitted 6th November 1948.

Dankert untraced.

Kiske, Paul killed at Breslau.

Knappe killed at Breslau.

Kreuzer untraced, probably killed 1945.

Kuhnel killed at Breslau.

Lang untraced, probably killed 1945.

Läuffer suicide reported, not confirmed.

Pattke, Walter untraced, probably killed 1945.

Prosse died 1944.

Schmauser, Ernst captured by Soviet Army.

Hampel, Walter arrested 1st September 1948; charge not proceeded with according to Government's new war crimes policy.

Schröder, Robert not charged, used as a material witness.

Brno/Zlín

Römer, Hugo untraced.

Nölle, Wilhelm arrested 10th June 1948; charge not proceeded with.

Ziegler, Hans suicide by cutting his throat 3rd February 1948.

Schauschütz, Franz executed in Czechoslovakia 1947.

Koslowsky, Otto executed in Czechoslovakia 1947.

Knippelberg, Adolf prematurely released from Russian camp 1945.

Zacharias, Erich executed at Hameln 27th February 1948.

Kiowsky, Friedrich executed in Czechoslovakia 1947.

Schwartzer, Friedrich executed in Czechoslovakia 1947.

Reichenberg

Baatz, Bernhard prematurely released from Russian camp.

Weyland, Robert refuge in Russian zone.

Weissman, Robert Held by French authorities but not transferred.

Munich

Schäfer, Oswald charge thrown out 11th December 1968.

	Schermer, Martin suicide by hanging 25th April 1945.
	Schneider, Johann executed at Hameln 27th February 1948.
	Geith, Eduard executed at Hameln 27th February 1948.
	Weil, Emil executed at Hameln 27th February 1948.
Saarbrücken	**Spann, Leopold** killed in air raid on Linz 25th April 1945.
	Schulz, Emil executed at Hameln 27th February 1948.
	Breithaupt, Walter sentenced to life imprisonment 3rd September 1947.
Kiel	**Schmidt, Friedrich (Fritz)** sentenced to two years' imprisonment May 1968.
	Post, Johannes executed at Hameln 27th February 1948.
	Schmidt, Oskar executed at Hameln 27th February 1948.
	Kähler, Hans executed at Hameln 27th February 1948.
	Jacobs, Walter executed at Hameln 27th February 1948.
	Schmidt, Franz suicide by hanging 27th October 1946.
	Denkmann, Artur sentenced to ten years' imprisonment 3rd September 1947.
	Struve, Wilhelm sentenced to ten years' imprisonment 3rd September 1947.
Karlsruhe	**Gmeiner, Josef** executed at Hameln 27th February 1948.
	Preiss, Otto executed at Hameln 27th February 1948.
	Herberg, Walter executed at Hameln 27th February 1948.
	Boschert, Heinrich sentenced to death 3rd September 1947; commuted to life imprisonment on review.
	Ganninger, Otto suicide by haemorrhage 26th April 1946.
	Wochner, Magnus sentenced to ten years' imprisonment for atrocities at Natzweiler.

Danzig

Venediger, Günther sentenced to two years' imprisonment after four years of appeals 17th December 1957.

Bruchardt, Reinhold sentenced to death 6th November 1948; commuted to life imprisonment when Britain experimentally abandoned the death sentence.

Kilpe, Max arrested 27th August 1948: charge not proceeded with.

Sasse, Walter escaped from internment camp.

Voelz, Walter untraced, believed killed.

Wenzler, Herbert arrested 1948: charge not proceeded with.

Witt, Harry arrested September 1948: charge not proceeded with.

Hug, Julius untraced.

Strasbourg

Schimmel, Alfred executed at Hameln 27th February 1948.

Dissner, Max suicide by hanging 11th May 1948.

Hilker, Heinrich prematurely released from French camp: charged with the Strasbourg crime and the case was dismissed, 23rd December 1966: died 11th April 1968.

Isselhorst, Erich condemned to death and executed for other atrocities.

Appendix VI

Chronology of the inquiry

1944

February German High Command issued Stufe Römisch III Order: recaptured officer prisoners of war to be dealt with secretly by the Gestapo.
Brünner visited Sagan, acquiesced in the counter-escape buried microphones remaining inoperative.

24 Officers in Sagan were privately warned against mass escapes.

March 6 Müller signed Bullet Order (Aktion Kugel), Top Secret order codifying Gestapo action under Stufe Römisch III.

mid-March Colonel Lindeiner, Commandant at Sagan, imprecisely warned Senior British Officer of consequences of escape.

24/25 79 officers escaped from Sagan. The last three gave themselves up and diverted pursuit.

26 After an angry conference with Keitel, Göring and Himmler, Hitler said more than half the officers must be shot.

27 Himmler fixed the number of deaths at 50, and organized them through Kaltenbrunner and Müller.

28 Nebe began to select officers to be shot.

29 There died: Flight Lieutenant Brettell; Flight Lieutenant Bull; Squadron Leader Bushell; Squadron Leader Catanach; Flying

Officer Christensen; Lieutenant Espelid; Lieutenant Fuglesang; Lieutenant Gouws; Flying Officer Kidder; Flying Officer Kierath; Squadron Leader Kirby-Green; Flight Lieutenant Marcinkus; Flying Officer Mondschein; Flight Lieutenant Picard; Lieutenant Scheidhauer; Lieutenant Stevens; Flight Lieutenant Walenn; Squadron Leader Williams.

Flying Officer Pawluk was last seen alive.

30 There died: Flight Lieutenant Hall; Pilot Officer Skanzikas; Flight Lieutenant Wernham.

31 There died: Flight Lieutenant Casey; Flying Officer Cochran; Squadron Leader Cross; Flight Lieutenant Hake; Flight Lieutenant Kiewnarski; Flight Lieutenant Leigh; Flying Officer Pohe; Flying Officer Stower; Flight Lieutenant Wiley.

Flying Officer Birkland, Flight Lieutenant Evans, Flight Lieutenant Humphreys, Flight Lieutenant Kolanowski, Flight Lieutenant Langford, Flight Lieutenant McGill, Flying Officer Stewart, Flight Lieutenant Swain and Flight Lieutenant Valenta were last seen alive.

April 2 Flying Officer Tobolski last seen alive.

3 Mohr saw 10–15 urns in Wielen's office in Breslau.

6 Flight Lieutenant Grisman, Flight Lieutenant Gunn, Lieutenant McGarr, Flight Lieutenant Milford, Flying Officer Street and Flight Lieutenant Williams were last seen alive.

Flight Lieutenant Hayter was shot (Maundy Thursday).

Group Captain Massey was informed at Sagan that 41 officers had been shot.

9 Easter Day. Memorial Service at Sagan.

12 Flying Officer Krol last seen alive.

13 Flight Lieutenant Long last seen alive.

15 Group Captain Wilson, new Senior British Officer at Sagan, was given 47 names of officers shot.

17 M. Naville, of the Swiss Protecting Power, paid a routine visit to Sagan which the German authorities decided not to stop.

May 12 Switzerland reported 47 dead to London.

19 Mr Eden's first statement in the House of Commons.

27 Wielen returned to Sagan the urns of 29 officers shot in the Breslau Military District.

June 6 The Swiss Government forwarded the German Note to London.

16 The Air Ministry announced the death of three more officers.

23 Mr Eden's second statement in the House of Commons.

25 Müller, Wielen and Scharpwinkel began the 'whitewash conferences' in Berlin.

July 14 The last of the 50 urns was returned to Sagan.

15 Sagan prisoners began to build a memorial to the Fifty.

20 The Bomb Plot against Hitler. (Nebe involved, and later simulated suicide.)

22 The German Government refused the promised further Note to Great Britain via Switzerland.

23 German Press carried the first official account of the Sagan escape, except for news items of the *Grossfahndung* in March.

August 8 The Swiss forwarded to London the findings of the Senior British Officer's Court of Inquiry at Sagan, entrusted to the Protecting Power.

26 The first MI9 assessment named Scharpwinkel, Schmauser and Seetzen.

September 9 Colonel von Lindeiner-Wildau was court-martialled over the Sagan escape.

December 4 Dedication of the Sagan Memorial in the presence of Swiss representatives.

1945

February Nebe was executed by the Gestapo for his part in the Bomb Plot.

March 5 Sagan having been overrun, the British Government urgently requested assistance

	in the investigation from the Soviet Government.
29	United Nations War Crimes Commission passed the case to the Judge Advocate General for prosecution.
April 25	Spann (Saarbrücken) killed in an air raid in Linz.
	Schermer (Munich) committed suicide.
26	Wielen (Breslau) made first statement to British interrogators.
30	Hitler committed suicide.
May 5	Geith arrested.
9	Römer (Brno) arrested by American Army.
10	Scharpwinkel (Breslau) arrested by Russian Army.
18	Römer (Brno) released by Americans to the Russians as the result of international decision over the spheres of influence in Czechoslovakia.
23	Himmler committed suicide after capture by the British Army.
24	Judge Advocate General's assessment absolved the Luftwaffe (but not Göring) for the Sagan crime and named RSHA Berlin and the Gestapo Breslau as the immediate targets of investigation.
May–June	JAG investigators took statements from the survivors of the Stalag Luft III escape.
August 7	Judge Advocate General made an interim report.
14	Colonel von Lindeiner-Wildau, in the London Cage, named Kaltenbrunner, Wielen, Absalon.
15	Royal Air Force Intelligence in Berlin began to seek Absalon.
31	The Czechs were already working on the Reichenberg murders.
September 3	Flight Lieutenant McKenna and Flight Sergeant Williams flew to Germany on attachment to SIB, BAFO.
	Judge Advocate General circulated a Wanted List of 106 persons.

16	Squadron Leader Thomas and Flight Sergeant Hicks arrived in Germany.
26	Kah (Berlin and Breslau) arrested in Hamburg.
27	Kah identified Seetzen (Breslau).
28	0100 hours. Seetzen (Breslau) committed suicide.
29	McKenna took statements from the Zembrodts relating to the arrest of Scharpwinkel (Breslau).
October 1	Flight Lieutenant Courtney and Sergeant Brocksom joined the SIB detachment.
23	A Czech memo on the Zlín murders named Schwartzer, Kiowsky, Zacharias and Ziegler.
November 13	Chief of Staff BAOR wrote regarding Scharpwinkel, Schmauser and Absalon to Colonel General Serov, Russian Army of Occupation, Berlin.
18	Courtney at work in the American zone listed 230 000 prisoners in American camps.
December 2	Dr van der Bijl, a Service acquaintance of Squadron Leader Kirby-Green, wrote to the British Ambassador in Prague with details of the Zlín murders.
14	Dr van der Bijl's statement reached the Air Ministry.
16	Squadron Leader Thomas was posted from Rinteln.
17	Chief of Staff BAOR wrote a further letter to Colonel General Serov regarding Scharpwinkel, Schmauser and Absalon.
	Wing Commander Bowes took over SIB BAFO. McKeena was promoted Squadron Leader and posted to SIB BAFO instead of attachment.
	SIB team temporarily enlarged to 12 NCOs and 12 interpreters to comb the internment camps.

1946

January 21	Czechs sent further report to British Embassy. Negotiations begun for British SIB visit to Czechoslovakia.
27	Williams interrogated Dingermann (Saar-

brücken Kripo). Spann (Saarbrücken Gestapo) incriminated.

February 6 Flight Lieutenant Lyon joined the SIB team.

13 French took statement on Saarbrücken murders, (withheld for three months).

14 Daniel confirmed suicide of Schermer (Munich), interrogated Weil (Munich) in Dachau, sought Schäfer (Munich) previously reported to have committed suicide.

February 15 – March 5 Bowes and Lyon worked in Czechoslovakia and took full statements incriminating all involved in the Zlín murders.

March 7 Williams got evidence on Schneider (Munich).

8 Bowes and Lyon raided Landhaus Brichta for Ziegler and Knippelberg.

9 Daniel at Dachau got evidence on Spann and Breithaupt (Saarbrücken).

11 Zacharias arrested in American enclave at Wesermünde.

12 Field-Marshal Milch, interviewed by Courtney at Nuremberg, 'remembered nothing' of Göring's implication in the Sagan murders and went on to give similar evidence at Nuremberg.
Zacharias escaped.

15 Göring, giving voluble evidence at Nuremberg, said he was completely innocent of the Sagan murders.

18 Schneider (Munich) arrested.

20/21 Göring, under cross-examination at Nuremberg, denied previous evidence that he had been present at Hitler's conference ordering the shootings, said he could not have stopped them anyway, conceded that the German Note declaring the prisoners had been shot whilst escaping was a lie, said he considered the Sagan affair 'the worst matter during the whole war'.

April 1 Zacharias recaptured on border of Russian zone.

early April Bowes and Lyon in Czechoslovakia investigating Reichenberg murders.

April 13–May 6 Bowes and Lyon in Poland.

April 26	Bowes and Lyon at Sagan.
	Ganninger (Natzweiler) committed suicide.
May 14	Daniel found Hampel (Breslau), got first eye-witness account of the first Breslau murders. Got names of Scharpwinkel's murder squad.
15	Flight Lieutenant Harrison joined the SIB team.
16	Weil arrested.
28	Herberg arrested: incriminated for the Karlsruhe murder Gmeiner, Preiss, Boschert, Ganninger, Wochner.
June 8	Boschert was seen in hospital and made a full statement.
11	Gmeiner located.
14	Preiss arrested.
July	Russians admitted Scharpwinkel held in Moscow.
10	Breithaupt (Saarbrücken) arrested.
18	Bruchardt (Danzig) arrested.
August 3	Gmeiner (Karlsruhe) arrested after conditional handover by the French.
10	Schulz (Saarbrücken) arrested.
15	Captain Cornish flew to Moscow.
20	Geith (Munich) arrested.
31	Scharpwinkel's first statement to Cornish.
September	McKenna hunted Venediger (Danzig) in Berlin, Hameln, Harz Mountains.
	Lyon and Harrison searching north Germany for evidence on the murders of Catanach, Christensen, Espelid and Fuglesang.
19	Scharpwinkel's second statement in Moscow.
25	Lyon and Harrison discovered four blank entries in Kiel crematorium register, and conducted intense inquiries.
October	Daniel operated against families of Ziegler (Zlín) and Müller (Berlin).
6	Jacobs, Kähler, Franz Schmidt and Oskar Schmidt (Kiel) arrested.
8	Struve (Kiel) arrested.
16	Göring committed suicide, Keitel and Kaltenbrunner executed at Nuremberg.
20	Denkmann (Kiel) arrested.

27	Franz Schmidt (Kiel) committed suicide.
November	Herberg (Karlsruhe) incriminated Hilker (Strasbourg) in a breakthrough on the Strasbourg murder.
December 12	Harrison instituted mail censorship for Hilker.
14	Harrison interviewed Julius Gehrum, the Strasbourg Gestapo executioner.
19	McKenna attempted to chase Venediger (Danzig) into the Russian zone: operation forbidden.
1947	
January 14	McKenna and Lyon in Hamburg hunting Post (Kiel).
	Schimmel interrogated in Dachau. Said he was in Oslo in March 1944.
23	Soviets offered to exchange Scharpwinkel for Baron von Walter.
February 27	Judge Advocate General got full information on Hayter's arrest.
March 10	Schimmel, reinterrogated, said he was still in command at Strasbourg at the operative time, but was absent in Berlin. Blamed Hilker.
12	McKenna got eye-witness confirmation that Schimmel was in Strasbourg at the time of the murder.
April 9	Peters (Gestapo Strasbourg) incriminated Schimmel, Hilker, Dissner.
25	Schimmel retired to hospital in Dachau.
29	Wieczorek (Breslau) found in American camp.
mid-May	Baron von Walter repatriated to Rhineland.
May 19	Post (Kiel) arrested.
	Wieczorek arrested, in American zone.
	Schimmel made full confession.
July 1	First trial of 18 defendants began at Hamburg.
29	McKenna distributed 10 000 photosheets of men still wanted.
early August	McKenna interviews mother of Fritz Schmidt (Kiel) and wife of Schäfer (Munich).
1948	
September 3	Verdicts and sentences in first trial.

October 17	Scharpwinkel reported to have died in Moscow.
1948	
February 3	Ziegler (Zlín) committed suicide.
27	Geith (Munich), Gmeiner (Karlsruhe), Herberg (Karlsruhe), Jacobs (Kiel), Kahler (Kiel), Post (Kiel), Preiss (Karlsruhe), Schimmel (Strasbourg), Oskar Schmidt (Kiel), Schneider (Munich), Schulz (Saarbrücken), Weil (Munich), Zacharias (Zlín) executed.
May 10	Absalon reported dead.
11	Dissner (Strasbourg) committed suicide.
24	Schröder (driver to Scharpwinkel, Breslau) arrested
July 26	Reimer and Bontenbroich (drivers, Danzig) arrested and incriminate Bruchardt with Venediger.
September 22	Ernest Bevin, Foreign Secretary, announced Cabinet decision to prosecute no more war criminals after 31 August 1948.
October 11	Second trial began in Hamburg.
November 6	Verdicts and sentences in second trial.
1949	
January 26	Bowes listed current list of Wanted Men.
1950	
March 24	Schäfer (Munich) acquitted by German court on charges of separate atrocities.
October 3	RAF trace Schäfer to British zone and urge renewed prosecution.
1952	Venediger (Danzig) emerges from Russian zone.
1954	
September 4	Venediger acquitted: prosecution appealed.
1955	
November 4	Venediger won appeal.
April 8	Venediger sentenced to two years: appealed.
December 17	Venediger's sentence confirmed.

1966	
December 23	Case dismissed against Hilker (Strasbourg).
1967	
January	Fritz Schmidt (Kiel) put on trial: pleaded superior orders.
1968	
March 16	Massacre at My Lai.
May	Fritz Schmidt (Kiel) sentenced to two years.
December 11	Case against Schäfer thrown out—after eighteen years.

Index